## USPA Values Statement

USPA is committed to promoting an atmosphere that allows our sport to be safe, inclusive and fun. We advocate for the dignity and well-being of all individuals and respect diverse traditions, heritages, and experiences. We value inclusivity and reject discrimination based on race, ethnicity, gender, sexual orientation, religious belief, or any other attribute not related to performance or merit. USPA affirms its vision of a safe and healthy skydiving environment free of violence and any form of discrimination, including sexual or racial harassment.

For additional information, refer to the USPA Policy Regarding Discrimination and Harassment in the USPA Governance Manual Section 1-9.

### 2025 Skydiver's Information Manual

©2025 United States Parachute Association®. All rights reserved. May not be reproduced without the express permission of USPA.

ISBN: 9798310558960

This version was produced by the following contributors and authors: Brandon Radcliff (SIM Rewrite Task Force Lead, 2024), Ron Bell (USPA Director of Safety and Training since 2018), Sherry Butcher, Darlene Kellner, Rob Laidlaw, Brian Naiman, Jen Sharp Ph.D., Mel Schock, and Michael Wadkins.

The following subject matter experts reviewed portions of this version related to their areas of expertise: Marie J. Clark, Jim Cowan, Niklas Daniel, Daniel Darby, George Hargis, Ray Lallo Jr., Nikko Mamallo, Alex Swindle, and Andrew Velasquez.

Other content originated from many talented skydivers, including but not limited to: Luke Aikins, Wade Baird, Thomas Baker, Glenn Bangs, Jim Crouch, Douglas Spotted Eagle, Wendy Faulkner, Jack Gregory, Kevin Gibson, Michael Johnston, Norman Kent, Nancy Koreen, Jim Mowrey, Madolyn Murdock, Chris Needels, Melissa Nelson, Luis Prinetto, Jack Pyland IV, and Mike Truffer.

### If found, please return to:

Name: Stephen Loyd

Address:

City, State, Zip:

Phone:

Email:

### Cover photos (clockwise from top):

**by Mark Kirschenbaum/Hypoxic | D-28511**

From left: Charles Knott, Robert Doughty and Ryan Clough fly a 3-way during the Chicks Rock boogie at Skydive Elsinore in California.

**by Bert Navarrete | D-19159**

A 9-way head-down skydive builds during the July 4 Boogie at Skydive Cross Keys in Williamstown, New Jersey.

**by Eddie Phillips | Member #317981**

Dana Bjorn (foreground), Eric Bjorn and Reed Welch prepare to land at Skydive Tennessee in Tullahoma.

# WARNING

**IMPORTANT NOTICE**

**SPORT PARACHUTING OR SKYDIVING IS A POTENTIALLY DANGEROUS ACTIVITY THAT CAN RESULT IN INJURY OR DEATH. EACH INDIVIDUAL PARTICIPANT, REGARDLESS OF EXPERIENCE, HAS FINAL RESPONSIBILITY FOR HIS OR HER OWN SAFETY.**

**THE FOLLOWING INFORMATION IS PRESENTED AS A MEMBERSHIP SERVICE BY THE UNITED STATES PARACHUTE ASSOCIATION (USPA). USPA MAKES NO WARRANTIES OR REPRESENTATIONS AND ASSUMES NO LIABILITY CONCERNING THE VALIDITY OF ANY ADVICE, OPINION OR RECOMMENDATION EXPRESSED IN THIS MATERIAL. ALL INDIVIDUALS RELYING ON THIS MATERIAL DO SO AT THEIR OWN RISK.**

An individual's safety can be enhanced by exercising proper precautions and procedures. This manual contains some of the knowledge and practices that, in the opinion of USPA, will promote the safe enjoyment of skydiving. The UNITED STATES PARACHUTE ASSOCIATION is a nonprofit, voluntary membership organization of the participants and supporters of the sport of parachuting. The sport is also referred to as skydiving. USPA has no involvement in the conduct or operations of any skydiving center, parachute center, or drop zone.

**USPA, AS A PRIVATE, NON-REGULATORY ORGANIZATION WHICH HAS NO LEGAL AUTHORITY TO REGULATE OR CONTROL INDIVIDUALS OR CORPORATIONS, CANNOT BE HELD LIABLE FOR ANY JUMP OR TRAINING OPERATIONS THAT RESULT IN INJURY OR DEATH TO ANY PARTY.**

Regardless of any statements made in any USPA publications, USPA has neither been given nor has it assumed any duty to anyone. USPA has no obligation to anyone concerning his or her skydiving activities. All references by USPA to self-regulation refer to each individual person regulating or being responsible for him or herself. USPA issues various licenses, ratings, awards, and appointments and provides various types of information, advice, and training but does not authorize anyone in any capacity to act for USPA as an agent or representative in connection with the regulation or control of skydiving operations. It is the responsibility of each student to ask whatever questions are necessary for him or her to have a thorough understanding of the actions and procedures that he or she must perform in order to make a safe jump. Each skydiver has the responsibility to exercise certain practices and perform certain actions to maintain safety for himself or herself and for other people.

---

**Looking for Forms or Applications?**
Download the most recent versions at
uspa.org/downloads

# Table of Contents

USPA Values Statement .................................................................................. I
**WARNING** ..................................................................................................... II

## Introduction: The United States Parachute Association ............... 2
The Association ........................................................................................... 2
Board of Directors and Leadership ........................................................... 2
Headquarters Staff ..................................................................................... 3
Your Role as a USPA Member .................................................................. 3

## About this Manual .............................................................................. 4
SIM Revisions .............................................................................................. 4

## Chapter 1: Integrated Student Program ........................................... 6
Overview ...................................................................................................... 6
About Your Training ................................................................................... 6
Regulations Pertaining to You .................................................................. 7
Category A (Arch) ....................................................................................... 8
Category B (Basics) ................................................................................... 22
Category C (Control) ................................................................................ 27
Category D (Direction) ............................................................................. 34
Category E (Explore) ................................................................................ 39
Category F (Flat Track) ............................................................................. 47
Category G (Groups) ................................................................................ 52
Category H (Hone) ................................................................................... 58
Applying for Your A License ................................................................... 63

## Chapter 2: Requirements and Regulations ..................................... 66
Overview of the BSRs .............................................................................. 66
2-1: Basic Safety Requirements .............................................................. 67
2-2: Waivers to the Basic Safety Requirements .................................... 70
2-3: Federal Aviation Regulations .......................................................... 71

## Chapter 3: Licenses, Ratings, and Awards ...................................... 74
3-1: Licenses .............................................................................................. 74
3-2: Ratings ................................................................................................ 79
3-3: Awards ................................................................................................ 79

## Chapter 4: Recommendations for Everyone .................................. 84
4-1: Skydiving Emergencies ..................................................................... 84
4-2: Currency Training .............................................................................. 90
4-3: Equipment .......................................................................................... 91
4-4: Pre-Jump Safety Checks and Briefings .......................................... 95
4-5: Weather .............................................................................................. 97
4-6: Aircraft ................................................................................................ 98
4-7: Spotting .............................................................................................. 99
4-8: Incident Reports .............................................................................. 101

## Chapter 5: Discipline-Specific Recommendations ...................... 104
5-1: Formation Skydiving ....................................................................... 104
5-2: Freeflying, Freestyle, and Skysurfing ........................................... 105
5-3: Night Jumps ..................................................................................... 106
5-4: Water Landings ............................................................................... 108
5-5: Canopy Formations ........................................................................ 109
5-6: High-Altitude Jumps ....................................................................... 112
5-7: Camera Flying .................................................................................. 112
5-8: Wingsuit Flying ................................................................................ 115
5-9: Canopy Piloting ............................................................................... 118
5-10: Movement Jumps .......................................................................... 129
5-11: Speed Skydiving ............................................................................ 131

## Chapter 6: Exhibition Jumping and PRO Rating ........................... 134
6-1: Exhibition Jumping ......................................................................... 134
6-2: Professional Exhibition Rating ...................................................... 137
6-3: FAA Form 7711-2 ............................................................................ 141

## Glossary ............................................................................................. 142
## Appendix: License Study Guide Index ........................................... 154

# Introduction: The United States Parachute Association

Although you may have heard talk of USPA, you may still wonder what USPA *is* exactly and have questions about your role in it. USPA is an internationally recognized skydiving organization that is governed by a volunteer board of directors consisting of members of the skydiving community. The board, supported by paid staff at headquarters, serves USPA's rating holders and members. USPA's mission is three-fold:

- to promote safe skydiving through training, licensing, and instructor qualification programs
- to ensure skydiving's rightful place on airports and in the airspace system
- to promote competition and record-setting programs

## The Association

The United States Parachute Association is a voluntary, not-for-profit membership organization of individuals who enjoy and support the sport of skydiving. In 1946, USPA—then called National Parachute Jumpers and Riggers—was first incorporated in New York with an estimated 100 members. Now, USPA has tens of thousands of members across the globe, and many countries use USPA's materials, standards, and credentials as the foundation for skydiving in their nations.

In its **sporting role**, USPA is the official U.S. skydiving representative recognized by the National Aeronautic Association (NAA) and the official skydiving representative of the Fédération Aéronautique Internationale (FAI) in the U.S.

In its **governing role**, USPA is officially recognized by the Federal Aviation Administration (FAA) as the representative of skydivers in the United States. Although the FAA does not mandate that sport skydivers have USPA membership to jump in the United States, the agency does recognize USPA as the skydiving authority in the U.S. As a result, most drop zones in the U.S. affiliate with USPA, adhere to USPA policies and guidelines, and require USPA membership.

USPA operates under a constitution and bylaws that define the organization's purpose. They are contained in the USPA Governance Manual, available on the downloads page on USPA's website or from USPA Headquarters.

United States Parachute Association
5401 Southpoint Centre Blvd.
Fredericksburg, Virginia 22407
(540) 604-9740
uspa@uspa.org
www.uspa.org

## Board of Directors and Leadership

USPA is governed by a board of directors, elected by USPA members every three years. The USPA Board of Directors meets twice a year to address concerns from the membership and review guidelines and regulations. These board members are volunteers who are active skydivers, drop zone owners, jump pilots, and other members of the skydiving community from across the country. USPA members can attend these biannual board meetings in person or via live broadcast.

The USPA Board consists of 22 members in total. This includes eight **National Directors**, elected by the USPA membership at large, and 14 **Regional Directors**, one from each designated geographical region of the U.S. Regional Directors and their jurisdictions can be found at uspa.org/regions.

The Board makes procedures and policy via the **committee system** following an agenda set prior to each meeting. To each committee, the president appoints committee chairs, who then appoint committee members and non-voting advisors. These committees research agenda items before meetings, discuss these in person at the meeting, then recommend additions, changes, deletions, and waivers for full board vote. Any USPA member can request that items of interest be put on the agenda of the appropriate committee by contacting their Regional Director or completing the Proposed Agenda Item form found at uspa.org/bod.

The board of directors elects its **Executive Committee**—president, vice president, secretary, treasurer, chairman of the board, and a member at large—from its membership. Other committees are Competition, Finance & Budget, Governance, Group Membership, Membership Services, Regional Directors, and Safety & Training. You can find contact information for members of the board and the committees at uspa.org/bod.

Nearly all drop zones have at least one USPA **Safety & Training Advisor** (S&TA) who is appointed by and serves as the direct link to their USPA Regional Director. The S&TA is a local jumper who is available to the drop zone's members to provide administrative services and information.

## Headquarters Staff

The USPA staff are paid employees whom the USPA Executive Director hires to implement the vision of the board and to serve members with administrative needs such as membership applications and renewals, ratings, licenses, and awards. The Executive Committee of the USPA Board hires the executive director, who reports to the board president. Staff headquarters is located in **Fredericksburg, Virginia.** You can find contact information for headquarters departments and staff at uspa.org/staff.

## Your Role as a USPA Member

As a member-led association, USPA is comprised of board members, staff, rating holders, appointees and regular jumpers. USPA members determine who sits on the board of directors and therefore, the direction of the organization. So, in a sense, *you* are USPA. In the U.S., you can skydive without a USPA membership, but USPA makes skydiving in the U.S. possible. You can support skydiving by being a member in good standing and striving to follow the Federal Aviation Administration's Federal Aviation Regulations (FARs) and USPA's Basic Safety Requirements (BSRs).

What happens if you don't follow the FARs and BSRs? The **Compliance Group** investigates purported violations of the FARs and BSRs, as well as misconduct as defined in the USPA Governance Manual. The group consists of four members of your elected board as well as the USPA Director of Safety and Training at USPA Headquarters. If you willfully violate the BSRs or FARs as a member or an instructional rating holder, the Compliance Group could bring disciplinary actions, such as suspending or even revoking your ratings or membership, against you. For more information on this process, see the **USPA Governance Manual** Section 1-6.

Skydivers can only continue to enjoy self-governance if each is aware of their role, as well as the roles of others, in the community. Continue to follow USPA guidance as best practices. Continue to adhere to FAA regulations. Continue to respect local authority with an air of collaboration. And most importantly, continue to update your knowledge and develop your own good judgment.

# About this Manual

The Skydiver's Information Manual (SIM) provides basic skydiving standards—the Basic Safety Requirements (BSRs) and recommendations that USPA members have agreed upon as providing for the conduct of safe and enjoyable skydiving. It also describes the programs USPA administers to recognize individuals for their expertise, ability to train others, and proficiency or tenure in the sport.

Although the SIM provides much basic information for skydivers, each jumper should research further and consult USPA and industry officials, documents, and other media, as well as other reliable individuals for clarification and additional information.

Although USPA is a voluntary membership association with no regulatory authority, USPA can suspend or revoke any USPA license, rating, award, appointment, or membership it issues, according to terms and conditions stated in the USPA Governance Manual. Compliance with the Basic Safety Requirements contained herein is mandatory for participation in USPA programs. The BSRs represent the commonly accepted standards for a reasonable level of safety.

However, the recommendations contained herein, unless otherwise stated (such as in the case of compliance with a Federal Aviation Regulation), are put forth as guidance and are not mandatory. Moreover, a deviation from these recommendations does not necessarily imply negligence and is not to be used in a court of law to demonstrate negligence.

Voluntary compliance with rules, recommendations, and standards within the SIM demonstrates that jumpers and drop zone operators are exercising self-regulation.

## SIM Revisions

As a living document reflecting best practices in skydiving, the Skydiver's Information Manual requires continuous updating. It is the responsibility of SIM holders to keep their version current. Users can purchase the most current physical or digital copies or download free copies from the USPA website at uspa.org/sim. Change documents that highlight differences from the previous version are available at uspa.org/downloads. The SIM is also available as a mobile app through Google Play and the App Store.

Third-party translators prepare translations of the SIM to make USPA documents accessible to those who may not read English. The official and binding documents that govern USPA are the English versions.

Readers are encouraged to submit comments or recommended changes in writing to:

USPA

5401 Southpoint Centre Blvd.

Fredericksburg, VA 22407;

or by email to uspa@uspa.org.

This manual provides procedures to address many foreseeable situations, but each situation is different. Deviations from these recommendations do not imply negligence.

# Chapter 1:
# Integrated Student Program

## Overview

USPA developed the Integrated Student Program (ISP) as a comprehensive student training outline that meets the Basic Safety Requirements (BSRs). It includes all methods of instruction (see below) used to train students from their first jumps through their A licenses. Some schools have developed equivalent programs that train students to meet all the qualifications of the USPA A license. If your drop zone follows a program by a different name, you can still use the ISP to find appropriate guidance for training.

USPA recognizes the following training methods:

1. Accelerated Freefall (AFF or harness hold), where the student exits with at least one instructor who holds the student by the harness
2. Instructor-Assisted Deployment (IAD), where an instructor in the aircraft deploys the pilot chute as the student falls away
3. Static Line (SL), where a line connected to the aircraft deploys the student's parachute
4. Tandem, where the student's harness attaches to the instructor's harness, and they share one parachute system

## About Your Training

The **A-License Progression** Card charts your individual progress as you make your way through this journey. All licenses, quizzes, and training materials are available in online and paper formats. You can download a PDF of this card at uspa.org/downloads in the License Applications folder. If you join USPA as a member, you can take advantage of the **online A-License Progression Card** at uspa.org/mya.

Following each jump during which you meet an A-license requirement, your coach or instructor signs off the appropriate spot on your A-License Progression Card, either online or on paper. At the end of each category, you complete the category quiz online or verbally with a coach or an instructor. Especially in Categories A through D, you will be expected to complete all the objectives of one category before making any jumps in the next. Recommended dive flows for freefall and canopy flight are at the end of each category.

According to the Basic Safety Requirements (Chapter 2-1G) all students must jump under the direct supervision of an appropriately rated **USPA Instructor** until demonstrating stability and heading control prior to and within 5 seconds of initiating two intentional disorienting maneuvers involving a back-to-earth orientation (e.g., barrel roll, front loop, back loop), which occurs in Category E. A **USPA Coach**—that is, an instructional rating holder who teaches students under the supervision of an instructor—may conduct freefall training and supervise jumps for students in Categories E through H. A coach may also supervise IAD and static-line students who have successfully deployed their own parachutes. Until USPA issues the student an A license, all training remains the responsibility of an instructor.

**CANOPY:** Canopy, parachute, and wing are interchangeable terms.

Before receiving your license, you will complete a check dive and oral and written exams.

Integrated Student Program

# Regulations Pertaining to You

All participants in skydiving must meet the USPA Basic Safety Requirement (BSR) for **medical fitness** (Chapter 2-1.C):

**MEDICAL REQUIREMENTS**

1. All persons engaging in skydiving must:
    a. Possess at least a current FAA Third-Class Medical Certificate; or
    b. Carry a certificate of physical and mental fitness for skydiving from a registered physician; or
    c. Agree with the USPA-recommended medical statement:
    "I represent and warrant that I have no known physical or mental infirmities that would impair my ability to participate in skydiving, or if I do have any such infirmities, that they have been or are being successfully treated so that they do not represent any foreseeable risk while skydiving. I also represent and warrant that I am not taking any medications or substances, prescription or otherwise, that would impair my ability to participate in skydiving."

A person should be in good health and physical condition to skydive and should not be on medication; however, many conditions can be properly managed if the instructor knows about them. In some cases, you may need to provide an FAA flight physical or a doctor's statement of fitness for skydiving. Your instructor will also need to know about any medical history that may affect your ability to skydive safely (e.g., recent blood donations, joint dislocations or recent dental work). People who participate in scuba diving should not skydive for at least 24 hours afterward.

All participants in skydiving must meet **the BSR for age** (Chapter 2-1.D).

For skydives made within the U.S. and its territories and possessions, no skydive may be made in violation of **FAA regulations** (Chapter 2-1.B).

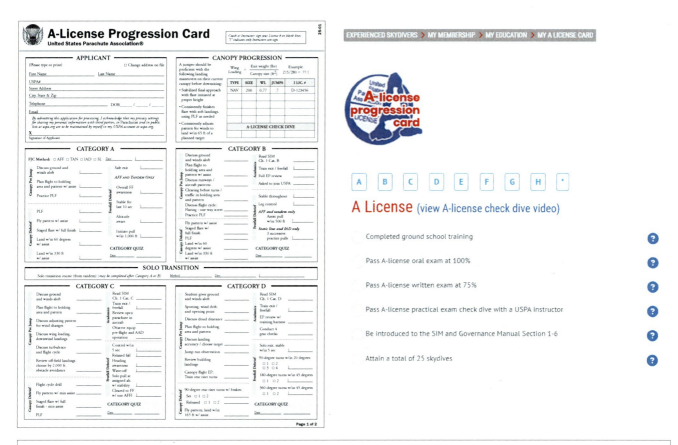

**Sample A-License Progression Cards:** Print (left) and online (right).

Integrated Student Program | Category A (Arch)

# Category A (Arch)

| AFF AND TANDEM<br>**1 Jump** | IAD/STATIC LINE<br>**2 Jumps** | DEPLOYMENT-INITIATION ALTITUDES<br>AFF: **5,500** feet<br>IAD and static line: **4,000** feet<br>Tandem: **6,000** feet |
|---|---|---|

In Category **A**, you take an active role in your skydive and perform the first basic body position, the **A**rch!

This category contains information about your first-jump course. Check out USPA's free online ground school to help you study ahead at skydiveschool.org.

## Category at a Glance

### First-Jump-Course Advancement Criteria (IAD, Static Line and AFF)

#### Equipment
- ☐ Find and operate main-deployment, cutaway and reserve-activation handles (or single-operating-system handle)
- ☐ Explain the use of the altimeter and the importance of altitude awareness
- ☐ State how many gear checks you will receive

#### Aircraft
- ☐ Approach the plane from behind (away from propeller) and with an instructor
- ☐ Demonstrate correct procedure for landing with the plane in an emergency
- ☐ Demonstrate correct procedures for emergency exit (exit using main parachute, exit using reserve parachute)
- ☐ Respond correctly to questions about how to handle an open parachute in the aircraft with the door open and with the door closed

#### Freefall
- ☐ Demonstrate the basic arch position
- ☐ Demonstrate proper arm and leg position and positive leg extension with symmetry
- ☐ Demonstrate the correct deployment and practice-deployment procedures, including cue words (e.g., "arch, reach, touch!") and symmetrical movement
- ☐ Understand and respond with the correct body position to freefall hand signals
- ☐ Explain your three pull priorities (if taught during ground school)
- ☐ Demonstrate the correct technique to handle both a hard pull and an inability to find the handle for the main deployment
- ☐ Demonstrate how to clear a pilot-chute hesitation (main or reserve)

#### Canopy
- ☐ Respond correctly and within 5 seconds to malfunction scenarios, including line twists, slider up, end-cell closures, and the four types of two-canopies-out configurations
- ☐ Name and explain "decision altitude" and "cutaway hard deck"
- ☐ Solve canopy descent problems from opening to 1,000 feet

#### Landing
- ☐ Explain your landing priorities
- ☐ Identify the wind direction and draw your landing pattern on an aerial map
- ☐ Describe how to handle a downwind landing and why you should avoid low turns
- ☐ Demonstrate the flare and a proper parachute landing fall (PLF)
- ☐ Explain the correct procedure for these landing obstacles: power lines, water, trees, buildings, and hazards specific to the drop zone

# Category-A Advancement Criteria

## Canopy Pre-Jump
- ☐ Discuss ground winds and winds aloft for the day
- ☐ Plan your flight to the holding area and in the pattern with assistance
- ☐ Practice a PLF

## Academics
- ☐ Attend ground school

## Canopy Debrief
- ☐ Prepare to perform a parachute landing fall (PLF) on final approach and perform a PLF if needed
- ☐ Fly your pattern with assistance
- ☐ Perform a staged flare with a full finish
- ☐ Land within 60 degrees of your intended heading with assistance
- ☐ Land within 330 feet (100 meters) of your intended target with assistance

## Freefall Debrief
- ☐ Perform a safe exit
- ☐ Show overall freefall awareness (AFF and tandem)
- ☐ Be stable for the last 10 seconds of freefall (AFF and tandem)
- ☐ Be altitude aware throughout the freefall (AFF and tandem)
- ☐ Initiate the pull within 1,000 feet of your assigned altitude (AFF and tandem)

# Category-A Tandem Training Requirements

*A USPA Tandem Instructor must teach this section.*

Before boarding the aircraft, the instructor should brief you on:

- ☐ Emergency procedures (stay calm and follow instructor's directions)
- ☐ Exit and freefall procedures (safety position)
- ☐ Operating the parachute
- ☐ Landing procedures

You will learn how to do the following:

1. perform the safety position used for exit and emergencies
2. maintain an arch in freefall
3. read the altimeter
4. deploy the main parachute
5. fly a landing pattern
6. flare for landing

Category-A skills and training are mostly **the same as for solo students**, described in the Academics section below. Here are the differences:

- **Climb-Out and Exit:** Your instructor will teach you the exit that best suits your tandem jump.
- **Freefall:** Exit with both hands in the safety position. Your instructor will signal you to move them into a neutral body position once in freefall, where you will start your dive flow. You will receive further instructions regarding main-canopy deployment.
- **Canopy:** Your instructor will perform the canopy-control check, then hand you the toggles and introduce you to basic canopy flight, including altitude awareness and landing pattern.
- **Landing:** Your instructor will teach you landing procedures with techniques specific to tandem jumping.

# Integrated Student Program | Category A (Arch)

## Academics

*The topics appear here in chronological order; however, your school's first-jump course may teach them in a different order. Unless otherwise indicated at the beginning of a section, a current USPA Coach under the supervision of any USPA Instructor may teach the first-jump course.*

## Equipment

Your equipment will consist of a harness-and-container system, commonly referred to as "a rig," which contains a main parachute and a reserve parachute. The rig will have three handles: a **main deployment handle** to open your main parachute, a **cutaway handle** to release the main parachute in an emergency, and a **reserve handle** to deploy your reserve parachute.

Your **main parachute** is divided into a series of cells that trap air. You will be suspended under the canopy by a set of suspension lines that attach to risers, which are connected to the harness-and-container system. There are also two toggles, which are attached to steering lines, that you'll use to steer the canopy.

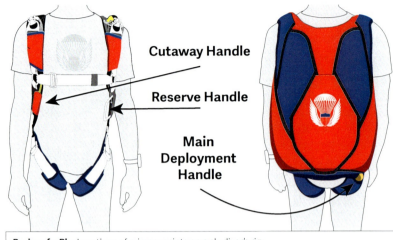

**Basics of a Rig:** Locations of primary points on a skydiver's rig.

A **parachute** opens in three stages:

1. Activation—by throwing the pilot chute, by pulling the ripcord, or by static line
2. Deployment—the parachute comes out of the container
3. Inflation—the parachute fills with air

Your rig also includes two important safety devices. The **reserve static line** is a connection between the main parachute risers and the reserve pin that activates your reserve parachute when you release a malfunctioning main parachute. The **automatic activation device** initiates deployment of your reserve parachute at a pre-set altitude and speed. Both are only back-up devices. It is always your job to pull the handles in case of a malfunction.

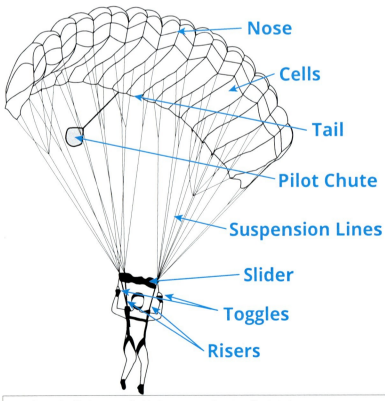

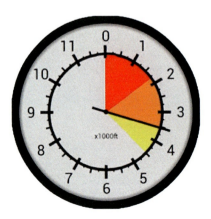

**Parachute:** Familiarize yourself with the names and parts as illustrated.

**Visual Altimeters:** digital (top) and analog (bottom)

Integrated Student Program | Category A (Arch)

You will also be equipped with an **altimeter**, which indicates your approximate altitude in thousands of feet above the ground. Handle it with care. Altitude awareness is your most important task until you open your parachute. You also use your altimeter throughout your canopy flight.

In freefall, you should **check your altitude**:

- every three seconds
- after each maneuver
- whenever you encounter something unexpected

In Category A, the USPA Instructor takes responsibility for putting your equipment on you, adjusting it correctly, and **checking it**:

1. before you put it on
2. immediately after you put it on
3. before boarding the plane
4. in the aircraft shortly before exit

# Aircraft

Your instructor must accompany you anytime you approach, enter, and move about the aircraft, whether the engine is running or not. Always approach fixed-wing aircraft from the rear to avoid contact with the propeller. Protect your gear by being mindful of the parachute rig on your back when climbing into and moving about the aircraft. According to Federal Aviation Regulations (FARs), the pilot and the jumper are jointly responsible for ensuring that the jumper wears seat belts or restraints during taxi, takeoff, and landing.

## Aircraft Emergencies

*A USPA Coach, under the supervision of a USPA Instructor, may teach this section.*

The probability of an aircraft emergency is low. In an emergency, your first response is to **stay calm and wait** for a command from your instructor. The pilot will tell your instructor to either prepare for landing or to exit the plane. Your instructor will tell you which of these actions you need to perform:

- land in the aircraft
- exit and use your reserve parachute
- exit and use your main parachute
- perform a routine exit with or without instructor assistance

If you land with the aircraft in an emergency:

- ensure your helmet and seat belt or restraint are on
- assume a safety position taught by your instructor
- clasp your hands behind your head to reinforce your neck
- after landing, unfasten your seat belt or restraint and immediately exit in an orderly fashion and walk at least 100 feet away from the plane

If you exit the aircraft after an emergency:

- ensure your parachute is open immediately
- look for your instructor's parachute
- follow them to a clear, open landing area and prepare to perform a parachute landing fall (PLF)

Select any clear area if you can't find your instructor.

**If any parachute opens in the aircraft**, attempt to contain the parachute and inform the instructor. If your parachute goes out the door, follow immediately to prevent damage to the plane and injury to yourself or others. If anyone else's parachute goes out the door, immediately push them to and through the door for the same reason.

# 1      Integrated Student Program | Category A (Arch)

## Exit and Freefall

*A USPA Instructor rated for the method-specific discipline in which you are training must teach this portion.*

It's important to plan your dive, then dive your plan.

### Exit

A good **exit** from the aircraft makes best use of learning time and provides a safer, more controlled experience. Mentally breaking the exit into three parts can help you be more aware and responsive during the exit and help you perform better, allowing for more working time in freefall. The three parts are:

**THE SETUP**     **THE LAUNCH**     **THE FLYAWAY**

**Set** yourself **up** for success by placing your hips, head, feet, and hands in the easiest position to get to the next picture …

As soon as you leave the plane, **launch** your hips into the relative wind, keeping your head and eyes up, relaxing as you get to the next picture …

Hold a relaxed arch as you **fly away** and shift from the relative wind to the terminal wind, a transitional state known as "the hill."

**Setup** procedures prepare you to exit in a stable, belly-first freefall body position. The setup position should place your belly (pelvis) facing forward into the supporting wind, known as the **relative wind**. As you exit, you will feel the relative wind coming from the front of the airplane. During the first several seconds of freefall, you will naturally transition to a belly-to earth position and will feel the relative wind supporting you from below. Presenting your belly to the relative wind on exit increases your stability during the exit.

Your setup will vary based on the aircraft from which you are exiting, but your launch and **flyaway** will be essentially the same, regardless of aircraft. To time the **launch**, you will either perform a count or respond to a "go" command.

> **Tandem students:** Your instructor will rehearse your exit and exit commands with you.
>
> **AFF students:** Verify that the instructors are ready. Call, "Check in!" to the inside instructor, who responds, "OK!" Call, "Check out!" to the outside instructor, who responds, "OK!" Take a deep breath to relax and then begin a count with a verbal and physical cadence "Up, down, arch!" or "Out, in, arch!" to help the instructors leave simultaneously with you.
>
> **IAD and static-line students:** Climb into position and wait for the instructor's command. Look for signals from your instructor. On "Go!" take a breath to relax and look up. Release from the plane, count out loud by thousands to 5,000, then check the parachute.

You must exit soon after climbing out to ensure that you open the parachute over the correct place on the ground.

During the first few seconds after your launch, you will experience what is known as the **flyaway**—the transition from your vertical position to your belly-to-earth position. This happens naturally when you maintain a relaxed, arched body position with your hips facing the relative wind.

> **AFF students:** In case of instability, check your altitude, arch until the horizon comes flat into view, and follow your instructors' signals. If you lose one instructor, continue as usual. If you lose both instructors, pull immediately.
>
> **Tandem, IAD, and static-line students:** In case of instability on exit, arch.

Integrated Student Program | Category A (Arch)

## Body Position

You will learn to fall belly first into the relative wind in a neutral, arched body position. An arched body position creates stability and results in a more reliable deployment of the parachute.

Arching and extending the legs slightly while relaxing the rest of the body results in a smooth, on-heading freefall. The key elements of a **neutral body position** include:

- hips forward with back arched
- knees at shoulder-width apart
- legs extended slightly, knees bent 45 degrees, toes pointed
- upper arms positioned 90 degrees or less from the torso and relaxed
- elbows bent 90-120 degrees and relaxed
- chin up

Neutral Body Position

You will practice this body position until it becomes more natural. Consciously breathing will help you relax.

Your instructor may use **hand signals** to correct your body position and to provide dive-flow reminders. You should respond to all adjustments smoothly and slowly and maintain your new body position.

## Hand Signals

Pelvis Forward (arch)

Circle of Awareness (altitude check)

OK

Deploy the Parachute (pull)

Legs In (retract legs slightly)

Extend Legs Six Inches and Hold

Open Hand (release pilot chute)

Check Arm Position

Knees Together Slightly –or– Toe Taps

Perform the Practice Deployment Sequence

Relax (breathe)

Integrated Student Program | Category A (Arch)

## Freefall-Dive-Flow Skills (AFF)

*If you are training via the AFF method or another harness-hold method, a USPA Coach may introduce these skills and the sequence, but a USPA AFF Instructor is responsible for directly supervising practice and ensuring proficiency.*

After exiting, take a breath and relax, making sure you are in the correct freefall body position. Then, perform a **circle of awareness**:

1. look at the horizon to check your heading
2. read your altimeter
3. look first to the reserve-side instructor and then to the main-side instructor for signals

Then, perform **three practice deployments**:

- practice slowly and deliberately, moving only your arms
- verbalize each action
- pause to feel the deployment handle each time
- check that your body position is correct before, during, and after each practice deployment

Perform a second **circle-of-awareness check**. Then monitor your altitude and body position for the remainder of the freefall using **HAALR**:

- Heading (look at the horizon)
- Altitude (most important)
- Arch (hips forward, chin up)
- Legs (ensure neutral leg position)
- Relax (take a deep breath)

> **DIVE FLOW:** is the planned sequence of events. There is a freefall dive flow and a canopy dive flow for every skydive.
>
> **COA:** Circle of awareness consists of checks to ensure you are aware of heading, altitude, and instructor signals.
>
> **HEADING:** is the direction you are facing.
>
> **PRACTICE DEPLOYMENT:** is a movement that mimics the pull sequence so you can practice finding the handle with the right timing and body position.

While receiving video of your jump may be of benefit during training, you must pay attention to your altitude not the camera flyer.

At 6,000 feet, **lock on** to your altimeter and keep looking at it until you see it read 5,500 feet. At 5,500 feet, **wave off** by waving both arms smoothly overhead, which signals to your instructors that you know your altitude and intend to pull. Remember that the **wave off** is the beginning of a slow, smooth, pull sequence that will take approximately 1,000 feet from start to finish. **Initiate deployment** with the wave off, arch, reach, and pull sequence, and deploy your parachute as practiced. The instructor may assist you.

## Main Deployment

*A USPA Coach can teach this section under the supervision of a USPA Instructor.*

### Body Position for Deployment

Establish a neutral body position, then locate the main deployment handle. Look up while reaching for your handle and maintain your arch while keeping your spine straight.

For balance, stretch your left hand overhead (like you are raising your hand to ask a question) as you reach with your right hand for the deployment handle. Pull the handle, then return to your neutral body position. Verbalize each action.

**Deployment:** From a neutral arch, reach back while staying symmetrical, and pull the handle, throwing it briskly. Then, return to a neutral arch.

After you pull, remain flat and stable with your shoulders level throughout the deployment, counting by thousands to 3,000. After the count of three, visually check for pilot-chute and main-canopy deployment.

Integrated Student Program | Category A (Arch)

## Pull Priorities

**1** Pull → **2** Pull at the proper altitude → **3** Pull, preferably while stable

The number-one priority on any skydive is to pull. You can pull at any time during the skydive when encountering difficulty or experiencing something unexpected. The second priority is to pull at the assigned altitude, and the third priority is to preferably pull in a stable body position. A stable, face-to-earth body position improves opening reliability but is less important than opening at the assigned altitude. Always prioritize altitude over stability.

### STOP AND CHECK YOURSELF:

What should you do anytime you see your instructor pull? Answer: **Pull**.

What should you do if you are on your back at pull altitude? Answer: **Pull**. Pulling at the proper altitude is more important than pulling while stable.

> **IAD and static-line students:** As you exit the plane, remain arched and stable with your feet extended slightly, toes pointed, and shoulders level through deployment, counting to five by thousands. Look over your shoulder for the pilot chute (if used) and main-canopy deployment.

## Deployment Problems

If you **cannot find the main deployment handle**, feel across the bottom of the container to the corner, then down the side to the corner. Attempt to locate it no more than twice or for 5 seconds, whichever comes first. If you cannot find it, initiate emergency procedures.

If you find the main deployment handle but it is stuck, often referred to as a **hard pull**, attempt to throw the pilot chute no more than twice or for 5 seconds, whichever comes first. If you are unsuccessful, initiate emergency procedures.

If you throw the pilot chute but it gets stuck in the burble behind your back, clear this **pilot-chute hesitation** by twisting at the waist and looking over your shoulder to change the airflow. Attempt to clear the pilot chute no more than twice or for 5 seconds, whichever comes first. If the pilot chute does not launch off your back, initiate emergency procedures.

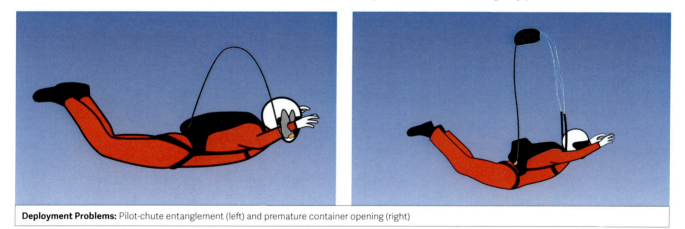

**Deployment Problems:** Pilot-chute entanglement (left) and premature container opening (right)

If you throw the pilot chute but the bridle wraps around a body part, arch harder for stability and attempt to clear the **pilot-chute entanglement** by pointing the limb that's entangled to the sky to shake it off. Attempt this no more than twice or for 5 seconds, whichever comes first. If that fails, initiate emergency procedures.

If your **container opens prematurely** in freefall, attempt to locate and deploy the pilot chute no more than two times or for 5 seconds, whichever comes first. If you can't locate the pilot chute after two tries or within five seconds, cut away and deploy the reserve. Alternatively, if you find and throw the pilot chute and it results in a partial malfunction, cut away and deploy the reserve.

> **IAD and static-line students:** If the static line fails to disconnect from the parachute system and you are being towed behind the aircraft, a situation known as **student-in-tow**, arch and signal to your instructor that you are ready for them to cut your static line. After the static line is cut, deploy your reserve.
>
> **IAD students:** Ensure that you look over your shoulder once you have exited the plane after counting to 5 seconds. If the pilot chute gets caught on your hand or arm, attempt to clear it twice; if it does not clear, execute your emergency procedures.

Integrated Student Program | Category A (Arch)

# Canopy

## Canopy Basics

A canopy is an inflatable wing that performs like the wing of an airplane. Once it is open and inflated, the canopy will start gliding forward and down through the air. The airflow around the canopy creates lift.

With both toggles all the way up, the canopy should glide straight ahead at full speed. To turn, look in the direction you want to turn, then pull that toggle down.

Pulling one toggle down a small amount produces a slow turn with a relatively small amount of dive. Small toggle inputs can be used to make minor heading corrections at any point in the canopy flight. Pulling one toggle down farther will produce a faster turn and cause the canopy to dive. Pulling both toggles down, known as a **flare**, decreases the rate of descent and forward speed of the canopy.

When flying into the wind, you will fly more slowly across the ground. When flying with the wind, you will move more quickly across the ground. When flying perpendicularly to the wind, known as **crabbing**, you will move in the direction you are facing with some sideways drift, and these effects will increase as wind speed increases.

**FLARE:** is a maneuver you perform under canopy in which you pull both toggles down to slow your forward speed and descent rate.

**CANOPY-CONTROL CHECK:** refers to the physical part of a canopy check and is often also called the controllability check. It consists of turning and flaring to assess the canopy's flight capabilities.

**DECISION ALTITUDE:** is the lowest altitude by which you must decide whether your canopy is safe to land. For students, this altitude is 2,500 feet.

**FULL FLIGHT:** is when the parachute is flying at its natural forward speed and descent rate with the toggles all the way up.

## Canopy Check

Immediately after deployment, you need to complete a canopy check to see whether you have a good canopy. Common questions used to assess your canopy include: "Is it there? Is it square? Is it steerable?" Or, "Is it square? Is it stable? Is it steerable?" During your first jump course, your instructor will cover what each question means specifically and help you practice applying them to several scenarios. For example:

**There?** Check the canopy for proper inflation after the deployment. The canopy should be large and fully inflated.

**Square?** It should have four well-defined edges that create a rectangular shape. The suspension lines should cascade down in four neat line groups to each riser, and the slider should be down to the tops of the risers. The canopy should be stable; it is flying level toward the horizon, not turning or spinning, with only fixable problems left to be solved.

**Steerable?** You must perform a canopy-control check to ensure the canopy flies straight in full flight, is steerable and can be flared. First, unstow your toggles and confirm the canopy is flying straight. To confirm the parachute will brake properly for landing, flare by pulling both toggles all the way down. Smoothly raise the toggles back up to full flight. To confirm the parachute is steerable, look right, turn right at least 90 degrees, then stop the turn by going back to full flight. Finally, look left, turn left, then stop the turn by going back to full flight.

Decide whether the canopy is controllable and safe to land by 2,500 feet, which is your **decision altitude**. If it is not, you must immediately initiate emergency procedures.

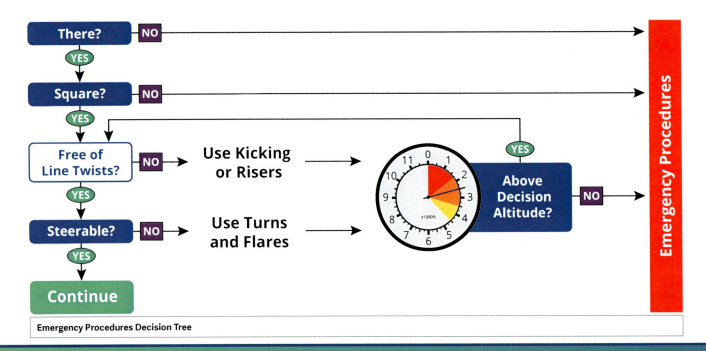

Emergency Procedures Decision Tree

Integrated Student Program | Category A (Arch)

## Fixable Problems

Problems that are usually minor include end cells of the canopy that stay closed, a slider that stays up near the canopy, an unintended turn, line twists, or other issues involving an inflated canopy. Line twists must be fixed first. To untwist the lines, spread the risers and kick, but release the brakes only after clearing the twist. Except for line twists, you can solve most minor problems with a canopy-control check. If the problem continues or gets worse, initiate your emergency procedures by 2,500 feet. If in doubt, initiate your emergency procedures. It is not advisable to try to land a compromised parachute.

## Canopy Malfunctions

*Your instructor will provide you with practice on the proper procedures for the equipment you will be jumping.*

**LINE TWISTS:** are a common problem in which the canopy has inflated but the lines or risers have developed one or more complete twists. This situation is usually easily remedied.

**CUTAWAY HARD DECK:** is 1,000 feet, the altitude where it becomes too low for a safe cutaway. Instead of cutting away, you must deploy the reserve and land both canopies.

### Emergency Procedures

If you have a canopy malfunction, check your altitude to make sure you are above your cutaway hard deck of 1,000 feet, then cut away and pull your reserve. Below 1,000 feet it becomes too low to safely cut away, and you must deploy the reserve and land both parachutes.

### Two Parachutes Out

You can prevent a two-parachutes-out malfunction by staying altitude aware and protecting your handles and closing pins. There are two possible actions you can take in a two-out situation: land both canopies or cut away.

You should land both canopies if you have a stable **biplane**, a **side-by-side**, or a **main-reserve entanglement.** If all toggles are stowed, leave them stowed. If the toggles have been unstowed on one canopy, unstow the toggles on the other. For a biplane, gently steer the front parachute by pulling down gently on the rear riser in the direction you wish to go. For a side-by-side, gently steer the parachute that is more directly overhead, also using the rear risers. Land without flaring and perform a parachute landing fall. In the rare case of a main-reserve entanglement, never give up trying to clear the entanglement or inflate the parachutes. Do your best to make the parachutes fly straight for landing, and perform a PLF.

If you have a **downplane**, you must **cut away** regardless of altitude. A downplane occurs when the two parachutes separate and begin flying toward the ground. *This is the only exception to the 1,000-foot cutaway hard deck.*

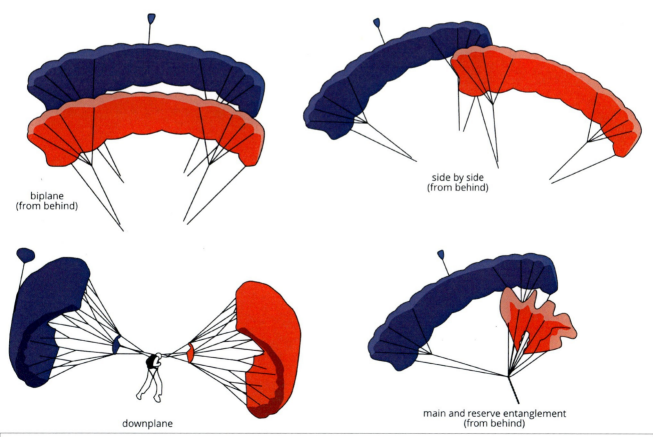

Two-Parachutes-Out Scenarios

Integrated Student Program | Category A (Arch)

## Canopy Flight

After making sure you have a good canopy, check your altitude, then observe your position over the ground. Following your canopy inspection, you must locate the airport and the planned **holding area**. Once you have identified the holding area, fly directly to it. Arriving at the holding area at or above 2,000 feet will set you up to be in the right place to enter your landing pattern.

While you are in canopy flight, regularly check your **altitude** and **position** over the ground while working toward your pattern-entry point and watch for other canopy **traffic (APT)**.

All jumpers must also avoid **canopy collisions** (i.e., collisions with other jumpers under open parachutes). If a collision is imminent, in most cases both jumpers should **steer to the right**. If two jumpers collide and entangle, they must communicate their intentions before taking further action. If it is too low for a safe cutaway (below 1,000 feet) and the canopies are uncontrollable, both jumpers should deploy their reserves.

## Landing

### Landing Pattern

Your landing pattern is a deliberate flight path, usually rectangular, that you use during the final phase of descent under canopy. It usually starts at 900 feet at a predetermined pattern-entry point. There are three legs to the pattern: downwind, base, and final. Before each jump, your instructor will determine your landing pattern and review it with you using an aerial map of your drop zone. It's important to plan your flight, then fly your plan.

The pattern consists of checkpoints at the start of each leg. Each checkpoint consists of an altitude and a landmark. Your **downwind** leg starts at 900 feet above the ground, **base** leg at 600 feet, and **final approach** at 300 feet. For each leg you must turn at your altitude or landmark, whichever comes first.

> Note: Your instructor may adjust the shape of the pattern, the altitudes, or the landmarks to account for various conditions or your drop zone's policies.

**DOWNWIND, BASE, AND FINAL:** are the three legs of your landing pattern.

**CROSSWIND LEG:** and "base leg" are interchangeable terms.

**HOLDING AREA:** is a predetermined, general location upwind of your landing area and near your pattern-entry point. You aim to stay in the holding area above 1,000 feet to stage your entry into the pattern and ensure you can land in the landing area.

**PATTERN-ENTRY POINT:** is the altitude and landmark where you start your landing pattern, generally at 1,000 feet and upwind of the target.

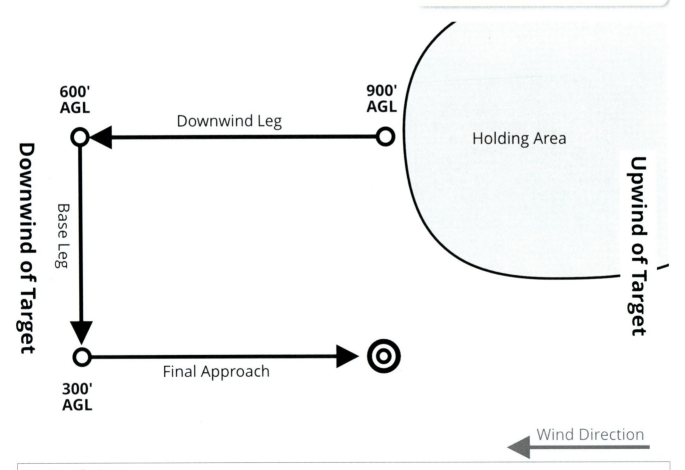

Example Landing Pattern

Integrated Student Program | Category A (Arch)

## Final Approach and Landing
### Landing Priorities

| **1** Land with a level wing | ➡ | **2** Land in a clear and open area | ➡ | **3** Flare and PLF |

On final, your main priority is to land with a **level wing**, while flying straight toward a **clear and open area**, **flaring** before touching down and performing a **PLF**. You may use minimal toggle inputs to avoid obstacles on the ground and give yourself a longer, obstacle-free runway for landing, but you must keep your wing level. If the canopy begins to drift right or left, use the appropriate input to stop the drift and keep the canopy flying straight toward a clear area. The best way to avoid obstacles is to look toward a clear area and guide the canopy there rather than focusing on an obstacle. Landing into the wind is desirable but is not one of your landing priorities.

To slow your forward speed and descent rate, you will **flare** when your feet are above the ground at approximately twice your height. Prepare to land during the last part of the final approach by putting your feet and knees together in a parachute landing fall (PLF) position. Except for small corrections, keep your toggles all the way up in the full-glide position when on final approach. This will help the canopy produce more lift when you flare. Judge the flare height by looking forward and down at a 45-degree angle.

> Note: Your instructor may vary the exact flare technique based on the type of canopy you will be using or other factors.

Think of flaring as driving down a one-way street. You can stop at any point but cannot go back. If you start the flare too high, stop flaring and hold the toggles where they are. Letting the toggles up abruptly causes a steep dive toward the ground, known as a "flight cycle." (You will learn more about flight cycles in Category B.) Quickly assess your height above the ground. Keep looking ahead and keep the canopy flying straight. When you are closer to the ground, push the toggles forcefully the rest of the way down to finish the flare before touching the ground.

**PLF:** stands for "parachute landing fall" and is a technique used to prevent injury on landing.

You should be prepared to **PLF** every time you land. You should only attempt a stand-up landing if you touch down softly and are confident that you can comfortably remain on your feet.

### Parachute Landing Fall (PLF)

Performing a PLF can help you reduce the risk of injury during landing by distributing the impact across five points of your body. To prepare for a PLF, press your feet and knees together with your knees slightly bent. Flare completely with both hands together and close to the front of your body to help prevent wrist and hand injuries. Keep your chin to your chest to help prevent neck injuries. Allow your feet to contact the ground first. Maintain the PLF position throughout the entire landing roll.

As the balls of your **feet** touch the ground:

1. Lean into the direction of the landing to roll down one side of the body
2. Lay over to the side of one **calf**
3. Continue to roll to the **thigh** on the same side
4. Continue rolling through the small of your **back** to the opposite **shoulder**

Allow your body to continue rolling and absorb the energy of the fall

The **PLF position** is also the proper way to prepare for a stand-up landing as it keeps your weight balanced in the harness and your hands even when the toggles are all the way down in the flare. If you touch down softly, you can step out of the PLF position and remain on your feet.

## Landing Problems

**Alternate Landing Areas:** You should be prepared to make correct decisions and land safely without assistance, whether you land in the intended landing area or an alternate one. If you are not in your holding area or close to it when the canopy opens, be prepared to **choose an alternate landing area by 2,000 feet.** Maintain altitude awareness while flying back toward your 900-foot pattern-entry point.

At or above 2,000 feet, you should determine whether you will be able to reach your 900-foot pattern-entry point. If it is obvious that the 900-foot point is unreachable, look for your 600-foot and 300-foot points. If you are sure that you will be able to reach one of those points, fly toward it and remain over that point until you reach the correct altitude to begin that leg of your pattern. If it is obvious that you will not reach any point in your pattern by the correct altitude, then plan to land in an open area that is free of obstacles. Keep in mind that your best alternate landing area may be behind you. Choose your new holding area and visually transfer the intended landing pattern to the new landing area.

**Landing Off Field:** Any time you must land in an alternate area, on or off the airport property, look carefully for obstacles. You can look closely during the downwind leg of the pattern because you are closer to the ground. Avoid the obstacles by looking and steering the canopy toward a **clear and open area**, avoiding straight lines in the terrain that may indicate power lines, fences, or ditches. PLF and wait for assistance or further instructions. Be polite to property owners. If possible, contact the drop zone to give them your status and location.

**LOOK AWAY - STEER AWAY:** Skydiving is just as much a mental sport as it is physical. There is a natural tendency to steer or move in the direction in which you are looking. "You go where your eyes go." Capitalize on this.

**Recovering the Canopy in Higher Winds:** When you are on the ground, pull in one toggle and steering line to assist in collapsing the canopy, especially if it is dragging you. Cut away the canopy as a last resort or if you're injured.

## Obstacle Landing

Potential obstacles during landing include water, trees, buildings, power lines, fences, and similar hazards. You can usually avoid these obstacles by preparing for the canopy flight by observing the winds and planning an appropriate landing pattern. Also, choosing an alternate landing area by 2,000 feet allows you to assess potential obstacles and plan your new pattern. Follow your **Landing Priorities**. You can find comprehensive best practices for obstacle landings in Chapter 4-1 G. Below are critical points listing actions you can take when landing in or on common obstacles.

- **Water:** Flare and PLF in case the water is shallow. After entering the water, try to stand up. If you cannot touch the bottom, swim out of your gear and leave it behind.
- **Trees:** Keep your arms close to your body and your legs together. Use a half flare as you enter the tree. Be prepared to finish your flare and PLF in case you drop all the way to the ground. If you remain suspended, hold on and stay in the tree. Wait for help; do not attempt to climb down.
- **Buildings:** If landing on a roof, flare and PLF. Once you've landed, disconnect the RSL and cut away. If landing under your reserve, contain it if it's windy. Wait for help; do not attempt to climb down. If hitting a building broadside, turn the canopy slightly to avoid a direct impact before flaring. Prepare to PLF, flare to slow down, and attempt to strike a glancing blow.
- **Power Lines:** Drop any handles. Flare and PLF. Touch no more than one wire at a time. Your parachute can conduct electricity, so if you are suspended in the wires, do not cut away and do not let anyone near you. Wait for qualified personnel to confirm the power is off. If your feet are on the ground, disconnect the RSL and cut away, leaving your main canopy behind.

Integrated Student Program | Category A (Arch)

## Category A Dive Flows

RED indicates Advancement Criteria
✔ indicates new skills

### AFF AND TANDEM

- **SAFE EXIT** ✔
- COA ✔
- PRACTICE DEPLOY (3x) ✔
- COA
- **6,000' LOCK ON** ✔ (6,500' for tandem)
- **5,500' WAVE OFF and PULL** ✔ (6,000' for tandem)
- CANOPY CHECK - APT ✔
- LOCATE HOLDING AREA ✔
- **FLY PATTERN** ✔
- **FLARE and PLF** if needed ✔

### IAD AND STATIC LINE (2 jumps from 4,000')

- **SAFE EXIT** ✔
- COUNT 1 – 2 – 3 – 4 – 5 ✔
- CANOPY CHECK - APT ✔
- LOCATE HOLDING AREA ✔
- **FLY PATTERN** ✔
- **FLARE and PLF** if needed ✔

**TAKE THE QUIZ:**

uspa.org/quiz/a

### ⟪⟪⟪ ACTION STEP ⟫⟫⟫

**Join USPA (uspa.org/register), login, and get credit automatically for all the quizzes you take online!**

Integrated Student Program | Category B (Basics)

# Category B (Basics)

| AFF<br>1 jump | TANDEM<br>1 jump | IAD-STATIC LINE<br>3 jumps |
|---|---|---|

**DEPLOYMENT-INITIATION ALTITUDES**
AFF: **5,500** feet
IAD and static line: **4,000** feet
Tandem: **6,000** feet

In Category **B**, you must practice the most **B**asic maneuver in freefall: pulling!

## Category at a Glance

## Advancement Criteria

### Canopy Pre-Jump
☐ Discuss ground winds and winds aloft for the day
☐ Plan your flight to the holding area and the pattern with assistance
☐ Discuss runways and aircraft patterns
☐ Practice clearing your airspace before turns and check for traffic in the holding area and in the pattern
☐ Discuss the flight cycle and how flaring is like a one-way street
☐ Practice a PLF

### Academics
☐ Read the Academics section for this category
☐ Pass the category quiz at 100%
☐ Train for exit and freefall
☐ Practice correct responses to deployment problems
☐ Consider joining USPA if you haven't already

### Canopy Debrief
☐ Fly your pattern with assistance
☐ Perform a staged flare with a full finish
☐ Prepare to PLF before landing and perform a PLF if needed
☐ Land within 60 degrees of your intended heading with assistance
☐ Land within 330 feet (100 meters) of your intended target with assistance

### Freefall Debrief
☐ Be stable throughout
☐ Demonstrate leg control
☐ Assist with the pull within 500 feet of your assigned altitude (AFF and Tandem)
☐ Successfully perform three practice pulls, three jumps in a row (SL and IAD)

Integrated Student Program | Category B (Basics)

## Academics

The Academics section of each category includes information on exit and freefall, canopy flight, emergency procedures, equipment, and standard operating procedures. Some of this information will review what you learned earlier, while some will be new and build on that foundation.

### A. Exit and Freefall

Review the exit procedures from Category A. For AFF students, your exit will be the same. IAD and static-line students perform the climb-out with little or no assistance from the instructor and exit promptly on the "Go!" command. Tandem students climb into position after the instructor's OK, check with the instructor once in position, and initiate the exit count.

During this category, you will improve your overall awareness and stability, reinforce muscle memory for your pull, and work on leg awareness and heading.

**LOCK ON:** is where you focus on your altimeter before pulling.

**WAVE OFF:** is where you signal with both hands that you are intending to pull. Your actual deployment usually occurs approximately 500 feet after waving off, given the time it takes to wave off, reach, and pull.

#### Heading, Altitude, Arch, Legs, Relax (HAALR)

Repeat this drill to establish and maintain awareness, stability, and control. First, recognize your **heading** to confirm you are not turning. Know your **altitude.**

> **IAD and static-line students:** Know your exit altitude and count to keep track of time after release from the aircraft.
>
> **Tandem and AFF students:** Make sure you check your altimeter. Check your **arch**, making sure your hips are forward a little. Check your **legs**; most beginners need to extend their legs a little and point their toes. **Relax** ... how? Breathe consciously, a full breath in and out, to release tension. Use this **HAALR** technique just before and after releasing from the aircraft.

#### Main Deployment

> **Tandem and AFF students:** Perform practice deployments in freefall until you can perform them smoothly and are comfortable with locating the deployment handle. At your assigned pull altitude, wave off to signal deployment, then pull at the correct altitude without prompting from the instructor.
>
> **IAD and static-line students:** Practice stable deployment within 5 seconds of exit. You must complete three jumps in a row with successful simulated deployments before moving to the solo freefall starting in Category C.

#### Leg Awareness

You can practice and improve your leg awareness by learning how to move forward in freefall. To move forward, extend your legs with your toes pointed while keeping your arms in a neutral position. Extending your legs from the neutral position adds more drag in the back, lifting your lower body to the relative wind. This off-level attitude causes you to move forward. It is less noticeable on a tandem jump. To practice in freefall, extend your legs smoothly and hold for three seconds, then relax your legs to neutral.

> **IAD and static-line students:** Increase your leg awareness during the exit set-up and after release from the plane. You can accomplish this with a little mental preparation on exit.

#### Maintaining a Heading

Staying stationary is key to having control. Relax in a neutral body position and find a point ahead on the horizon as a heading reference.

> **Tandem and AFF students:** Your instructor may have you perform turns together.
>
> **IAD and static-line students:** You must perform three successful practice deployments before moving on to a clear-and-pull jump, also called a "hop-and-pop," where you clear the aircraft then pull for yourself.

### B. Canopy

#### For Review

In your first-jump course you learned to prevent canopy collisions by always clearing your airspace both before and during any turn. Simply look in the direction of the turn both horizontally and below before you make the turn.

Review the wind direction and speed with your instructor. You'll develop your **descent strategy**, that is, determine the expected opening point and prepare your canopy flight plan. After opening and performing your canopy check, check your altitude, determine your position relative to the drop zone, and then monitor canopy traffic. Locate the holding area and establish your path to your 900-foot pattern-entry point. Fly directly to your holding area. Fly to the pattern-entry point and fly the planned pattern using downwind, base, and final-approach legs with checkpoints. Flare and PLF.

Integrated Student Program | Category B (Basics)

More about **canopy traffic in the pattern**: It is important to fly predictably so that canopies behind you in the pattern can determine your flight path and remain sufficiently separated from you. You do this by flying your pattern, staying in your lane and flying a straight final approach.

## New Stuff
### Flight Cycle

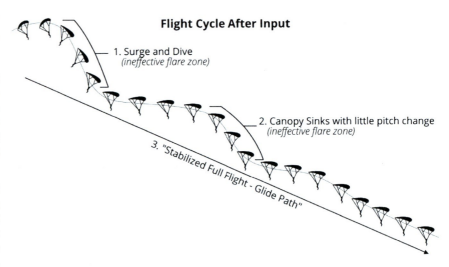

A flight cycle is the parachute's response during the period of time between an input and the parachute's return to stabilized full flight. It is important to understand how a flight cycle is created so that you can avoid entering one close to the ground just before landing. Flaring is a **one-way street**, meaning you can stop pulling down the toggles at any point during the flare stroke if you started it too high, but you cannot go back up.

Any input to a canopy, such as turning or pulling down the toggles and letting them back up, initiates a flight cycle. The flight cycle is a normal and predictable flight characteristic of all parachutes. When a flight cycle occurs, the parachute dives, its speed increases beyond that of full flight, and the jumper swings back behind the parachute. The parachute then slows down as the jumper swings forward under the parachute and it returns to full flight.

Experiencing a flight cycle up high can be fun. However, a flight cycle just before or during a flare is dangerous because the parachute dives forward and picks up speed, and the effectiveness of the flare is greatly reduced. This is why the proper response to a flare initiated too high is to stop and hold whenever you realize it is too high, then finish the flare forcefully when closer to the ground.

## C. Emergency Procedure Review

Review the correct responses to a **premature deployment in the aircraft**: Attempt to contain the open parachute and inform the instructor. If your parachute goes out the door, follow immediately to prevent damage to the plane and injury to yourself or others. If anyone else's parachute goes out the door, immediately push them to and through the door for the same reason.

### Review Pull Priorities:

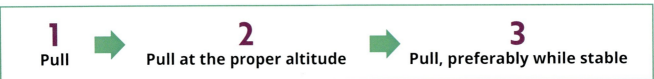

Review deployment problems and correct responses.

**IAD and static-line students:** this may be new to you.

Make no more than two attempts or take no longer than 5 seconds, whichever comes first, before initiating emergency procedures.

- **Premature container opening in freefall:** Attempt to locate and deploy the pilot chute first. If you can't locate the pilot chute after two tries or 5 seconds, or if deploying the pilot chute results in a partial malfunction, cut away and deploy the reserve.
- **Lost deployment handle:** Place your hand on the side of the container and slide it down to the bottom corner. Find the pilot chute and deploy. If you cannot find the pilot chute after two tries or 5 seconds, initiate emergency procedures.
- **Hard pull:** Place your elbow against the container for leverage. If you cannot throw the pilot chute after two tries or 5 seconds, initiate emergency procedures.
- **Pilot-chute hesitation:** Modify the airflow by twisting slightly while looking over your right shoulder. If that doesn't work, repeat over your left shoulder. If the pilot chute does not launch after two tries or 5 seconds, initiate emergency procedures.

**Static-line students:** Your instructor will review the **student-in-tow** procedures, which are: Arch and signal to your instructor that you are ready for them to cut your static line. After the static line is cut, deploy your reserve.

Remember these critical altitudes: You must **decide to cut away by 2,500 feet and then act immediately.** Also, if you find yourself below 1,000 feet without a functioning canopy, deploy the reserve without cutting away.

Integrated Student Program | Category B (Basics)

With your instructor, practice in the training harness to recognize and respond to **problems and malfunctions** using guidance from Category A—Academics in the first-jump-course topics.

Expanding on what you learned in Category A, if you have line twists and are also spinning, **don't delay, cut away.** Spinning main parachute malfunctions can cause you to lose altitude very quickly and require a rapid response You will also be unable to control the canopy due to it having line twists. For this reason, check your altitude to confirm you are **above the 1,000-foot cutaway hard deck** and initiate emergency procedures immediately.

## D. Equipment
### For Review
Review how to retrieve your parachute after landing.

## E. Standard Operating Procedures
### For Review
Minimal and careful movement in the aircraft helps protect your gear from a premature container opening.

### New Stuff

> **Tandem students:** your progression in the tandem method ends with Category B, and you will transition to a different method by attending a solo-equipment first-jump course in order to continue on to Category C.

**S&TA:** stands for Safety and Training Advisor, an appointed USPA position usually held by a highly experienced instructor. The S&TA at your drop zone represents your USPA Regional Director and is available to provide advice and administrative assistance to USPA members.

Student **wind limits** are 14 mph, waiverable by your S&TA, according to the BSRs (Chapter 2-1.H).

The minimum required **deployment altitude** for students and USPA A-License holders is 3,000 feet (Chapter 2-1.I).

At airports, normal flight practices **separate aircraft traffic from parachute traffic**, but you need to respect runways and aircraft landing patterns. Your instructor will explain your drop zone's policies about avoiding runways while flying your canopy and after you've landed.

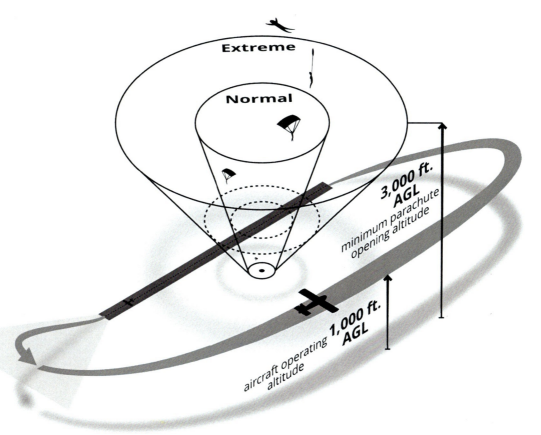

Aircraft and Parachute Traffic

## Category B Dive Flows

RED indicates Advancement Criteria
✔ indicates new skills

### AFF AND TANDEM

- **RELAXED EXIT**
- COA
- PRACTICE DEPLOY
- HAALR
- **EXTEND LEGS** ✔ (3 seconds)
- HAALR
- TEAM TURNS ✔ (if trained)
- **6,000'** LOCK ON (6,500' for tandem)
- **5,500'** WAVE OFF and PULL (6,000' for tandem)
- CANOPY CHECK - APT
- LOCATE HOLDING AREA
- **FLY PATTERN**
- **FLARE and PLF** if needed

### IAD AND STATIC LINE (3 jumps from 4,000')

- EXIT **WITH LEGS EXTENDED** ✔
- **PRACTICE DEPLOY** ✔ (with count)
  "Arch, Reach, Pull, Neutral, Check"
- CANOPY CHECK - APT
- LOCATE HOLDING AREA
- **FLY PATTERN**
- **FLARE and PLF if needed**

**TAKE THE QUIZ:**

uspa.org/quiz/b

Integrated Student Program | Category C (Control)

# Category C (Control)

| AFF | IAD-STATIC LINE | DEPLOYMENT-INITIATION ALTITUDE |
|---|---|---|
| **2 jumps** | **3 jumps** | **5,500** feet |

In Category **C**, you finally gain **C**ontrol over your skydive by pulling stable, solo, and unassisted!

## Category at a Glance

## Advancement Criteria
### Canopy Pre-Jump
☐ Discuss ground winds and winds aloft for the day
☐ Plan your flight to the holding area and the landing pattern
☐ Discuss adjusting landing pattern for wind changes
☐ Discuss wing loading and downwind landings
☐ Discuss turbulence and flight cycle
☐ Review off-field landings, including choosing an alternate area by 2,000 feet and obstacle avoidance

### Academics
☐ Read the Academics section for this category
☐ Pass the category quiz at 100%
☐ Train for exit and freefall
☐ Review what to do for an open parachute in the aircraft
☐ Observe equipment pre-flight check and AAD operation

### Canopy Debrief
☐ Perform a flight-cycle drill
☐ Fly your pattern with minimal assistance
☐ Perform a staged flare with a full finish with minimal assistance
☐ Prepare for a PLF and PLF if needed

### Freefall Debrief
☐ Establish control within 5 seconds of exit
☐ Perform a relaxed fall
☐ Show heading awareness
☐ Wave off before pulling
☐ Pull at the assigned altitude with stability
☐ Be cleared to freefall with one AFF Instructor (AFF only)

## Academics

## A. Exit and Freefall
### For Review
Review the **climb-out and exit** procedures. Improving your setup, launch, and flyaway on each jump will prepare you for a solo exit in Category D.

Review the stability recovery and maintenance procedure: **heading, altitude, arch, legs, relax (HAALR).** First recognize your **heading** to confirm you are not turning. Know your **altitude** by reading the altimeter (AFF and tandem) or counting from exit (IAD and static line). **Arch** at the hips to improve belly-to-wind stability. Check your **leg** position—extended to 45 degrees with toes pointed—and adjust as needed. **Relax** by taking a breath in and out, letting go of unwanted body tension.

> **IAD and static-line students:** HAALR might be new to you, as this applies only after you've made a successful clear and pull.

## Integrated Student Program | Category C (Control)

### New Stuff

**AFF students:** If you now have only one AFF instructor, the instructor will revise the climb-out procedure for your exit. With one instructor, you may prepare for slightly different results after the launch, as it typically flies vertically a little longer than it would with two instructors.

**AIR:** The freefall rule for Category A and B *was*: if your AFF instructors are not with you, you must pull immediately. This rule changes for Category C and forward. Now that you have demonstrated awareness and stability, your instructors may release you during the freefall. *The new rule is:* if you are **A**ltitude aware, **I**n control, and **R**elaxed (**AIR**), you may continue in freefall and deploy at the assigned altitude. However, if you are not **A**ltitude aware, **I**n control, and **R**elaxed (**AIR**), you have only 5 seconds to fix it. If unsuccessful after **5 seconds,** deploy your main canopy immediately.

**Roll out of Bed:** Check altitude (left). Arch, and start rollover (center). Neutral body position; check altitude (right).

If you are above your assigned deployment altitude and oriented back-to-earth, roll to one side to recover to a stable, belly-to-earth body position. To do so, first check your altitude, relax, arch, and hold it. Look toward the ground either to the right or left and bring the arm on that side across your chest. As your body rolls that direction and you face the ground, go back to the neutral body position. Check altitude. This is commonly called the **roll-out-of-bed** technique. If you are unsuccessful after **5 seconds**, deploy your main canopy immediately, even if you are on your back, spinning, or tumbling.

**IAD and static-line students:** After your first successful clear-and-pull jump, you will experience more freefall time by performing two stable 10-second delays. The transition of the relative wind from opposite the aircraft heading to below will be a new experience. Use HAALR to control stability. Add a **wave-off** prior to deployment, which is a signal to other jumpers that you are getting ready to pull.

## B. Canopy

### New Stuff

#### Wing Loading and Canopy Size

The wing-loading ratio is the jumper's exit weight (geared up) divided by the square footage of the canopy. Canopy manufacturers publish wing-loading recommendations for each model of canopy in their owner's manuals and often on their websites. Take the time now to calculate your wing loading for the canopy you are about to jump next.

**Wing loading** affects the performance and speed of your canopy. **With higher wing loadings**, expect faster forward speeds and descent rates, quicker turns, steeper and longer dives from turns, and more violent malfunctions. Canopies at higher wing loadings require more skill to flare correctly. **With lighter wing loadings**, expect less drive against a strong wind, slower turns, and more forgiveness of landing errors.

| WING LOADING EXAMPLES | | |
|---|---|---|
| Jumper's exit weight | 215 | 215 |
| Divided by canopy size (sq ft) | 280 | 195 |
| Wing loading | .77:1 | 1.1:1 |

Integrated Student Program | Category C (Control)

## Turbulence on Landing

Turbulence is disturbed air that can affect canopy flight and integrity. Due to obstacles and wind direction, turbulence sometimes occurs in the landing area. Understanding and predicting turbulence will allow you to make safe landing choices. Managing unexpected turbulence on landing is an important skill, but avoiding a landing in turbulence is the best plan for safe landings.

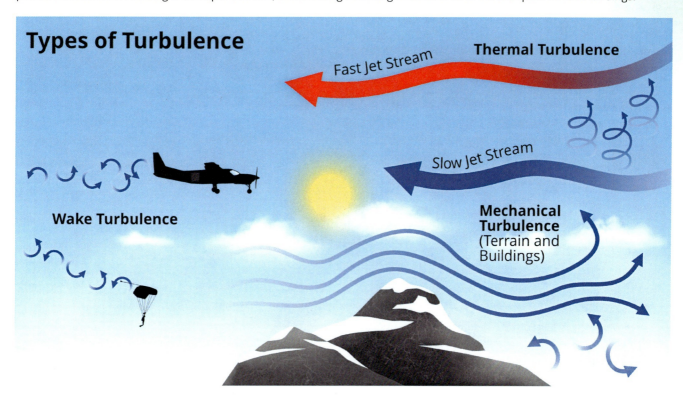

## Types of Turbulence

Anticipate turbulence 10-20 times the height of an obstacle on its downwind side. The effects and likelihood of turbulence increase with the surface-wind speed.

Other types of turbulence often occur near runways, alongside roads, behind other canopies, over irregular terrain, and anywhere the color of the ground changes. You can even find it downwind of the propeller wash of a aircraft.

When flying in turbulence at any altitude, maintain the desired heading using smooth but effective toggle input. Fly in full flight unless the canopy's owner's manual directs otherwise. If there is turbulence near the ground, prepare to respond quickly with a forceful flare and a PLF.

**Turbulence can create a flight cycle.** Category B introduced the concept of the flight cycle to reinforce that flaring a parachute is a one-way street, meaning you can always stop pulling down the toggles at any point during the flare stroke, but cannot go back up. A flight cycle is the parachute's response during the period of time between any input and the parachute's return to stabilized full flight.

**Mechanical Turbulence:** Anticipate turbulence 10 to 20 times the height of an obstacle on its downwind side.

Turbulent or gusty winds on landing can also initiate a flight cycle, causing your parachute to dive toward the ground. If this happens just before the flare, the effectiveness of the flare diminishes. Because the flight cycle will cause you to swing back from underneath the parachute as it dives and picks up speed, you must flare forcefully to get back under the parachute and in a position for landing. To help you recognize a flight cycle and respond effectively, you will perform a flight-cycle drill in this category and practice a forceful flare when in a flight cycle.

**Integrated Student Program | Category C (Control)**

## Comparing High-Wind to Low-Wind Landing Patterns

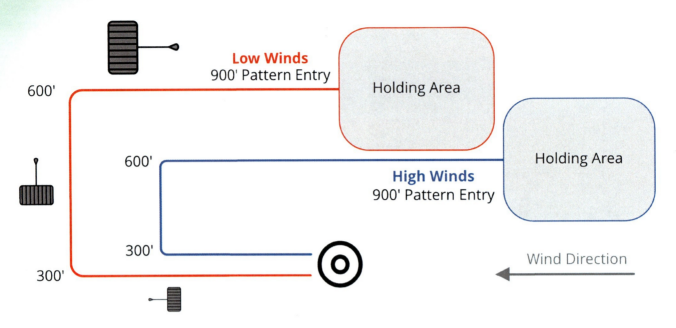

The location of each point and the shape of your landing pattern will vary based on the strength of the wind.

In lighter winds, your pattern will resemble a square, with the downwind leg, base leg, and final-approach leg being of similar length. Make sure you have plenty of clear space past the target in case you overshoot.

In stronger winds, the final-approach and base legs become shorter, and the downwind leg becomes longer. Turn over a clear area during your base leg and final approach in case you land short of the target.

*Note: Your USPA Instructor may adjust the shape of the pattern or the checkpoint altitudes or landmarks to account for various conditions.*

## Improving your Landing

**Downwind landings are better than low turns.** On calm days, unexpected wind shifts sometimes require you to land with the wind, instead of against it. Sometimes, jumpers become confused about the pattern and don't realize they are set up for a downwind landing until they're on final approach. When faced with deciding between a low turn or a downwind landing, apply your landing priorities and choose to land downwind. When making a downwind landing, flare at the normal altitude, regardless of ground speed, and PLF.

Flaring for landing can take a few seconds, so dissecting the parts of the flare can increase your awareness and improve your flare for better landings. During the flare, you are converting forward speed to lift. Flare the canopy quickly to the first stage to slow down and swing under your canopy, flattening the glide. Continue the flare to keep the flat glide. Continue flaring smoothly and completely until landing.

**TWO TYPES OF FLARES:** A staged flare uses **multiple stages**; a continuous flare uses a single continuous motion.

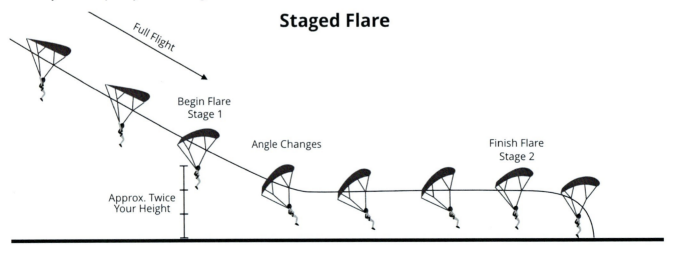

Integrated Student Program | Category C (Control)

## C. Emergency Procedure Review

**IAD and static-line students:** review procedures for deployment handle problems, premature container opening in freefall (hand deployment), and pilot-chute hesitations before making any jump in Category C.

### For Review

To prevent an **open parachute in the aircraft**, take care when you're leaning back against anything. Move carefully when you're near or outside the door. If a parachute opens in the plane and the door is closed, secure the parachute, notify your instructor and land with the plane. If the door is open, contain the parachute, close the door, and land with the plane. If the parachute goes out the door, follow immediately to prevent endangering yourself and others. A pre-jump gear check shortly before leaving the aircraft is essential to prevent these occurrences.

### Review Pull Priorities:

1. Pull
2. Pull at the proper altitude
3. Pull, preferably while stable

If you see your instructor pull, you should pull.

If **landing off the DZ** is unavoidable, look for an open, clear, accessible field as early as possible. Decide on an alternate landing area by 2,000 feet. Be aware that power lines often run along roads and between buildings, as well as randomly in open fields. A row of vegetation often hides a fence. Rocks, hills, and other terrain irregularities often remain invisible until just prior to touchdown. Inspect an unfamiliar landing area more closely at every 500-foot interval during descent and continuously below 500 feet. Fly a predictable landing pattern and attempt to land clear of turbulence and obstacles. Prepare for a PLF.

Be polite to property owners. Cross only at gates or reinforced areas and leave all gates as they were found. Do not disturb cattle. Walk parallel to and between any rows of crops until reaching the end of the field. Repair or replace any damaged property. If possible, contact the drop zone to give them your status and location.

Some skydiving schools are subject to state and local rules or restrictions concerning landing off. Your instructor will explain anything that pertains to you and your drop zone.

### Review Landing Priorities

1. Land with a level wing
2. Land in a clear and open area
3. Flare and PLF

After **landing in high winds**, pull in one toggle and steering line to assist in collapsing the canopy, especially if the canopy is dragging you. Cut away the canopy as a last resort or if you're injured.

### New Stuff

**IAD and static-line students:** Previously, in Categories A and B, if you needed to exit the plane in an aircraft emergency, you used your reserve. The new rule for Category C and forward is: if you are **above 3,000 feet, you can use your main** canopy if exiting the plane **in an aircraft emergency.**

## D. Equipment

### New Stuff

The automatic activation device—which you wear only as a backup—initiates reserve deployment when certain parameters are met. *Detailed AAD operation is explained in Category D.*

Observe the instructor performing the **pre-flight check**, that is, the equipment check that happens before you put your gear on.

**Back: top to bottom—**

- ☐ reserve pin in place and straight
- ☐ reserve closing loop must have no visible wear
- ☐ reserve ripcord cable movement in housing
- ☐ reserve packing data card and seal
- ☐ AAD on
- ☐ main activation cable or pin in place, free of nicks or kinks

- ☐ main closing loop not worn, near perfect
- ☐ pilot-chute-bridle routing or ripcord-cable movement
- ☐ main activation handle in place

Front: top to bottom—

- ☐ three-ring release system
- ☐ RSL connection and routing
- ☐ chest strap and hardware intact
- ☐ cutaway handle in position
- ☐ reserve handle in position
- ☐ leg straps and hardware operational and correctly threaded

## E. Standard Operating Procedures

As a student, you have certain mandatory **gear requirements** (BSR, Chapter 2-1.M.2-5 ).

The Federal Aviation Administration regulates the training and certification of **the FAA rigger** (FAR 65).

Your reserve parachute must have been packed by a certificated FAA rigger within the last **180 days**. Your main parachute must have been packed within the last 180 days, as well, and can be packed by a rigger, someone under the supervision of a rigger, or the person jumping it (FAR 105.43).

## Category C Dive Flows

RED indicates Advancement Criteria
✔ indicates new skills

### AFF
(2 jumps, first with two instructors, second with one instructor)

- RELAXED EXIT
- COA
- PRACTICE DEPLOY
- COA
- RELEASE ✔
- HAALR
- 6,000' LOCK ON
- 5,500' WAVE OFF and PULL
- CANOPY CHECK - APT
- LOCATE HOLDING AREA
- FLIGHT-CYCLE DRILL ✔
- FLY PATTERN
- FLARE and PLF if needed

### IAD AND STATIC LINE (1 jump from 4,500')

#### #1 CLEAR & PULL (1 jump from 4,500')

- EXIT WITH LEGS EXTENDED
- PULL ✔ (with count) "Arch, Reach, Pull, Neutral, Check"
- CANOPY CHECK - APT
- LOCATE HOLDING AREA
- FLY PATTERN
- FLARE and PLF if needed

#### #2 10-SECOND FREEFALL (2 jumps from 5,500')

- EXIT WITH LEGS EXTENDED
- RELAX INTO NEUTRAL
- COUNT TO 10
- 4,500' WAVE OFF (at 7 seconds)
- 4,000' PULL
- CANOPY CHECK - APT
- LOCATE HOLDING AREA
- FLIGHT-CYCLE DRILL ✔
- FLY PATTERN
- FLARE and PLF if needed

Integrated Student Program | Category C (Control)

## CANOPY DRILL: Experience a Flight Cycle

- Release brakes and address any routine opening problems.
- Look left, turn left.
- Look right, turn right.
- Flare.
- Check altitude, position, and traffic.
- Find the holding area, landing area and pattern-entry point.
- Fly directly to the holding area.
- Check altitude, position and traffic.
- Smoothly and evenly pull toggles to ¾ brakes (hip bones) and hold for 5 seconds.
- Quickly but smoothly raise the toggles back to full flight to induce the flight cycle.
- Take note of the canopy surge and dive as it picks up speed.
- Expect 5-7 seconds to pass for the canopy to recover to full flight.
- Repeat, if altitude permits, this time with a forceful flare to get back under the parachute for landing (to practice your response to turbulence close to the ground).
- Check altitude, position, and traffic.
- Stay in the holding area until starting the pattern at 900 feet.
- Fly the planned pattern following the landing priorities on final.
- Flare to land and PLF.

**TAKE THE QUIZ:**

uspa.org/quiz/c

Integrated Student Program | Category D (Direction)

# Category D (Direction)

| AFF | IAD-STATIC LINE | DEPLOYMENT-INITIATION ALTITUDE |
|---|---|---|
| **2 jumps** | **3 jumps** | **5,000** feet |

In Category **D**, you must perform turns in both **D**irections, right and left, in varying degrees!

## Category at a Glance

## Advancement Criteria

### Canopy Pre-Jump
☐ Provide the ground winds and winds aloft information for the day
☐ Discuss spotting, wind drift, and opening point
☐ Discuss cloud clearance and visibility requirements
☐ Plan your flight to the holding area and the pattern
☐ Discuss landing accuracy and choosing the landing target
☐ Discuss observing jump run
☐ Review EPs for landing on a building
☐ Train for rear-riser turns for canopy-flight EPs

### Academics
☐ Read the Academics section for this category
☐ Pass the category quiz at 100%
☐ Train for exit and freefall
☐ Review canopy-opening EPs in a training harness
☐ Conduct four gear checks with supervision

### Canopy Debrief
☐ Perform a 90-degree rear riser turn with brakes set (1st)
☐ Perform a 90-degree rear riser turn with brakes set (2nd)
☐ Perform a 90-degree rear riser turn with brakes released (1st)
☐ Perform a 90-degree rear riser turn with brakes released (2nd)
☐ Fly a proper pattern and land within 165 feet (50 meters) of your planned target with assistance

### Freefall Debrief
☐ Perform a solo exit and get stable within 5 seconds
☐ Perform a 90-degree left turn with a 20-degree heading tolerance (1st)
☐ Perform a 90-degree right turn with a 20-degree heading tolerance (1st)
☐ Perform a 90-degree left turn with a 20-degree heading tolerance (2nd)
☐ Perform a 90-degree right turn with a 20-degree heading tolerance (2nd)
☐ Perform a 180-degree left turn with a 45-degree heading tolerance
☐ Perform a 180-degree right turn with a 45-degree heading tolerance
☐ Perform a 360-degree left turn with a 45-degree heading tolerance
☐ Perform a 360-degree right turn with a 45-degree heading tolerance

Integrated Student Program | Category D (Direction)

## Academics

### A. Exit and Freefall

#### Solo Exit
In this category, you will perform a solo exit, achieving stability within 5 seconds. Remember tools to maintain control and stability, including HAALR and AIR.

#### Freefall Turns
To turn in freefall, first establish a comfortable, relaxed, neutral body position. Find a point ahead on the horizon as a primary **heading** reference. Use the **start-coast-stop (SCS)** technique to control your turn. Turns should begin from a neutral body position. Maintain symmetry in your arms and legs, a straight spine, and level shoulders. Breathe, relax, and initiate the turn:

**Start** by pressing one elbow down from the shoulder joint only. Press your arm down no more than 45 degrees. Maintain a neutral leg position during the turn.

**Coast** in the turn by returning to neutral before your desired heading comes into view. Your momentum will continue to turn you while you are neutral, much like your car continues to go forward after taking your foot off the accelerator. During the coast, assess your speed and the distance to your desired heading to determine when you should begin your stop movement.

**Stop** by countering the turn in the opposite direction, then return to a neutral body position.

If you go past your intended heading or encounter other difficulties, use HAALR and pick a new heading before starting another turn. Stop all maneuvers by 6,000 feet.

**SCS:** stands for start-coast-stop, and is a technique used in a variety of maneuvers where you start by moving a particular body part, coast by returning to neutral, and stop with the opposite motion.

**CANOPY-FLIGHT EMERGENCY:** is an emergency that happens while under a fully inflated canopy, anytime during the canopy descent or landing.

**CANOPY-FLIGHT EMERGENCY PROCEDURES (CEPs):** is a set of five skills you can use to respond to canopy-flight emergencies.

**STAY ALIVE – PRACTICE FIVE!**

### B. Canopy

#### Rear-Riser Steering
Learning to use your rear risers gives you more options to control your canopy. The rear risers operate the back half of your canopy, and steering with them with your brakes still stowed is the fastest way to change heading right after opening. Rear-riser steering is the first of several **Canopy-Flight Emergency Procedures (CEPs)** you will learn, because it can be useful for avoiding a canopy collision right after opening.

To steer with your rear risers, reach up and grab them firmly above where the toggles are stowed. Look in the direction you want to turn, check for traffic, and pull that riser down 4 to 6 inches. Once you have unstowed your toggles, keep them in your hands while performing rear-riser maneuvers.

In this category, you will perform 90-degree rear-riser turns after visually inspecting your canopy but before you unstow your toggles. You will perform them again with your toggles unstowed. Stop all rear-riser steering practice by 2,000 feet.

#### Accuracy
Before your jump, identify your target and draw a 165-foot (50-meter) radius circle around it on the aerial map. Use an interactive online map to help estimate the distance. Land within that area with minimal radio assistance and record the distance from the target in your logbook.

### C. Emergency Procedure Review

You will review **canopy problems and malfunctions** in the training harness to help you develop quicker recognition of malfunctions and improve your decision-making ability, especially as your assigned pull altitude lowers as you gain experience. The canopy must reliably fly straight, turn, and flare. Decide if your canopy is safe to land by the **2,500-foot decision altitude** and execute your emergency procedures if necessary.

You should be able to describe procedures for **landing on a building**: If landing on a roof, flare and PLF. Cut away once you've landed. If landing your reserve, contain it. Wait for help. If hitting a building broadside, turn the canopy slightly to avoid a direct impact before flaring. Prepare to PLF, flare to slow down, and attempt to strike a glancing blow.

### D. Equipment

#### AAD Operation
You will learn how to turn on your automatic activation device. Different brands of AADs have different operational modes that affect the firing altitude and speed. The owner's manual contains more information.

Integrated Student Program | Category D (Direction)

## Conducting Gear Checks

You should perform four gear checks supervised by your instructor before every jump.

1. Check your gear before putting it on (pre-flight)
2. Check your gear immediately after putting it on
3. Check your gear before loading the plane
4. Check your gear before exiting the plane

As you make more jumps, you will start taking more responsibility for your gear checks. The **"check of threes"** is a self-check commonly used for the pre-boarding and pre-exit gear checks. They include:

1. three-ring assembly and reserve static line (three rings)
2. three points of harness attachment for snap assembly and correct routing and adjustment (three straps)
3. three operation handles—main activation, cutaway, reserve (three handles)

Additionally, you should have another jumper check your **pins** on the back of the system from top to bottom:

1. AAD on
2. reserve pin in place
3. main pin in place
4. ripcord cable movement or correct bridle routing
5. reserve handle in place

Your **personal equipment** check includes SHAGG:

**S**hoes—tied, no hooks
**H**elmet—fit and adjustment and buckled
**A**ltimeter—set for zero
**G**oggles—tight and clean
**G**loves—lightweight and proper size (below 40 degrees F)

## E. Standard Operating Procedures

### Requirements

All student jumps, including tandems, must be completed between official **sunrise and sunset** according to the BSRs (Chapter 2-1.G.9).

You must maintain vertical and horizontal separation from clouds while jumping. FAR 105.17 lists the FAA's **cloud clearance and visibility minimums** for skydivers. You must be able to apply these requirements to your jumps, as the FAA places joint responsibility for cloud clearance and visibility on the jumper and the pilot.

The altitudes are given in mean sea level, or **MSL**, which is your true altitude using sea level as zero. Pilots use MSL to allow for consistent application of altitude requirements regardless of a location's elevation. The **elevation** is the altitude of a given location, like your drop zone, at ground level. Above ground level, or **AGL**, refers to your height above the ground. Using AGL allows for better understanding of your actual reference to the ground.

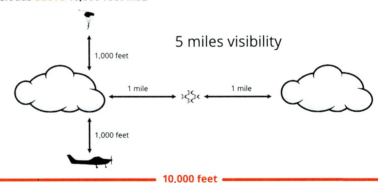

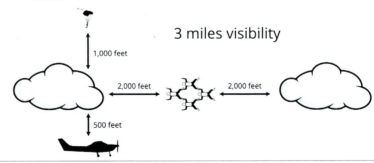

**Visual representation of FAR 105.17:** Cloud clearances above and below 10,000 ft.

Integrated Student Program | Category D (Direction)

## Spotting, Wind Drift, and Opening Point

You must determine the ground winds and winds aloft **before every skydive** according to the BSRs (Chapter 2-1.K). Having this information can help you plan your canopy flight and landing pattern. You can obtain current wind information from various weather apps. Ask your instructor which apps provide the most accurate information for your drop zone. The apps provide the direction and strength of the wind at ground level and at various altitudes in either miles per hour or knots. The description of winds includes their direction of origin expressed as a compass heading such as, "The ground winds are from two-seventy degrees." In this example, the winds are blowing from the west. Thus, your planned landing pattern will have the final approach going west, facing into the wind for landing.

To land on the drop zone, you must be able to determine the spot on the ground over which to exit the plane and know how to find that spot while on jump run in the aircraft. **Jump run** is the predetermined path the aircraft flies prior to exit. Your **exit point** is the point at which you exit the plane. The direction of jump run is determined by the strength and direction of the winds aloft. The stronger the winds aloft, the farther the exit point will be from the landing area. The wind pushes you during freefall from the exit point toward the landing area. This horizontal movement is known as **wind drift.** The winds, presence of clouds, the size of your group and your jump type, planned deployment altitude, and many other factors all go into determining your ideal exit point.

**Spotting** is the term for selecting an exit point while accounting for the effect of winds aloft in freefall and during canopy flight. The exit point is also known as **the spot.** Spotting starts with determining the best **opening point** for canopies, which is the ground point of reference over which you open your parachute. This point is determined from wind forecasts for different altitudes. The stronger the wind is at the exit altitude and during freefall, the farther upwind of the holding and landing area the exit point, or spot, will be. This is also true for the canopy opening point, as it also should be upwind of your holding and landing area. If you open upwind of your holding area, the wind will help you get there.

The pilot, instructors, and drop zone staff determine the direction of jump run and the location of the spot based upon the forecasted and observed winds. The direction of jump run and the location of the spot may change throughout the day as the weather and winds change.

The first step in learning to spot is determining what is "straight down" and predicting how the plane is moving across the ground. First, look straight out at the horizon and draw an imaginary line back to you. Then look forward toward where you are headed and draw an imaginary line back to you. The junction of the two perpendicular lines from the horizon marks the point straight below the aircraft. Before exiting, you must also verify that the area below you is clear of clouds and aircraft, and to do so effectively, you must get your head completely outside the aircraft.

You will observe your instructor's spotting procedures, and then you will demonstrate the technique for looking straight down from the aircraft during jump run. You should be able to determine whether the aircraft is on the intended jump run and when you are at your desired exit point.

## Estimating Freefall Time

You can note your freefall time in your logbook based on your exit altitude by assuming an average terminal velocity of 120 mph. The first 1,000 feet of your freefall takes approximately 10 seconds as you reach terminal velocity. Each 1,000 feet after that takes approximately 5 seconds. For example: You exit the airplane at 5,000 feet and deploy your canopy at 3,000 feet. The first 1,000 feet takes 10 seconds, and the next 1,000 feet takes 5 seconds. You can log 15 seconds of freefall time.

**GROUND WINDS:** are also called surface winds.

**WINDS ALOFT:** are the winds at various altitudes above the ground.

**WIND DRIFT:** is the horizontal movement caused by the wind, and understanding it is important for accurate navigation and landing.

**CARDINAL DIRECTIONS:** are North 360°, East 90°, South 180°, and West 270°.

# Integrated Student Program | Category D (Direction)

## Category D Dive Flows

RED indicates Advancement Criteria
✔ indicates new skills

## AFF

### #1 90° TURNS
- OBSERVE SPOTTING
- **RELAXED EXIT**
- COA
- PRACTICE DEPLOY (optional)
- HAALR
- Find reference, ask to turn
- 90° TURNS SCS ✔
- (repeat until 6,000' no more)
- 5,000' WAVE OFF and PULL
- CANOPY CHECK - APT
- LOCATE HOLDING AREA
- REAR-RISER TURNS ✔
- FLY PATTERN
- FLARE and PLF if needed

### #2 180° and 360° TURNS
- OBSERVE SPOTTING
- **RELAXED EXIT**
- COA
- PRACTICE DEPLOY (optional)
- HAALR
- Find reference, ask to turn
- 180° and 360° TURNS SCS ✔
- (repeat until 6,000', no more)
- 5000' WAVE OFF and PULL
- CANOPY CHECK - APT
- LOCATE HOLDING AREA
- REAR-RISER TURNS ✔
- FLY PATTERN
- FLARE and PLF if needed

## IAD AND STATIC LINE

### #1 15-SECOND FREEFALL (2 jumps from 7,500')
- OBSERVE SPOTTING
- **RELAXED EXIT**
- COA
- PRACTICE DEPLOY (optional)
- HAALR
- 90° TURNS SCS ✔
- 5,000' WAVE OFF and PULL
- CANOPY CHECK - APT
- LOCATE HOLDING AREA
- REAR-RISER TURNS ✔
- FLY PATTERN
- FLARE and PLF if needed

### #2 30-SECOND FREEFALL (2 jumps from 9,500')
- OBSERVE SPOTTING
- **RELAXED EXIT**
- COA
- PRACTICE DEPLOY (optional)
- HAALR
- 180° and 360° TURNS SCS ✔
- 5,000' WAVE OFF and PULL
- CANOPY CHECK - APT
- LOCATE HOLDING AREA
- REAR-RISER TURNS ✔
- FLY PATTERN
- FLARE and PLF if needed

## CANOPY DRILL: Rear-Riser Turns

- Correct minor canopy problems (line twist, slider, end cells) using rear risers with brakes stowed.
- Check altitude, position, and traffic.
- Locate the holding area and turn toward it. Reach to the top of the risers and grab where the lines meet the risers.
- Look right, turn right 90 degrees using rear riser.
- Check altitude, position, and traffic.
- Repeat to the left.
- Check altitude, position, and traffic.
- Repeat turns if altitude permits.
- Unstow the brakes above 2,500 feet, do a controllability check and fly to the holding area.
- With your hands in your toggles, reach to the top of the risers and grab the risers where the lines meet the risers.
- Look right, turn right 90 degrees using rear riser.
- Check altitude, position, and traffic.
- Repeat to the left.
- Check altitude, position, and traffic.
- Repeat turns right and left if altitude permits.
- Return to steering with the toggles by 2,000 feet.
- Fly the planned pattern, flare and PLF if needed.

**TAKE THE QUIZ:**

uspa.org/quiz/d

Integrated Student Program | Category E (Explore)

# Category E (Explore)

| 2 jumps | DEPLOYMENT-INITIATION ALTITUDE  4,500 feet |

In Category **E**, you **E**xperiment with intentionally disorienting maneuvers: barrel roll, front loop, and back loop!

## Category at a Glance

## Advancement Criteria

### Canopy Pre-Jump
☐ Provide the ground winds and winds aloft for the day
☐ Discuss time between groups and spotting techniques
☐ Plan the spot accounting for exit separation, wind drift, and opening point
☐ Plan your flight to the holding area and the pattern, including traffic avoidance
☐ Discuss landing accuracy and choosing the landing target
☐ Discuss two common flare techniques: staged (sweet spot) and continuous.
☐ Train for sweet-spot drill
☐ Train for stall-point drill

### Academics
☐ Read the Academics section for this category
☐ Pass the category quiz at 100%
☐ Train for exit and freefall
☐ Expand on the causes of having two parachutes out and review high-wind landings
☐ Identify the components, their functions, and potential malfunctions of your parachute system
☐ Join USPA if you haven't already

### Canopy Debrief
☐ Participate with spotting during jump run using SPACE
☐ Practice finding the sweet spot
☐ Practice finding the stall point (above 2,500 feet)
☐ Perform a flare technique appropriate for your canopy
☐ Land within 165 feet (50 meters) of your planned target without assistance

### Freefall Debrief
☐ Perform a barrel roll, recovering within 5 seconds
☐ Perform a back loop, recovering within 5 seconds
☐ Perform a front loop, recovering within 5 seconds
☐ Be cleared to jump without freefall supervision by recovering twice from intentional instability (barrel roll, back loop, or front loop) within 5 seconds

## Academics

## A. Exit & Freefall

### For Review

You will perform a stable solo exit. Set up your position for the best launch that will present the front of your hips to the relative wind. Exit in a neutral position with your legs slightly extended for better stability. Maintain your arch as the relative wind changes from ahead to below after exit. As always, you can recover from exit and freefall instability by using HAALR, AIR, and the roll-out-of-bed technique.

### New Stuff

In Category E, you will purposely experiment outside of the neutral stable position by performing barrel rolls, back loops, and front loops. When you recover from any two

**SELF-SUPERVISION:** is the point in your training where you are cleared by an instructor to jump without supervision in freefall. An instructor or coach will continue to supervise your activities on the ground.

of these within 5 seconds, you qualify for **self-supervision** in freefall. The BSRs state: "All students must jump under the direct supervision of an appropriately rated USPA Instructor until demonstrating stability and heading control prior to and within 5 seconds after initiating two intentional disorienting maneuvers involving a back-to-earth presentation." (Chapter 2-1.G.4)

Being cleared for self-supervision indicates that an instructor authorizes you to jump without direct oversight. However, an instructor or coach will still supervise your pre-jump preparations and must give you a gear check before boarding the aircraft. It is your responsibility to check your gear before you exit but it is highly recommended to do a mutual gear check with an experienced jumper before exiting. (see Chapter 4-4.A)

An analog altimeter may read high when it is in your burble during inverted positions such as loops and barrel rolls, so you may be lower than the altimeter indicates.

## Barrel roll

The barrel roll is a fun maneuver, as well as the best technique for returning to a belly-to-earth position. Start the barrel roll in a neutral body position. Become narrow by bringing your knees together and stretching both arms out in front of your head. Keep your eyes on the horizon. Aggressively drive one arm across your chest in a punching motion to create momentum. Create a scissoring action with your arms and legs to twist around the imaginary axis that runs from your head to your feet. Recover by returning to the neutral body position. Relax and check your altimeter.

## Back loops

The back loop is a dynamic maneuver that challenges you to use your entire body. Start the back loop by bringing your knees up into a sitting position. Stretch your arms out to the side and widen your leg stance. Next, push your legs out and look back in the direction of the loop. Keep your head back as you roll over until you see the horizon. Recover by returning to the neutral body position. Relax and check your altimeter.

## Front loops

The front loop is also a dynamic maneuver that requires more aggressive action at the beginning and end. Start the front loop by forcefully bending at the waist while throwing your head forward toward your knees and tucking your legs in. Hold this position until you feel the wind in your face again. Recover by throwing your knees back out and returning to the neutral body position. Relax and check your altimeter.

# B. Canopy

## For Review

Before you meet with your instructor for your training, you can check ground winds and winds aloft and construct your flight plan so you're ready to discuss it.

Review your **traffic avoidance** procedures: watch for other canopy traffic, especially upon entering the landing pattern. The most dangerous point of the pattern occurs when two jumpers who are flying in opposite directions on their base legs turn to final approach. The lower canopy has the right of way, but one jumper should not maneuver to assert right of way over another. It takes two people to have a collision, but only one to avoid it.

## New Stuff
### Flare techniques

Effective flare techniques vary depending on the design and size of a parachute, but the basics of flaring apply to any technique. You can refine your flare technique by expanding on the basics using the following strategies:

**SIGHT PICTURE:** refers to the visual cues you observe to judge your altitude, speed, and trajectory as you approach your landing.

**RAM-AIR PARACHUTE:** is a canopy characterized by its design which includes a series of cells that inflate to create an airfoil shape. It needs to be moving forward and have air flow in the nose in order to fly.

Being in the PLF position for landing allows you to maintain your heading and stay level in your harness during the landing flare. Except for small corrections on final approach, keep your toggles all the way up, in full glide, for 8 to 10 seconds before starting your flare. This will help the canopy produce more lift when you flare. Keep your chin level, looking at the point mid-way to the horizon, to better judge the flare height. Start the flare when your feet reach an altitude of approximately twice your height above the ground. Flare with your hands close to your body, bringing your elbows back as your hands come down. Continue to push your hands evenly down the side of your thighs to full arm extension. **It is important to fully finish your flare**. Finish with your feet approximately 12 inches above the ground. Hold the flare all the way down during a PLF or for a few steps after touch down.

Two common flare techniques are the **continuous flare** and the **staged flare.** Most larger canopies, those 220 square feet or more, flare effectively with either technique.

The **continuous flare** is one smooth motion that should take about the same time that it takes to count to five. You may count slower or faster depending on wind conditions or your sight picture. Regardless of the speed of your flare, you should time it to be smooth and consistent overall, responding to how your canopy is performing.

The **staged flare** consists of points where you may pause during the flare stroke. The flare your instructor taught you may have two, three, or even more stages. Many canopies flare most effectively using a two-stage flare. The first stage of this two-stage flare is called the **sweet spot**, the point where your wing is in level flight. You can find the sweet spot several ways, including by noticing at what point in your flare the nose of your canopy is directly above you; or by locating where the locking loops on the steering lines are even with the steering-line rings on the riser. Note the position of your hands in relation to your body so you can find this spot again easily. Once you reach this point in your flare, pause and assess your height above the ground. Start the second stage of this two-stage flare when you are at the proper height to smoothly and fully finish the flare with your feet approximately 12 inches above the ground.

Your instructor will determine the best flare technique for your canopy and practice with you for the landing on your next jump. You will practice finding the sweet spot above 2,500 feet on your next jump, even if you use a continuous flare for landing.

## Stalls

A stall is an aerodynamic event where the wing loses its ability to produce lift. When a ram-air parachute stalls, it also loses pressurization, and the canopy will no longer be able to support the weight of the jumper. To avoid stalling close to the ground in a flare, you should know the **stall point** on any canopy you jump, especially if the canopy is new to you. *For this reason, you need to perform all stall practice above your 2,500-foot decision altitude.*

Too much input or input applied too abruptly using either the **toggles** or the **rear risers** can cause a stall. Applying too much input is associated with a slow-speed stall, where the canopy loses airspeed and eventually stalls. Applying input too abruptly is associated with a high-speed stall, where the stall occurs more suddenly and at a higher airspeed.

Before intentionally stalling with **toggles**, make sure your canopy is in full flight and flying straight. Slowly pull the toggles down to full arm extension until you feel the onset of the stall, a feeling similar to rocking back in a chair and falling backward. After holding the toggles all the way down for 5 to 6 seconds, the stall will develop further, and the canopy will become bowtie shaped. The air will leave the canopy, and you will begin descending at a high rate. Some student canopies are configured to prevent a toggle stall, so your canopy may not develop a full one. Recover from a fully developed toggle stall by slowly raising the toggles up a few inches until the canopy inflates and returns to slow flight. Avoid raising the toggles too quickly, which can cause the canopy to surge, dive, or spin into line twists.

Stalling using the **rear risers** works similarly, except that you need to pull down only 5 or 6 inches on both risers. For now, you will **practice only toggle stalls**; your B-license canopy training addresses rear-riser stalls.

**Finding the sweet spot:** Here, the locking loop on the steering lines are even with the steering-line ring on the riser.

## C. Emergency Procedure Review

### Two Open Canopies

You will review detailed procedures for having two canopies out with your instructor, expanding on your first-jump-course knowledge by looking at the guidance in Chapter 4: Recommendations for Everyone. A two-canopies-out malfunction can be caused by your AAD firing if you fail to deploy at the planned deployment altitude or by deploying your reserve without cutting away if you are below your 1,000-foot cutaway hard deck.

**STALL POINT:** is the position of your input at which your canopy stalls. The stall point will differ from canopy to canopy, jumper to jumper, and at different speeds with different maneuvers. Your student canopy may not stall using toggles, even after holding your toggles all the way down for several seconds.

### Procedures for High-Wind Landings

Winds can change from the time you leave the plane to when you are under canopy. If you land in high winds, PLF and then pull one toggle all the way in as quickly as possible until the canopy collapses. You risk injury when being dragged after landing in high winds. When you land and the canopy is dragging you and you cannot collapse it, disconnect your RSL, if possible, and cut away.

Your canopy may dive or collapse behind any **obstacle** that generates turbulence. Thus, if landing in high winds, plan your final approach and choose a landing spot with the least potential for turbulence and the greatest distance between you and any obstacle.

## D. Equipment

### Open-Parachute Orientation

If you have not already been involved in packing, you should begin packing lessons in this category. A rigger or instructor will expand on your knowledge of the parachute system by slowly opening a packed rig, highlighting how your parachute ideally deploys in a specific order. A malfunction happens when the deployment is delayed, halted, or happens out of sequence. You should identify your rig's components, their functions during deployment, and how malfunctions might happen.

# Integrated Student Program | Category E (Explore)

## Components

- pilot chute, bridle, and collapsing system
- deployment bag
- pilot-chute attachment
- top skin, bottom skin, ribs, and crossports
- nose and tail (leading and trailing edges)
- stabilizers and slider stops
- A, B, C, D, and brake lines
- line cascades, including brake lines
- slider and slider grommets
- connector links and link protectors
- risers and toggles
- AAD
- standard RSL or MARD

## Potential Malfunctions

- lost or unrecoverable deployment handle
- hard pull
- pack closure
- pilot-chute hesitation
- pilot chute in tow
- premature deployment (hand deploy)
- pilot-chute entanglement
- bag lock
- streamer
- line over
- fabric or line failure sufficient to interfere with control and flare
- slider hang-up
- control-line entanglement

## RSL and MARD

A **reserve static line (RSL)** is a back-up safety device meant to automatically deploy the reserve canopy following a cutaway. On an RSL-equipped rig, one end of the RSL lanyard attaches to a main riser, and then the lanyard runs to the reserve ripcord cable, where the other end attaches. When the main risers depart following a cutaway, the RSL lanyard pulls the reserve pin and releases the reserve pilot chute, which deploys the reserve parachute. When the RSL includes a **main-assisted-reserve-deployment (MARD)** device, the RSL lanyard hooks to the reserve-pilot-chute bridle, which allows the departing main parachute to assist in extracting the reserve, speeding up its deployment. RSLs help to both ensure and speed up reserve deployment when fractions of a second matter; MARDS speed up the deployment even further. (See Chapter 4-3: Equipment for more details.)

**USPA requires all students to use an RSL** and recommends that all experienced jumpers use an RSL with a MARD. The RSL must be attached and routed correctly to function properly.

## E. Standard Operating Procedures

According to the BSRs (Chapter 2-1 H), students are limited to jumping when surface winds are **14 mph or less**. An S&TA may file a waiver for students to jump in higher winds. Licensed jumpers have no established wind limit, so they must exercise good judgment.

FAR 91.107 establishes that you must wear a **seat belt** during taxi, takeoff, and landing. Drop zones establish their own policies regarding the altitude at which you may remove your seat belt.

**Review aircraft EPs** from Category A. In an aircraft emergency, you can choose one of these actions: land in the plane, exit on your reserve, or exit on your main parachute. When choosing which action is appropriate, consider your drop zone's policy on the altitude at which you take off your seat belt. If an aircraft emergency occurs below that altitude, land in the plane. Further, consider your decision altitude when choosing when you use your main rather than your reserve. If an aircraft emergency occurs above seat-belt-off altitude and below your decision altitude, use your reserve.

### Spotting, Winds Aloft, Opening and Exit Points, Exit Separation, and SPACE

Previously, you learned that **spotting** is the process of selecting an exit point while accounting for the effect of winds aloft in freefall and during your canopy flight. The exit point is known as "**the spot**." You will take a more active role in spotting by calculating the spot and participating during jump run. Determining the spot involves multiple steps, which include obtaining the winds-aloft information, calculating the effect of wind on your canopy flight and calculating your freefall drift.

### Finding the Winds Aloft

Accurately determining the spot will allow you to arrive at your pattern-entry point at 900 feet. Ground winds are often not the same as winds at higher altitudes. **Winds aloft** cause jumpers to drift across the ground both when in freefall and under canopy. You must account for winds aloft to determine your ideal **exit and opening points**.

Use an app recommended by your instructor to find a winds-aloft report, which might look like this:

The data provided includes the altitude in feet above the ground (AGL), a heading in degrees indicating where the winds are coming from, and the wind speed in either mph or knots. You can convert knots to mph by multiplying by 1.15. Degrees are expressed as a position on a compass:

Keep in mind that the winds-aloft report is only a forecast and can differ from what you actually experience. To assess the accuracy of the forecasted winds, observe other jumpers' opening points and canopy flights from the ground. Ask them about their flights and how the winds aloft affected their canopy flights.

Integrated Student Program | Category E (Explore)

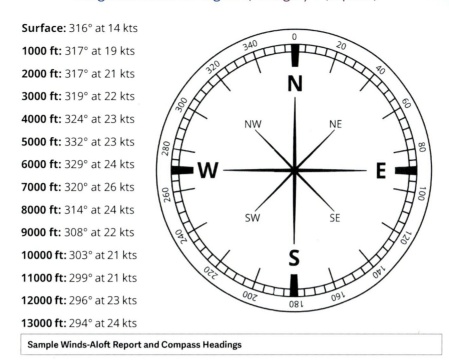

**Surface:** 316° at 14 kts
**1000 ft:** 317° at 19 kts
**2000 ft:** 317° at 21 kts
**3000 ft:** 319° at 22 kts
**4000 ft:** 324° at 23 kts
**5000 ft:** 332° at 23 kts
**6000 ft:** 329° at 24 kts
**7000 ft:** 320° at 26 kts
**8000 ft:** 314° at 24 kts
**9000 ft:** 308° at 22 kts
**10000 ft:** 303° at 21 kts
**11000 ft:** 299° at 21 kts
**12000 ft:** 296° at 23 kts
**13000 ft:** 294° at 24 kts

Sample Winds-Aloft Report and Compass Headings

## Determining Opening Point

Using the winds-aloft report, first consider the effect of winds during canopy descent. **A student canopy descends at approximately 1,000 feet per minute.** We can convert the strength of the wind in miles per hour to distance drifted per minute by dividing by 60, like this:

| AVERAGE WIND IN MILES PER HOUR | DISTANCE PER MINUTE (in miles) |
|---|---|
| 60 | 1 |
| 30 | 1/2 |
| 20 | 1/3 |
| 15 | 1/4 |
| 10 | 1/6 |
| 5 | 1/12 |

To determine the opening point, start by calculating how many minutes you will spend under canopy from opening point to pattern-entry point.

**For example**, at a descent rate of 1,000 feet per minute, if you are **open at 3,000 feet**, your time from opening to pattern entry at 900 feet would be approximately two minutes.

Now, average the winds-aloft report for altitudes from 3,000 feet AGL to 1,000 feet AGL.

For example, if the reported winds aloft were:

- **1,000 ft:** 260° at 10 mph
- **2,000 ft:** 270° at 15 mph
- **3,000 ft:** 280° at 20 mph

The average would be 270° at 15 mph.

# Integrated Student Program | Category E (Explore)

To determine the distance of your drift from 3,000 feet to the pattern-entry point, find the average wind speed in the first column, multiply the distance per minute column by two minutes under canopy.

| AVERAGE WIND IN MILES PER HOUR | DISTANCE PER MINUTE (in miles) | **Example:** drift from 3,000 feet to 900-foot pattern entry.(approximately 2 minutes). |
|---|---|---|
| 60 | 1 | 2 miles |
| 30 | 1/2 | 1 mile |
| 20 | 1/3 | 2/3 mile |
| 15 | 1/4 | 1/2 mile |
| 10 | 1/6 | 1/3 mile |
| 5 | 1/12 | 1/6 mile |

According to the above chart, from 3,000 feet to the pattern entry point, this 15-mph average translates to a ½ mile of drift. The direction 270° is wind from the west. Thus, the ideal **opening point** would be 1/2 mile to the west of the entry point of your landing pattern. Use an aerial map to determine a landmark at this calculated opening point. You can use your runway as a ruler to estimate the distance from your opening point to your pattern-entry point by converting your runway's length to miles.

## Determining Exit Point

After calculating the ideal opening point, which is the ideal spot to open your canopy, calculate the **exit point**, which is the ideal spot to leave the plane. This requires adding the drift experienced in freefall to the drift experienced under canopy.

Start by computing your time in freefall, where the first 1,000 feet takes approximately 10 seconds and each 1,000 feet after that takes approximately 5 seconds.

**The example below uses 1 minute of freefall.**

| AVERAGE WINDS IN MILES PER HOUR | DISTANCE PER MINUTE (in miles) |
|---|---|
| 60 | 1 |
| 30 | 1/2 |
| 20 | 1/3 |
| 15 | 1/4 |
| 10 | 1/6 |
| 5 | 1/12 |

Now, determine the average winds aloft during freefall. If the reported winds aloft were:

- **3,000 ft:** 280° at 20 mph
- **6,000 ft:** 290° at 27 mph
- **9,000 ft:** 270° at 31 mph
- **12,000 ft:** 240° at 42 mph

The average would be 270° at 30 mph.

According to the above chart, from 12,000 feet to 3,000 feet, this 30-mph average translates to a freefall drift of 1/2 mile in one minute of freefall. The direction 270° is wind from the west. Add this freefall drift distance on top of the opening point of 1/2 mile west, so the ideal **exit point** would be one mile to the west.

**EXIT SEPARATION:** is the practice of spacing out exits of groups of skydivers, based on the strength of the upper winds, to maintain a safe distance between them in air.

## Participating in Jump Run

Establish what communication with the pilot you might use for spotting corrections or the go-ahead to open the door and jump. Commonly, jumpers use verbal or physical communication like hand signals, shoulder taps, or yelling "door!" for smaller aircraft, and electronic (e.g., spotting buttons) and lights for larger aircraft. Regardless, the pilot determines when the door may be opened and may prefer to operate the door.

Integrated Student Program | Category E (Explore)

## Clearing your SPACE

Using the acronym **SPACE** can help you quickly remember what to look for while clearing your airspace before exiting.

### Skydivers

**Exit separation** between groups of **skydivers** is a critical part of clearing the space on exit and can change according to winds at altitude, size of the groups, and the skydiving disciplines they are engaging in. Generally, the stronger the winds aloft, the more time between groups is needed for proper exit separation. Chapter 4-7 explains how to determine the time between exiting groups.

### Planes

According to FAR 105.5, the jumper and the pilot are jointly responsible for making sure the space is clear of other **planes** before jumping.

### Airport

Make sure you see the **airport** in the space below you and orient it to the direction of jump run. Ensure it is in the expected location based on your previously determined exit point.

### Clouds

The FAA prohibits skydiving through or near clouds. Make sure the distance between clouds is sufficient according to what you learned in Category D.

### Exit Light

In larger aircraft, wait for the green light to exit. In smaller aircraft, confirm with your pilot. At any time during jump run, the pilot may have to remove their OK for the jump due to traffic, instructions from air traffic control, or other reasons.

**Integrated Student Program | Category E (Explore)**

## Category E Dive Flows

RED indicates Advancement Criteria
✓ indicates new skills

### #1 BARREL ROLL/RECOVERY

- SPOT (with assistance)
- **SOLO UNGRIPPED EXIT** ✓
- HAALR
- **BARREL ROLL** ✓
- (recover w/in 5 sec) HAALR
- (repeat until 6,000' no more)
- **4,500' WAVE OFF and PULL**
- CANOPY CHECK - APT
- LOCATE HOLDING AREA
- **SWEET-SPOT DRILL** ✓
- **FLY PATTERN**
- **FLARE and PLF** if needed

### #2 FRONT & BACK LOOPS

- SPOT (with assistance)
- **CHOICE OF EXIT**
- HAALR
- **FRONT LOOP** ✓
- (recover w/in 5 sec) HAALR
- **BACK LOOP** ✓
- (recover w/in 5 sec) HAALR
- (repeat until 6,000' no more)
- **4,500' WAVE OFF and PULL**
- CANOPY CHECK - APT
- LOCATE HOLDING AREA
- **STALL-POINT DRILL** ✓
- **FLY PATTERN**
- **FLARE and PLF** if needed

### CANOPY DRILL #1: Sweet-Spot Practice

- Altitude–Position–Traffic
- Full flight, flare to chest strap (or until steering-line locking loops are even with rings on riser) and hold
- Is the nose of the canopy directly above? (meaning canopy is in level flight)
- If not:
  - full flight for 10 seconds
  - flare to slightly lower than chest strap
  - hold and assess for level flight
- If so:
  - note the position of your hands in relation to your body so you can find this **sweet spot** again
  - Full flight for 10 seconds
  - Practice full flare, pausing at sweet spot, then finish
- Repeat if altitude and position permit
- Stop all practice by 2,000 feet
- Fly pattern and land within 165 feet (50 meters) of target
- Measure your distance from the planned landing point

TAKE THE QUIZ:

uspa.org/quiz/e

### CANOPY DRILL #2: Toggle-Stall-Point Practice

- Check altitude, position, and traffic
- From full flight, slowly pull the toggles down to full arm extension
- Hold the toggles down for 5-6 seconds until you feel the onset of the stall, a feeling like rocking back in a chair and falling backward, which signals that you have found the stall point
- As the stall develops further and the canopy begins to look like a bowtie, the air will leave the canopy, and you will begin descending at a high rate.
- Recover from a fully developed toggle stall by slowly and symmetrically raising the toggles up a few inches until the canopy inflates and returns to slow flight
- Continue to raise the toggles up 6 inches at a time to return to full flight
- Repeat if altitude and position permit
- Stop all maneuvers above your decision altitude of 2,500 feet
- Fly the planned pattern and land within 165 feet (50 meters) of target
- Measure your distance from the planned landing point and log it
- **Note:** Some student canopies are configured to prevent a toggle stall, so even with your toggles down at full arm extension for more than 5-6 seconds, a full toggle stall may not develop.

Integrated Student Program | Category F (Flat Track)

# Category F (Flat Track)

| 2 tracking jumps and  2 clear-and-pulls (if not already done) | **DEPLOYMENT-INITIATION ALTITUDE**  **4,500** feet |

In Category **F**, you must perform a **F**lat track, among other skills, in preparation for jumping with others.

## Category at a Glance

## Advancement Criteria

### Canopy Pre-Jump
- [ ] Provide the ground winds and winds aloft for the day
- [ ] Plan the spot accounting for exit separation, wind drift, and opening point
- [ ] Plan your flight to the holding area and the landing pattern
- [ ] Train on braked turns for canopy-flight EPs
- [ ] Train on half-braked flares for canopy-flight EPs
- [ ] Train on braked pattern for canopy-flight EPs

### Academics
- [ ] Read the Academics section for this category
- [ ] Pass the category quiz at 100%
- [ ] Train for exit and freefall
- [ ] Review EPs for landing in power lines
- [ ] Review SHAGG for checking accessories
- [ ] Pack with assistance
- [ ] Check another jumper's gear before boarding
- [ ] Discuss aircraft weight and balance

### Canopy Debrief
- [ ] Spot providing for appropriate exit separation with minimal assistance
- [ ] Perform a 90-degree braked turn (1st)
- [ ] Perform a 90-degree braked turn (2nd)
- [ ] Perform a 90-degree braked turn (3rd)
- [ ] Perform a 90-degree braked turn (4th)
- [ ] Above 2,000 feet, perform a half-braked flare (1st)
- [ ] Above 2,000 feet, perform a half-braked flare (2nd)
- [ ] Fly your landing pattern in half brakes on downwind and base legs, returning to full flight on final
- [ ] Land within 82 feet (25 meters) of your planned target without assistance

### Freefall Debrief
- [ ] Flat track for 5 seconds with a 30-degree heading tolerance (1st)
- [ ] Flat track for 5 seconds with a 30-degree heading tolerance (2nd)
- [ ] Flat track for 5 seconds with a 30-degree heading tolerance (3rd)
- [ ] Perform a stable clear-and-pull exit from 5,500 feet
- [ ] Perform a stable clear-and-pull exit from 3,500 feet

## Academics

## A. Exit and Freefall

### The Flat Track

Before beginning to jump with others, you need to learn to generate horizontal speed with minimal altitude loss, a skill called "tracking." This skill allows you to create separation from others before opening your parachute. You will perform a flat track, maintaining heading within 30 degrees. Focus on **heading** first, then **pitch**; **speed** will come with practice.

First, locate a point on the horizon to establish your **heading**. Smoothly and fully extend both legs with your toes pointed to initiate forward motion, and steer to maintain heading. Roll your shoulders and flatten your arch to control your **pitch**. Fully extend

## Integrated Student Program | Category F (Flat Track)

your arms to the side, pressing them down level with your hips. Once you can control your heading and pitch, you can **speed** up your track by extending your legs more quickly and sweeping your arms back slightly.

**Stop** your track by passing through neutral, extending your arms forward and down slightly. Return to neutral.

Practice entering and refining an on-heading 5-second track, turning 180 degrees after each attempt and repeating as altitude permits. Exit from a position facing up the line of flight, such as a **floater exit**. Turn 90 degrees to start tracking perpendicularly to the line of flight. This allows you to avoid those who exited before or after you, up and down the **line of flight**. Always plan tracking dives with other groups in mind.

### Clear-and-Pull

> **IAD and static-line students:** You have already met the clear-and-pull requirement in Category C.
>
> **AFF students:** You will perform a clear-and-pull jump from 5,500 feet and, once successful, another from 3,500 feet. A clear-and-pull is used during emergency exits and pre-planned low-altitude jumps. You may want to practice the clear-and-pull on full-altitude jumps by doing a practice throw right after exit, then continuing your planned freefall.

On the clear-and-pull, use a familiar, stable exit technique. To deploy within 5 seconds of exit, present your hips to the relative wind and execute normal pull procedures without the wave-off. Expect the parachute to open in relation to the relative wind, not overhead as usual.

> Although they are included in Category F, you may complete these two clear-and-pull jumps anytime during your A-license progression and can continue to Category G without them at the discretion of your drop zone and instructor.

**LINE OF FLIGHT:** is the path that the aircraft follows over the ground while on jump run dropping skydivers.

**FLOATER EXIT:** is an exit where you set up outside the aircraft to achieve a stable entry into the relative wind, facing the line of flight. Three common positions in the door are front, center and rear floater on a side-door aircraft.

**POISED EXIT:** is an exit where you set up using the aircraft door frame or strut for stability to achieve a stable entry into the relative wind with your hips presented into the relative wind.

**CLEAR-AND-PULL:** is interchangeable with "hop-and-pop." It refers to exiting and clearing the aircraft, then deploying immediately.

## B. Canopy

### CEP—Braked Turns

Braked turns are one of the most important **canopy-flight emergency procedures** (CEPs) you can practice. Using braked turns, also called "flat turns," you can change direction under canopy while losing as little altitude as possible. A braked turn also slows your forward speed while maintaining a stable, level wing. If you find yourself landing in a tight or unfamiliar landing area and you must turn to avoid an obstacle at a low altitude, you can use a braked turn. In this emergency situation, executing a braked turn instead of a turn from full flight allows you to change heading and still honor the first landing priority: landing with a level wing.

Start by pulling both toggles down evenly to the half-braked position and hold for a few seconds. Push one toggle down slightly to initiate a 90-degree turn. Practice changing heading as quickly as possible while keeping the wing level. You will practice 90-degree braked turns in this category, but you may need only a 45-degree turn or less, followed by a braked flare, to avoid an obstacle on landing.

### CEP—Half-Braked Flares

Practicing braked flares can help you discover the effectiveness of the flare when finishing from a braked position. This CEP is useful in several situations, including when you initially flare too high and need to hold in brakes for a few seconds before finishing; after you use a braked turn to avoid an obstacle on landing; or when you turn too close to the ground.

First, for reference, start by performing a flare from full flight using your normal landing technique. Note the pitch change of your parachute and your swing forward under the parachute at the bottom of your flare stroke. Start a half-braked flare by pulling the toggles to a half-braked position and hold for a few seconds. Then, from that position, flare more quickly and forcefully than you would for your normal flare stroke. Compare the flares you just practiced, especially the parachute's pitch change and your swing forward. Practice another braked flare, adjusting the speed and force to most closely match the effect of your flare from full flight. Braked flares generally need to be faster and more forceful than a flare from full flight to get an equivalent response.

### Braked Landing Pattern

Knowing how your canopy flies in different modes of flight can be useful for adjusting your descent, which allows you to keep a safe vertical distance from other canopies, as well as flatten your glide to conserve altitude on the downwind leg of your pattern.

Fly the downwind and base legs of your landing pattern in at least half brakes to determine the effect on your glide path. Expect a different a glide path than what you normally experience, and plan for a longer final approach to avoid overshooting the target. Once you turn onto your final approach, go into full flight and land as usual.

### Accuracy

You must accumulate two unassisted landings within 82 feet (25 meters) of the planned target.

## C. Emergency Procedure Review

Explain to your coach or instructor the procedure for an emergency power-line landing. Power lines are difficult to see under canopy, but you can expect them along roads, between buildings, and in clearcut passages for utilities in the forest.

## D. Equipment

### Packing Your Main

You will pack at least one parachute with assistance. Remember the most important points of packing: the lines are straight and in place in the center of the completed pack job, the slider is quartered and at the slider stops at the top of the lines, and the line stows are tight to prevent premature line deployment.

### Pre-Jump Equipment Check

You will perform a pre-jump equipment check on another jumper who is in full gear, applying the principles you learned in Category D.

"Check of threes" in the front

1. three-ring assembly and reserve static line (three rings)
2. three points of harness attachment for snap assembly and correct routing, adjustment, and stowing of excess (three straps)
3. three operation handles—main activation, cutaway, reserve (three handles)

Pin check back of system, top to bottom:

1. AAD on
2. reserve pin in place
3. main pin in place
4. ripcord cable movement or correct bridle routing
5. reserve handle in place

Also check personal equipment ("SHAGG")

**S**hoes—tied, no hooks
**H**elmet—fit and adjustment and buckled
**A**ltimeter—set to zero
**G**oggles—tight and clean
**G**loves—lightweight and proper size (below 40 degrees F)

## E. Standard Operating Procedures

Having supplementary **oxygen** available on the aircraft is mandatory for skydives made from higher than 15,000 feet MSL (Chapter 2-1.N)

### Aircraft Weight and Balance

An aircraft needs to maintain proper **weight and balance** for the pilot to be able to control its flight. Each aircraft has a specified maximum weight it can carry, and that weight must be distributed properly for it to be in balance. Jumpers moving around the aircraft improperly can place the load out of balance. For example, in aircraft with a door in the rear, some jumpers must remain forward as groups congregate near the door. Large groups planning to exit together should inform the pilot. Your instructor or pilot will answer any specific questions you may have about the aircraft your drop zone flies.

### Winds on Jump Run

Winds at altitude can affect jump run. **Airspeed** is the speed the aircraft is flying. Flying into or with the wind can change its **ground speed**, that is, the speed it is traveling across the ground. Subtract the speed of the headwind on jump run from the airspeed of the aircraft to determine the ground speed.

There is also a consideration called **forward throw**. Jumpers first get thrown forward on exit approximately 0.2 miles in calm winds, less with headwind, from residual aircraft speed before they fall straight down.

## Exit Separation

Slower-falling jumpers and groups are exposed to upper headwinds longer and are blown farther downwind than faster-falling jumpers and groups. Slower-falling groups should exit before faster-falling groups if jump run is flying into the wind.

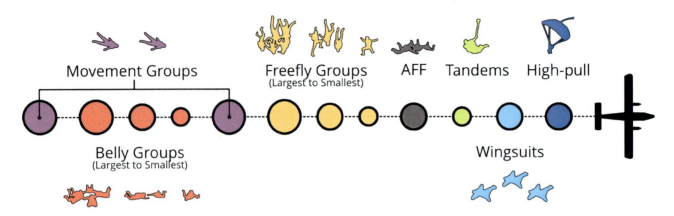

As upper winds get stronger and group sizes get larger, more time between groups is necessary for them to get sufficient horizontal separation over the ground. Provide at least 1,000 feet of ground separation between individuals jumping solo. Provide at least 1,500 feet of ground separation between small groups, adding more as the size of the groups increase.

Many drop zones post in the aircraft a chart of calculated separation times based on the aircraft's ground speed.

| Aircraft Ground Speed (knots) | Time in seconds for 1,000' separation between individuals | Time in seconds for 1,500' separation between groups |
|---|---|---|
| 115 | 5 | 8 |
| 110 | 6 | 8 |
| 105 | 6 | 8 |
| 100 | 6 | 9 |
| 95 | 7 | 9 |
| 90 | 7 | 10 |
| 85 | 7 | 11 |
| 80 | 8 | 11 |
| 75 | 8 | 12 |
| 70 | 9 | 13 |
| 65 | 10 | 14 |
| 60 | 10 | 15 |
| 55 | 11 | 16 |
| 50 | 12 | 18 |

Once your parachute has opened, fly perpendicularly to the line of flight to promote more separation under canopy from the groups that exited before and after you.

Integrated Student Program | Category F (Flat Track)

## Category F Dive Flows

RED indicates Advancement Criteria
✓ indicates new skills

### FLAT TRACKING
(2 jumps, first focusing on heading and pitch, second focusing on speed if ready)
- SPOT (with minimal assistance)
- **CHOICE OF EXIT**
- **TRACK** ✓ (for 5 seconds)
- TURN 180
- HAALR
- (repeat until 6,000' no more)
- **4,500'** WAVE OFF AND PULL
- CANOPY CHECK - APT
- LOCATE HOLDING AREA
- **BRAKED TURNS** ✓
- **FLY PATTERN**
- **FLARE and PLF** if needed

### CLEAR and PULL
(2 jumps, first from 5,500', second from 3,500' if not already done)
- SPOT (with minimal assistance)
- **FLOATER OR POISED EXIT**
- **PULL** ✓ (within 5 seconds)
- CANOPY CHECK - APT
- LOCATE HOLDING AREA
- **HALF-BRAKED FLARES** ✓
- **FLY PATTERN**
- **FLARE and PLF** if needed

## CANOPY DRILL #1: Braked Turns (CEP)
- ☐ Check altitude, position, and traffic
- ☐ Pull toggles smoothly and evenly to half-braked position
- ☐ Perform a 90-degree-braked turn by pushing down one toggle slightly
- ☐ Stop the turn by bringing the toggle back to the half-braked position
- ☐ Check altitude, position, and traffic
- ☐ Perform a 90-degree-braked turn in the other direction
- ☐ Return to full flight
- ☐ Check altitude, position, and traffic
- ☐ Repeat to no lower than 2,000 feet
- ☐ Fly the planned landing pattern and flare
- ☐ Measure your landing distance from the planned target

## CANOPY DRILL #2: Half-Braked Flares (CEP)
- ☐ Check altitude, position, and traffic
- ☐ For reference, start by doing a flare from full flight, using your normal landing technique.
- ☐ Note the pitch change of your parachute and your swing forward under the parachute when at the bottom of your flare stroke
- ☐ Return to full flight for 10 seconds
- ☐ Start a half-braked flare by pulling the toggles to a half-braked position and hold for 3 seconds
- ☐ Flare from that position more quickly and forcefully than you would for your normal flare stroke.
- ☐ Compare the braked and normal flares you just practiced, especially the parachute's pitch change and your swing forward under it.
- ☐ Return to full flight for 10 seconds and check altitude, position, and traffic
- ☐ Practice another half-braked flare, adjusting the speed and force to most closely match the effect of a flare from full flight.
- ☐ Repeat to no lower than 2,000 feet
- ☐ Fly the planned landing pattern and flare
- ☐ Measure your landing distance from the planned target

**TAKE THE QUIZ:**

uspa.org/quiz/f

Integrated Student Program | Category G (Groups)

# Category G (Groups)

| 3 jumps | BREAKOFF ALTITUDE **5,500** feet | DEPLOYMENT BY **4,000** feet |

In Category **G**, you must perform skills relating to jumping with **G**roups, such as moving forward to dock, changing levels, performing the breakoff sequence, and canopy traffic considerations!

## Category at a Glance

## Advancement Criteria

### Canopy Pre-Jump
☐ Provide the ground winds and winds aloft for the day
☐ Plan the spot, accounting for exit separation, wind drift, and opening point
☐ Plan your flight to the holding area and the landing pattern, choosing your target for landing
☐ Discuss maximum rate of turn under canopy
☐ Train on turn reversal, a canopy-flight EP, for collision avoidance
☐ Train for adjusting your glide path

### Academics
☐ Read the Academics section for this category
☐ Pass the category quiz at 100%
☐ Train for exit and freefall
☐ Review tree-landing EPs
☐ Discuss high-wear equipment items and gear maintenance that requires a rigger
☐ Pack without assistance

### Canopy Debrief
☐ Spot with minimal assistance
☐ Adjust the glide path on your canopy
☐ Perform the turn-reversal drill (1st) above 2,500 feet
☐ Perform the turn-reversal drill (2nd) above 2,500 feet
☐ Perform the turn-reversal drill (3rd) above 2,500 feet
☐ Perform the turn-reversal drill (4th) above 2,500 feet
☐ Land within 65 feet (20 meters) of your planned target without assistance (1st)
☐ Land within 65 feet (20 meters) of your planned target without assistance (2nd)

### Freefall Debrief
☐ Re-dock from 10 feet using start-coast-stop (1st)
☐ Re-dock from 10 feet using start-coast-stop (2nd)
☐ Match level—"up" from 6 feet using start-coast-stop
☐ Match level—"down" from 6 feet using start-coast-stop
☐ Re-dock with level adjustment using start-coast-stop (1st)
☐ Re-dock with level adjustment using start-coast-stop (2nd)
☐ Break off at your assigned altitude without being prompted
☐ Track at least 50 feet within a 10-degree heading tolerance

## Academics

### A. Exit and Freefall

#### Group Exits
You will practice for an efficient group exit using the same key elements you have used for your solo exits: setup, launch, and flyaway.

In the **setup**, each jumper in a group has an assigned exit position and should know that position before climb-out. This exit position should include specific foot and hand placement to support **presentation of hips into the relative wind** during the

# Integrated Student Program | Category G (Groups)

launch and flyaway. You can exit in a group with or without grips on other jumpers. If you are making a gripped exit, presentation to the relative wind in a neutral body position is the largest contributor to success.

To coordinate the **launch**, one person in the group will give the count. The movements of the count should be pronounced and given with a smooth cadence so that all jumpers can follow it and leave at the right time. Launch using a neutral body position, presenting to the relative wind.

During the **flyaway**, maintain eye contact across the center of the group. Looking toward the center of the group will keep you close to the others and support a stable flyaway, preventing the exit from funneling.

**FUNNEL:** happens when a formation collapses or fails. A group exit is susceptible to funneling.

**Front Float Exit:** Setup and Launch

**Rear Float Exit:** Setup and Launch

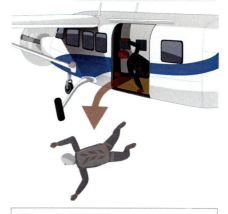
**Diving Exit:** Setup and Launch

## Forward Movement to Dock

Just as you did for turns in Category D, you will use the concept of start-coast-stop when performing forward movement.

**Start** forward movement by extending both legs. This will tilt you slightly head-low and initiate forward movement. Use your legs for forward movement, keeping your arms neutral. Maintain your heading by steering with your arms or legs.

**Coast** by returning to neutral before your desired stopping point. Your momentum from the start movement will continue to carry you forward while you are in neutral, much like your car continues to move forward after removing your foot from the accelerator. During the coast phase, assess your speed and distance to your target to determine when you should begin your stop movement.

**Stop** by briefly extending both arms and pushing down slightly, which produces backward movement. Keep your legs neutral during the stop. Fly on level all the way to the **grips**. If you stop prematurely, extend your legs slightly to take the grip.

**"Docking"** is the term for taking grips, which you'll do on your coach at the end of your forward movement. Take the **grip** on your coach's wrist. Check that your **elbows** are back to neutral after your stop movement. Extend your **feet** slightly to maintain positive pressure and counter any tension you feel in the grips, and check altitude. Once you feel no tension, you can loosen your grips and open your **palms**.

## Levels

When jumping with others, you need to get level with the formation prior to docking. Getting level before docking allows for a smooth approach and prevents vertical collisions with other jumpers. You will practice getting level by going up or down relative to your coach.

Just as with turns and forward movement, use **start-coast-stop** to control your level relative to your coach. Start your movement with the appropriate body position indicated below, coast by going back to neutral, and, if needed, stop by applying movement in the opposite direction.

To **start downward** movement, temporarily increase your vertical freefall speed by pushing your hips forward, raising your chin, and lifting your shoulders and knees to spill air.

To **start upward** movement, temporarily decrease your vertical freefall speed by rounding your spine, widening and dropping your knees, cupping your shoulders and chest, and extending your arms and pushing down slightly. Your legs will remain neutral.

When jumping with others, you will likely have to combine the skills of moving up or down with moving forward to dock. First, make sure you are on **level**, move forward into your position, which is called your "**slot**," then take your **dock**.

**FALL RATE:** is the speed at which you are falling, which can be increased or decreased by changing your neutral body position. In this category, you will go up and down to match the level of your coach. Later, you will learn how to fly in an adjusted neutral body position to match other jumpers' fall rates for entire skydives.

**LONG SPOT:** is the term for being far from the drop zone with the wind mostly at your back.

# Integrated Student Program | Category G (Groups)

## Breakoff

Breaking off is the term for tracking away from other jumpers in your group to create horizontal separation before pulling. This assures you have clear airspace when you open your canopy, avoiding a collision with another jumper.

Breakoff occurs at a pre-planned altitude on every skydive. This should be at least **1,500 feet above** the planned deployment altitude. At the breakoff, turn 180 degrees from the center of the group, track away, stop, and deploy. It should take approximately 8 seconds from the time you turn and start your track to the time you stop and pull.

Wave off and deploy at the planned altitude whether or not you have turned and tracked. Follow your pull priorities. You are always responsible to breakoff and open at the planned altitude on jumps both with your coach and with others once you get your license.

## B. Canopy

### Extending Glide

Extending the glide of your canopy allows you to cover a greater distance than full flight. This is important when you are coming back from a long spot.

You can use your brakes or rear risers to extend your glide. Many other variables, such as wind strength, wind direction, and canopy design and size, also affect your glide path. In this category, you will practice using your toggles to extend your glide path. You will learn more about using your rear risers in your B-license canopy proficiency training.

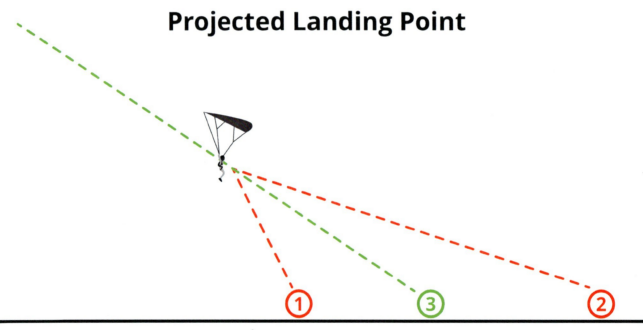

**To find your projected landing point:**

Pick a point in front of you on the ground and fly toward it.

1. If that point falls relative to the horizon or appears to move closer to you, you will fly past this point. You will overshoot this point.
2. If that point rises relative to the horizon or appears to move farther from you, you will not make it there. You will undershoot this point.
3. If the point stays stationary, this is your project landing point. You will land there.

**To adjust your glide path:**

Find your projected landing point in full flight. Then pull the toggles down slightly and find the new projected landing point for your new glide path. If the new projected landing point rises or appears to move farther relative to the original projected landing point then your glide path has flattened, and the canopy will cover more distance. If not, your glide path is steeper, and the canopy will cover less distance.

### CEP—Turn Reversals with Max Rate of Turn

A turn reversal is when you make a toggle turn in one direction then immediately in the opposite direction, with the goal of maintaining line tension and stability under the canopy throughout the turns. Turn reversal is another canopy-flight emergency procedure (CEP) used for collision avoidance during canopy flight.

Unexpected line twists can occur if you switch too aggressively or rapidly between left and right toggle inputs. Practicing **turn reversals** will help you discover how far and how fast you can do so without creating line twists. Knowing your maximum safe rate of turn can help you avoid line twists when reacting to avoid an imminent canopy collision. A canopy collision can happen anytime during a canopy descent or in the landing pattern. The potential for collision with other jumpers increases when in the holding area and pattern because other jumpers may be focused more on the target than on traffic. Line twists at landing-pattern altitude may be unrecoverable in time for a safe landing, particularly with a higher wing loading. For these reasons, you must practice all turn reversals above your decision altitude, just in case you induce a line twist.

**To practice turn reversals**, make a smooth but deep turn at least 90 degrees to the left, then reverse toggle positions smoothly but quickly for a 180-degree turn to the right. Enter a turn only as quickly as the canopy can maintain balance and line tension during the turn. Surging, lurching, or line twists indicate a turn entered too quickly. The canopy dives sharply after a maximum-performance turn.

## Accuracy

You will accumulate two unassisted landings within 65 feet (20 meters) of a planned target. Remember, you need five total to complete the requirements for your A license.

# C. Emergency Procedure Review

## CEP for Canopy-Collision Avoidance - Rear-Riser Steering

Know where other nearby jumpers are during opening and steer with the back risers to avoid them. If a head-on collision is pending, both jumpers should turn right. For expanded collision-avoidance training, look up the USPA-recommended procedures in Chapter 4-1.

## Tree-Landing Avoidance

As a review, your coach or instructor will ask you to describe the tree-landing emergency procedure that you learned in the Category A first-jump course.

# D. Equipment

By the end of this category, you should be able to pack at least one main parachute without assistance.

## Inspecting Gear

You should be able to inspect your gear to identify areas susceptible to high wear. If you find items requiring maintenance, you should alert your coach or instructor. Many of these items must be addressed only by an **FAA rigger**.

### pilot chute, bridle, and deployment handle

- Look for broken stitching around the apex and the seam where the pilot chute's fabric and mesh meet.
- Check for security at the bridle's attachment point.
- Look for damage to the fabric and mesh.

### deployment bag

- Look for distortion in the grommets, especially at the bridle, and fabric damage around their edges.
- Check the loops that hold the line-stow rubber bands.

### closing pin

- Check for nicks or corrosion on the pin.

### pilot-chute attachment

- Look for wear where the bridle attaches to the canopy.
- Look for broken stitching on the canopy itself where it is reinforced for the bridle-attachment loop or ring.

### parachute fabric

- Check for small holes on the top skin where the bridle attaches to the parachute
- Look for wear on the top skin and end cells caused by contact with sharp objects or corrosive materials.
- Look for wear in and around the reinforcements in the stabilizers that contain the slider stops.
- Look for broken or missing stitching along the seams.

### slider

- Inspect for nicks or sharp edges in the slider grommets and fabric pulling out of the grommets.
- Look at the fabric for damage.

### lines

- Look for wear anywhere along the lines, but especially where the slider grommets contact metal connector links.

- Look for signs of line shrinkage that cause unequal lengths.

## slider bumpers and links
- Look for damage to slider bumpers.
- Check that the slider bumpers are tight on the link or secured with tack cord to prevent them from sliding up the lines and stopping the slider.
- Check accessible links for nicks and sharp edges. Ensure they are closed and tightened.
- Check soft links for wear.

## brake system
- Look for wear on the lower steering lines.
- Examine the toggle locking loops on the brake lines for damage and wear.
- Inspect toggle keepers and brake-line-excess keepers.
- Ensure that the toggle keepers hold the toggles securely.

## three-ring release system
- Look for wear in the loops holding the rings and the white retaining loop.
- Check the cutaway-cable housings for wear or damage and broken or loose tacking.
- Look for kinks in the cutaway cable where it contacts the white retaining loop.
- Check the front and back of the riser webbing for fraying or warping around the edges of the grommets.
- Check that riser-housing inserts are secure and excess cutaway cable is stowed in the riser housing.

## riser covers
- Confirm tuck tabs fit properly and stay in their pockets.
- Check that the stiffener in the tuck tab is not cracked or bent.

## main-container closing grommets
- Inspect for distortion, sharp edges or nicks, and fabric damage around the edges.
- Check for severe distortion or breakage of the plastic stiffener inside the fabric where the grommet is set.

## main- and reserve-pin covers
- Check the plastic stiffeners for distortion.

## reserve loop and pin
- Check that there is no fraying of the reserve loop.
- Check that the thread on the seal is not broken.
- Look at the condition of the reserve pin and grommet.

Store your parachute in a cool, dry, dark place. In the summer, cars are too hot for safe prolonged storage since heat weakens AAD batteries and rubber bands. The sun's ultraviolet rays degrade nylon. Moisture corrodes hardware, which is very dangerous, since rust degrades nylon. Moisture also promotes mildew, which is harmful to nylon. Many chemicals and acids damage parachute materials.

# E. Standard Operating Procedures

Only an **FAA Senior or Master Rigger** may **maintain and repair a parachute system**, but only an **FAA Master Rigger** may make **major repairs and alterations**. (FAR 65.125)

**AADs**, if installed, must be maintained according to the manufacturer's instructions (FAR 105.43.c).

## Weather Conditions

Refer to the information on **weather** in Chapter 4-5, Recommendations for Everyone. Some weather conditions can be hazardous for skydivers, but there are many practical methods of observing weather and obtaining forecasts that can help you avoid these hazards. In this category, you will perform all spotting procedures with assistance in routine weather conditions.

Integrated Student Program | Category G (Groups)

## Category G Dive Flows

RED indicates Advancement Criteria
✔ indicates new skills

### #1 FORWARD MOVEMENT
- TO DOCK
- SPOT (with minimal assistance)
- **REAR-FLOAT EXIT** ✔ (inside strut)
- Coach does the count
- Face direction of flight
- Coach docks, nods, backs up (5 to 10 feet)
- **FORWARD MVT TO DOCK** ✔
- COA
- (repeat until breakoff)
- **5,500' BREAKOFF SEQUENCE** ✔
- **PULL BY 4,000'**
- CANOPY CHECK - APT
- LOCATE HOLDING AREA
- **ADJUST GLIDE PATH** ✔
- **FLY PATTERN**
- **FLARE and PLF** if needed

### #2 LEVELS (UP & DOWN)
- SPOT (with minimal assistance)
- **FRONT-FLOAT EXIT** ✔ (outside strut)
- Student does the count
- Face direction of flight
- Coach docks, nods, backs up (5 to 10 feet)
- **DOWN TO MATCH LEVEL** ✔ (5 ft)
- COA
- **UP TO MATCH LEVEL** ✔ (5 ft)
- COA
- (repeat until breakoff)
- **5,500' BREAKOFF SEQUENCE**
- **PULL BY 4,000'**
- CANOPY CHECK - APT
- LOCATE HOLDING AREA
- **TURN REVERSALS** ✔
- **FLY PATTERN**
- **FLARE and PLF** if needed

### #3 LEVEL THEN DOCK
- SPOT (with minimal assistance)
- **CHOICE OF EXIT**
- Student does the count
- Face direction of flight
- Coach docks, nods, backs up and down (5 to 10 feet)
- **DOWN TO LEVEL and DOCK**
- COA
- Coach docks, nods, backs up and up (5 to 10 feet)
- **UP TO LEVEL and DOCK**
- COA (repeat until breakoff)
- **5,500' BREAKOFF SEQUENCE**
- **PULL BY 4,000'**
- CANOPY CHECK - APT
- LOCATE HOLDING AREA
- **CANOPY DRILLS as needed**
- **FLY PATTERN**
- **FLARE and PLF** if needed

## CANOPY DRILL #1: Adjusting Glide Path
- Check altitude, position and traffic
- Find projected landing point (PLP) for full flight
- Go to 1/4 brakes and find PLP for 1/4 brakes
- Compare full flight PLP with 1/4 brakes PLP
- While holding in 1/4 brakes, check altitude, position, and traffic
- Go to 1/2 brakes and find PLP for 1/2 brakes
- Compare 1/4 brakes PLP with 1/2 brakes PLP
- While holding in 1/2 brakes, check altitude, position, and traffic
- If altitude permits, go to 3/4 brakes and find PLP for 3/4 brakes
- Compare 1/2 brakes PLP with 3/4 brakes PLP
- Slowly return to full flight
- Check altitude, position, and traffic
- Fly planned pattern and flare
- Measure your landing distance from the planned target

## CANOPY DRILL #2: Turn Reversal with Max Rate of Turn (CEP)
- Check altitude, position, and traffic in both directions
- Make a quick but balanced 90-degree turn
- Reverse the toggle position aggressively and make a balanced 180-degree turn
- Check altitude, position, and traffic in both directions
- Repeat to no lower than 2,500 feet, in case of line twist
- Fly planned pattern and flare
- Measure your landing distance from a planned target

TAKE THE QUIZ:

uspa.org/quiz/g

Integrated Student Program | Category H (Hone)

# Category H (Hone)

| 2 jumps | BREAKOFF ALTITUDE<br>5,500 feet | DEPLOYMENT BY<br>4,000 feet |

In Category **H**, you must **H**one previously learned skills to higher measurable standards, blending skills such as diving and docking, using forward and down together over longer distances!

## Category at a Glance

## Advancement Criteria

### Pre-Jump
- [ ] Provide the ground winds and winds aloft for the day
- [ ] Plan the spot accounting for exit separation, wind drift, and opening point
- [ ] Plan your flight to the holding area and the landing pattern, choosing your target for landing
- [ ] Train for the low-turn recovery drill, a canopy-flight EP

### Academics
- [ ] Read the Academics section for this category
- [ ] Pass the category quiz at 100%
- [ ] Train for exit and freefall
- [ ] Review flotation-gear advice and EPs for water landings
- [ ] Discuss equipment maintenance you can perform
- [ ] Replace a main closing loop
- [ ] Assemble a three-ring-release system

### Canopy Debrief
- [ ] Spot without assistance
- [ ] Above 2,000 feet, perform a low-turn recovery drill (1st)
- [ ] Above 2,000 feet, perform a low-turn recovery drill (2nd)
- [ ] Land within 65 feet (20 meters) of your planned target without assistance (1st)
- [ ] Land within 65 feet (20 meters) of your planned target without assistance (2nd)
- [ ] Land within 65 feet (20 meters) of your planned target without assistance (3rd)

### Freefall Debrief
- [ ] Dive to dock using a stairstep approach, 100 feet to your coach/instructor (1st)
- [ ] Dive to dock using a stairstep approach, 100 feet to your coach/instructor (2nd)
- [ ] Break off at your assigned altitude without being prompted
- [ ] Track 100 feet within a 10-degree heading tolerance

## Academics

### A. Exit and Freefall

#### Diving Exit
A diving exit is where you launch out of an aircraft without climbing out and then achieve a stable entry into the relative wind. **Set up** in the door with your hips facing the relative wind as much as possible. **Launch** by placing your hips and chest into the relative wind in a neutral body position, oriented side-to-earth, looking at the wing tip. During the **flyaway**, turn your head left to look for your coach, who exited in the floater position.

#### Dive to Dock with Stairstep Approach
In larger groups, some jumpers will launch together or from a floating position outside the aircraft, but others will need to dive out of the plane from inside. The divers leave slightly after the floaters and dive down to the other jumpers to dock. Because divers often must cover long distances, they use a technique to safely dive to a formation that helps them manage their speed and descent. This is called the **stairstep approach.**

Integrated Student Program | Category H (Hone)

# Stairstep Approach

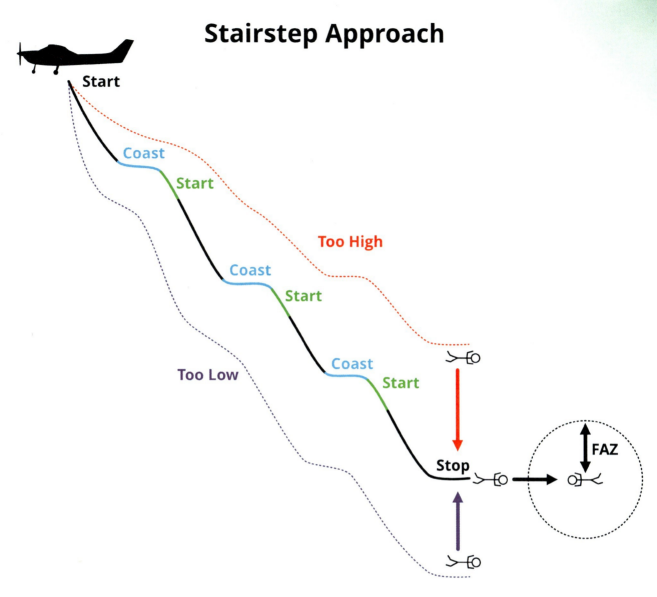

In this category, you will use the stairstep approach to practice diving to dock with your coach. After you exit but before starting to dive, hold the neutral body position for two to three seconds while slowly turning toward your coach. Use the **start-coast-stop** concept as you have before, but this time using start and coast repeatedly while diving, with a stop at the end.

To **start**, smoothly extend both legs fully with your toes pointed to initiate forward motion, steering to maintain heading. Arch more and sweep your arms back. Your hands should be above your hips. To **coast**, return to neutral and assess your horizontal and vertical distance from your coach.

**Start** again, adjusting your pitch based on the horizontal and vertical distance to your coach. To create a **steeper** pitch angle in your dive, arch more and sweep your arms up farther behind your hips. To create a **shallower** pitch angle in your dive, flatten your arch and move your arms slightly down toward your hips. After a few seconds, return to **coast** and assess your position. Repeat as necessary, maintaining altitude awareness.

To **stop**, extend both arms forward, flatten your arch, and drop your knees slightly, approximating the combination of the body positions for back and up movement. Aim to stop your dive on level with and approximately 20 feet away from your coach, just outside the **final-approach zone (FAZ)**. The FAZ is a buffer area that gives you room for error in case your approach is too fast, shallow, or steep. Before entering the FAZ you need to be level with your coach, then move forward to dock.

**FINAL-APPROACH ZONE (FAZ):** Once you earn your license and jump with larger groups, the FAZ helps you avoid a collision with other jumpers approaching the same formation. Remain clear of the area immediately below and above any group. Watch for traffic and dive in a straight line.

If you have built up too much speed in your approach, you will need to initiate your stop higher and more aggressively. If you go past the level of your coach, use the position for up movement while outside the FAZ to match the level of your coach and then move forward to dock.

If you stop in a position close to the FAZ, but higher than your coach, use the position for down movement to match the level of your coach. Once level, enter the FAZ and move forward to dock.

## Improving Your Breakoff and Track

After you earn your A license and begin to jump with larger groups, plan your breakoff altitude conservatively. The minimum breakoff altitude for **groups of five or fewer** should be at least 1,500 feet higher than the highest planned deployment altitude in the group. For **groups of six or more**, minimum breakoff altitude should be at least 2,000 feet higher than the highest planned deployment altitude in the group.

During your breakoff sequence, scan for and steer clear of jumpers ahead of and below you. Look sideways and above for other jumpers in the immediate area during wave-off and deployment so you can steer clear under canopy as soon as you open.

# B. Canopy

## CEP—Low-Turn Recovery

The low-turn-recovery technique is a canopy-flight emergency procedure. Practicing the skill will build muscle memory, allowing you to quickly **neutralize a turn**. Use low-turn recovery anytime you turn too low to the ground and do not have enough altitude to achieve a level wing without immediate input. A low-turn recovery requires neutralizing this turn.

**To practice low-turn recovery,** first check your canopy, altitude, position and traffic. From full flight, pull one toggle down to at least quarter brakes to initiate a 90-degree turn. To neutralize the turn, pull the toggle that is still in full-flight position to match the lower toggle, resulting in both toggles in a braked position. Hold the toggles even, then continue pushing them down evenly but forcefully for a braked flare. Anticipate that you may need more input than you expect to arrest the canopy descent. Slowly return to full flight for additional practice.

In a real low-turn emergency, immediately neutralize the turn, hold the toggles evenly in brakes, finish with a braked flare, and PLF.

**NEUTRALIZING A TURN** is different than just stopping a turn. Instead of just raising a toggle to stop a turn, you will pull down the toggle still in full flight so both toggles are in a braked position. This maneuver not only stops the turn, but it also slows the descent and forward speed.

## Accuracy

Perform the remaining unassisted landings within 65 feet (20 meters) of the planned target to meet the USPA A-License requirements (five total required).

# C. Emergency Procedure Review

Explain the procedure for an **emergency water landing** to your coach or instructor. Include when it is appropriate to have flotation devices. Look up USPA recommendations on procedures for an unintentional water landing in Chapter 5-4: Discipline-Specific Recommendations.

# D. Equipment

## Owner Maintenance of the Three-Ring Release System

You should disassemble the three-ring system every month to clean the cable and exercise the material between the rings to prevent the riser forming a memory of its shape. Clean the cables with silicone spray or according to the manufacturer's instructions to remove the sludge-like coating that develops on most three-ring release cables and causes them to bind, increasing the required pull force.

## Line Stows

Make sure your rubber bands are in good shape and hold your line stows securely. Replace stretched, worn, or broken rubber bands.

## Main Closing Loop

If your closing loop is worn and does not appear to be nearly perfect, it warrants replacement. The loop must have enough tension to keep the container closed in freefall. A loose closing loop could result in a premature deployment. Freeflying maneuvers increase the importance of closing-system security.

Adjust the closing-loop tension by moving the overhand knot or replacing the loop with the knot tied in the correct place. Use only closing-loop material approved by the harness-and-container manufacturer.

## Clothing and Accessories

Check your jumpsuit or clothes to ensure they allow access to your main, cutaway, and reserve handles. You should tuck in shirt tails, jackets, and sweatshirts and zip your pockets closed. Your clothing should provide protection during landing and provide you with the correct fall rate based on your physical size. Tighter fitting clothing will increase your fall rate, while baggier clothing will slow it.

## E. Standard Operating Procedures

All skydivers wearing a round main or reserve canopy and all solo students must wear **flotation gear** when the intended exit, opening, or landing point is within one mile of an open body of water (an open body of water is defined as one in which a skydiver could drown). (Chapter 2-1.M)

Look up USPA recommendations on training following **periods of inactivity** in Chapter 4-2. Students have different currency-training recommendations than licensed skydivers.

Study for your A-license exam.

### Aircraft-Radio-Use Requirements

Jump aircraft must have an operating **radio**, and the pilot must be in contact with air traffic control prior to jumping (FAR 105.13).

### Notification Before a Jump

A jumper or the pilot must **notify the appropriate air traffic control facility** at least one hour but no more than 24 hours prior to jumping. Some drop zones have a written notification renewed annually for that location only (FAR 105.25 and AC-105-2E).

### Aircraft Approved for Flight with Door Removed

Some aircraft are unsafe for flight with the door open or removed. Aircraft approved for flight with the door removed may require additional modifications and usually require additional **FAA field approval.** Other modifications to a jump aircraft, such as in-flight doors, hand holds, or steps, require additional field approval or a supplementary type certificate.

# Category H Dive Flows

RED indicates Advancement Criteria
✔ indicates new skills

## DIVE TO DOCK
### (2 jumps)

- SPOT (without assistance)
- **DIVING EXIT** ✔
- TURN TO COACH
- **DIVE TO DOCK** ✔
- Use stairstep approach*, stopping in FAZ ✔
    - First jump 10-20 ft out
    - Second jump 20-40 ft out
- (repeat if time after coach gets into position)
- **5,500' BREAKOFF SEQUENCE**
- **PULL BY 4,000'**
- CANOPY CHECK - APT
- LOCATE HOLDING AREA
- **LOW-TURN-RECOVERY PRACTICE** ✔
- **FLY PATTERN**
- **FLARE and PLF** if needed

## CANOPY DRILL: Low-Turn-Recovery Practice (CEP)

- Check altitude, position, and traffic
- From full flight, pull one toggle down to at least quarter brakes to initiate a 90-degree turn
- Neutralize the turn by pulling down the toggle still in full-flight position to match the lower toggle, resulting in both toggles in a braked position
- Hold the toggles even, then continue pushing them down evenly but forcefully for a braked flare
- Anticipate needing more input that you expect to arrest the canopy descent
- Slowly return to full flight for additional practice if altitude permits
- Fly your planned pattern and flare
- Measure your landing distance from a planned target

**TAKE THE QUIZ:**

uspa.org/quiz/h

Integrated Student Program | Applying for Your A License

# Applying for Your A License

## Before you apply for your license, you also will:

☐ Pass the A-license oral exam at 100%
☐ Pass the A-license written exam at 75%
☐ Pass the A-license practical exam (check dive) with a USPA Instructor
☐ Be introduced to USPA SIM and Governance Manual Section 1-6
☐ Attain a total of 25 skydives

The examining USPA Instructor will conduct a **40-question written** USPA A-license exam (available online). The applicant must score **at least 75% on this written exam.**

The examining USPA Instructor will also conduct an **oral quiz of at least 20 questions** taken from the USPA Integrated Student Program syllabus, with emphasis on the following:

- cloud-clearance and visibility requirements
- equipment operation and maintenance
  - wing loading and its effects
  - closing loop
  - Velcro and tuck flaps
  - packing and authorization to pack
- canopy flight
  - traffic patterns and collision avoidance
  - braked turns and obstacle avoidance
  - low-turn avoidance and recovery
  - downwind landing procedures
  - obstacle-landing-emergency-and-recovery procedures
- aircraft procedures
  - during jump run and exit to observe balance limits
  - distance between groups to maintain separation
  - aircraft emergency procedures
- group breakoff recommendations
- parachute emergency procedures
  - deployment malfunctions
  - cutaway decide-and-act altitude
  - two-canopies-deployed scenarios
- accountability for FAR compliance

The applicant must score **100% on this oral exam**. If the student fails to answer all questions in the oral quiz correctly, the examining USPA Instructor will conduct or arrange appropriate review training until passing.

The examining instructor will also conduct a **practical exam** by making a skydive (also referred to as the "A-license check dive") with the applicant to verify practical capabilities in the following areas:

- choosing the spot and selecting and guiding the pilot to the correct exit and opening point in routine conditions
- pre-jump equipment checks for self and others
- planning an effective group breakoff
- right 360-degree turn, left 360-degree turn, and a back loop (back loop to be completed within 60 degrees of the original heading)
- docking from 20 feet (evaluator flies into position)
- breakoff-altitude recognition and tracking for a minimum of 100 feet within 10 degrees of heading
- signal before deployment and overall awareness during and after deployment
- planning and flying a logical landing pattern that promotes a smooth traffic flow and avoids other jumpers
- packing and preparing equipment for the next jump

The applicant must score **satisfactorily on this practical exam**. If the student fails to demonstrate practical capabilities in any area, the examining USPA Instructor will conduct or arrange appropriate review training and re-jump until passing.

## Integrated Student Program | Applying for Your A License

## A-License Check Dive

- Stable exit
- 360° Right Turn SCS
- 360° Left Turn SCS
- Backloop
- Forward Movement to Dock
- 5,500' Breakoff Squence
- 3,500' Wave and Pull
- Canopy Check - APT
- Landing Pattern
- Pack for Self

This dive must be performed with a USPA Instructor.

# Chapter 2:
# Requirements and Regulations

USPA Members must follow the fundamentals contained in two interrelated documents—the USPA Basic Safety Requirements (BSRs) and the Federal Aviation Regulations (FARs) pertinent to skydiving.

The **Basic Safety Requirements** have been established as the cornerstone of a self-policing principle and represent the industry standard generally agreed upon as necessary for an adequate level of safety. Research can be conducted to develop and document new methods and procedures within the BSRs and, when necessary, under waivers to the BSRs, establish a justifiable basis to modify these standards.

The Federal Aviation Administration (FAA) of the U.S. Department of Transportation has the responsibility for regulating airspace usage in the United States. Concerning skydiving activities, the FAA fulfills this responsibility by specifically regulating certain aspects of skydiving through the **Federal Aviation Regulations** and by relying upon the guidelines and recommendations published by USPA.

## Overview of the BSRs

## A. How the BSRs Affect Safety

The BSRs promote practices aimed at eliminating incidents in skydiving and, by doing so, make skydiving safer and more enjoyable. USPA establishes the BSRs by evaluating incidents and identifying their root causes.

Safety is accomplished by reducing the risk factors, which requires everyone involved in skydiving to:

- acquire knowledge and make a continuing effort to increase and improve that knowledge
- practice and prepare for both the expected and the unexpected
- evaluate the risk factors
- accurately evaluate personal capabilities and limitations
- stay alert and aware of surroundings
- keep options open
- exercise good judgment

Failure to follow the BSRs may not always result in an incident, but many incidents are the result of not following these risk-reduction procedures.

## B. Waivers and Changes to the BSRs

Included in this chapter is a section titled "Waivers to the Basic Safety Requirements," which describes procedures for approving and documenting exceptions to the BSRs. Waivers provide for the responsible development of new techniques and methods.

- The BSRs are designed to establish safety standards for common situations; however, local circumstances may allow for greater tolerance in some cases.
- The purpose for filing a waiver is to document that the particular BSR has been evaluated in the individual case and that the prescribed deviation and conditions do not represent an unacceptable compromise of safety.
- Each BSR is categorized for the level of authority necessary for the approval of the waiver. Each BSR requires full board approval of a waiver, except for those designated with an [S] (S&TA or Examiner), or an [E] (Executive Committee).

From time to time, the USPA Board of Directors changes the BSRs as equipment and practices develop and evolve.

# 2-1: Basic Safety Requirements

*Note: Every BSR requires full board approval if a waiver is requested, unless the BSR has a marginal notation of [S] or [E], which identifies its waiverability by others as indicated.*

## A. Applicability

1. These procedures are applicable worldwide, apply to all jumps except those made under military orders, and those training personnel under military orders, and those made because of in-flight emergencies. However, USPA-licensed skydivers when jumping outside of the United States, its territories, and possessions, must comply with the USPA Basic Safety Requirements or the rules and regulations of the country where the jump is being made, but must comply with the USPA BSRs when instructing student skydivers unless the instructor simultaneously holds the appropriate instructional rating issued by the country where the jump is completed, in which case they must follow the USPA BSRs or they must follow the rules applicable to that rating as defined by the issuing body of that rating.
2. A "skydive" is defined as the descent of a person to the surface from an aircraft in flight when he or she uses or intends to use a parachute during all or part of that descent.
3. All persons participating in skydiving should be familiar with the Skydiver's Information Manual and all federal, state, and local regulations and rules pertaining to skydiving.

## B. Compliance with Federal Regulations

1. For skydives made within the U.S. and its territories and possessions, no skydive may be made in violation of Federal Aviation Administration (FAA) regulations.
2. FAA regulations include the use of restraint systems in the aircraft by all skydivers during movement on the surface, takeoff, and landing. [FAR 91.107]

## C. Medical Requirements

1. All persons engaging in skydiving must:
   a. Possess at least a current FAA Third-Class Medical Certificate; or
   b. Carry a certificate of physical and mental fitness for skydiving from a registered physician; or
   c. Agree with the USPA-recommended medical statement: "I represent and warrant that I have no known physical or mental infirmities that would impair my ability to participate in skydiving, or if I do have any such infirmities, that they have been or are being successfully treated so that they do not represent any foreseeable risk while skydiving. I also represent and warrant that I am not taking any medications or substances, prescription or otherwise, that would impair my ability to participate in skydiving."
2. Any skydiver acting as tandem parachutist in command must possess a current FAA Third-Class Medical or military flight or diver physicals that are required by their position or duty status by their military command authority. Alternatively, if acting as tandem parachutist in command outside the United States, its territories or possessions, a current medical certificate recognized by the civil aviation authority of the country where they will be exercising their tandem rating privileges may be substituted.
   a. A tandem parachutist in command with a medical condition that would not allow the use of their FAA medical certificate to act as a pilot in command of an aircraft may not act as a tandem parachutist in command.
   b. A tandem parachutist in command with a medical condition that would not allow the use of the privileges of their USPA-accepted-equivalent medical certificate may not act as a tandem parachutist in command.
3. Any foreign national in the United States, its territories or possessions for the purpose of qualifying as a tandem parachutist in command, or to fulfill rating renewal or currency requirements, must be under the direct supervision of a tandem examiner and must possess a current FAA Third-Class Medical Certificate or a current medical certificate recognized by the civil aviation authority of the country where they will be exercising their tandem rating privileges.

## D. Age Requirements

1. For skydives made within the U.S. and its territories and possessions, skydivers are to be at least 18 years of age. [E, during interim]
2. For skydives made outside the U.S. and its territories and possessions, the minimum age is specified by the country's (or its national airsport control's) requirements. Such skydivers who are under 16 years of age will not be issued a USPA license.
3. A waiver for tandem jumps may be issued to terminally ill persons under the age of 18 with manufacturer approval. The organizer of such jumps must submit a USPA Waiver Request form to the director of safety and training and the chair of the safety and training committee for approval prior to such jumps.

## E. Membership

USPA membership is required of any skydiver cleared for self-supervision at a USPA Group Member drop zone, except for non-resident foreign nationals who are members of their own national aeroclubs.

## F. Alcohol and Drugs

1. No person may make a parachute jump, or attempt to make a jump, if that person is or appears to be under the influence of either;
   a. alcohol.
   b. any drug that affects that person's faculties in any way contrary to safety.
2. No person may make a parachute jump, or attempt to make a jump, within 8 hours after the consumption of any alcoholic beverage.

## G. Student Skydivers

*Note: All references to USPA instructional rating holders apply to higher rating holders in that training discipline.*

1. General [E]
   a. All student training programs must be conducted under the supervision as required by an appropriately rated USPA Instructor until the student is issued a USPA A license.
   b. A person conducting, training, or supervising student jumps must hold a USPA instructional rating according to the requirements that follow.
   c. On any student jump, the supervising instructor or both instructors if a two-instructor jump, must submit a completed incident report to USPA within 48 hours if any automatic activation device (AAD) was activated on the jump. No disciplinary action will result from this self-report.
   d. Instructional rating holders must give each of their students a complete gear check before boarding the aircraft and verify that their student's gear is in proper jumping configuration.
2. First-jump course [E]
   a. All first-jump non-method-specific training must be conducted by a USPA Instructor or a USPA Coach under the supervision of a USPA Instructor.
   b. All method-specific training must be conducted by a USPA Instructor rated in the method for which the student is being trained.
3. All students must receive training in the following areas, sufficient to jump safely [E]:
   a. equipment
   b. aircraft and exit procedures
   c. freefall procedures (except IAD and static-line jumps)
   d. deployment procedures and parachute emergencies
   e. canopy flight procedures
   f. landing procedures and emergencies
4. Advancement criteria
   a. IAD and static line [E]
      (1) All jumps must be conducted by a USPA Instructor in that student's training method.
      (2) Before being cleared for freefall, all students must perform three successive jumps with practice deployments while demonstrating the ability to maintain stability and control from exit to opening.
      (3) All students must be under the direct supervision of an appropriately rated instructor until completing one successful clear-and-pull.
      (4) Following a successful clear-and-pull, each student must be supervised in the aircraft and in freefall by a USPA Coach or Instructor until demonstrating stability and heading control prior to and within five seconds after initiating two intentional disorienting maneuvers involving a back-to-earth presentation.
      (5) All ground training must be conducted by an instructor in that student's training method, until demonstrating stability and heading control prior to and within five seconds after initiating two intentional disorienting maneuvers involving a back-to-earth presentation.
   b. Harness-hold program
      (1) All students must jump with two USPA AFF rating holders until demonstrating the ability to reliably deploy in the belly-to-earth orientation at the correct altitude without assistance, except:
         i. Students who have been trained in a wind tunnel may jump with one AFF rating holder after demonstrating the following in the wind tunnel:
            - basic stability (neutral body position)
            - heading control
            - controlled forward and backward motion
            - controlled turns
            - proper response to hand signals
            - simulated altimeter checks and time awareness
            - wave-offs
            - simulated main parachute activation
         ii. The wind tunnel training and tunnel flight sessions must be conducted by an AFF rating holder, or a tunnel instructor who is under the direct supervision of an AFF rating holder. All training must be documented.
      (2) l students must jump with one USPA AFF rating holder, exit safely, maintain stability, and deploy at the planned altitude without assistance prior to attempting disorienting maneuvers.
      (3) All students must jump under the direct supervision of an appropriately rated USPA Instructor until demonstrating stability and heading control prior to and within five seconds after initiating two intentional disorienting maneuvers involving a back-to-earth presentation.
   c. Tandem training jumps [E]
      (1) Any USPA member conducting a tandem jump must have successfully completed a tandem instructor course conducted by the manufacturer of the tandem parachute system used in the parachute operation, been certified by the ap-

## Requirements and Regulations

propriate parachute manufacturer or tandem course provider as being properly trained on the use of the specific tandem parachute system to be used, and must hold a current USPA Tandem Instructor rating.

(2) For progressive training requirements following tandem jumps, refer to "Crossover training."

(3) Intentional back-to-earth or vertical orientations that cause tandem freefall speeds exceeding that of droguefall are prohibited.

(4) Tandem equipment instruction must be conducted by an individual approved by the tandem equipment manufacturer of that system.

(5) All student tandem skydives must be conducted in accordance with the specific manufacturer's age requirements for the tandem system used for that jump.

(6) Use of any extendable or fixed pole camera mounts, attached or handheld by the tandem instructor or student, is prohibited.

(7) Any person acting as parachutist in command on a tandem skydive is required to conduct system-handles checks as defined by the manufacturer of the specified tandem equipment being used immediately after deploying the drogue.

(8) Any person making a tandem skydive may not perform a turn of more than 90 degrees below 500 feet AGL.

(9) Tandem instructors must have at least 200 tandem skydives before any camera device may be used, held or attached to the tandem instructor or tandem student.

(10) Any person acting as a parachutist in command on a tandem skydive must meet the jump currency and retraining requirements defined by the manufacturer of the specified tandem equipment being used. A Tandem Designated Evaluator or Examiner rated on the equipment used, or an S&TA must supervise the currency training.

5. Crossover training [E]

   a. Students may transfer after the first or subsequent jumps to another training method after demonstrating sufficient knowledge and skill in the areas of equipment, aircraft, exits, freefall maneuvers, deployment, emergency procedures, canopy control, and rules and recommendations to enter into that program at a comparable level of proficiency and training.

   b. Students previously trained in a tandem program may continue in a harness-hold program or must demonstrate a solo exit and practice deployment with stability in the IAD or static-line program prior to advancing to freefall.

   c. Students who have completed at least two tandem jumps and demonstrated the ability to reliably pull the drogue release at the correct altitude, maintain heading and a stable body position, without requiring any control or altitude prompts from the tandem instructor, may progress to single-instructor AFF jumps after completion of solo ground training.

   d. Students previously trained in a harness-hold program must have exited stable without assistance or performed a stable IAD or static-line jump with a practice deployment supervised by a USPA IAD or Static-Line Instructor prior to performing freefall jumps with any non-AFF-rated USPA Instructor.

   e. Students previously trained in Categories A-C in SL, IAD and tandem programs may jump with one AFF instructor after demonstrating the AFF wind-tunnel requirements.

6. Students training for group freefall [E]

   a. Student freefall training for group freefall jumps must be conducted by either a USPA Coach or a D-license holder approved to make coach jumps by their S&TA, under the supervision of a USPA Instructor, and;

   b. The maximum number of participants in any skydive that includes a student on solo equipment is four. Students must not form the majority of the group, must be cleared for self-supervision and have successfully demonstrated the skills of ISP Category G. All other participants must be current USPA instructional rating holders.

7. Instruction of foreign students [E]

   a. Foreign non-resident instructional rating holders appropriately and currently rated by their national aero club may train students from that nation in the U.S., provided the instruction is conducted in accordance with the USPA Basic Safety Requirements.

   b. Appropriately and currently rated USPA instructional rating holders may assist in this training.

8. No skydiver will simultaneously perform the duties of a USPA instructional rating holder and pilot-in-command of an aircraft in flight.

9. All student jumps, including tandems, must be completed between official sunrise and sunset.

## H. Winds

Maximum ground winds

1. For all solo students [S]

   a. 14 mph for ram-air canopies

   b. 10 mph for round reserves

2. For licensed skydivers are unlimited

## I. Minimum Opening Altitudes

Minimum container opening altitudes above the ground for skydivers are:

1. Tandem jumps: 5,000 feet AGL [E]
2. All students and A-license holders: 3,000 feet AGL [E]
3. B-license holders: 2,500 feet AGL [E]
4. C- and D-license holders: 2,500 feet AGL [S] (waiverable to no lower than 2,000 feet AGL)

## J. Drop Zone Requirements

1. Areas used for skydiving should be unobstructed, with the following minimum radial distances to the nearest hazard:
   a. solo students and A-license holders: 330 feet
   b. B- and C-license holders and all tandem skydives: 165 feet
   c. D-license holders: 40 feet
   d. Or, landing areas that do not meet the minimum radial distance to the nearest hazard requirement, as described above, may be approved by the Regional Director and the Director of Safety and Training. These areas may be non-circular and similar in square footage to those described above.
2. Hazards are defined as telephone and power lines, towers, buildings, bodies of water, highways, vehicles, and clusters of trees covering more than 32,292 square feet. However, clusters of trees must not be greater than 10% of the designated landing area.
3. Manned ground-to-air communications (e.g., radios, panels, smoke, lights) are to be present on the drop zone during skydiving operations.

## K. Pre-Jump Requirements

The appropriate altitude and surface winds are to be determined prior to conducting any skydive.

## L. Extraordinary Skydives

1. Night, water, and demonstration jumps are to be performed only with the advice of the appropriate USPA S&TA, Examiner, or Regional Director.
2. Pre-planned breakaway jumps are to be made only by class C- and D-license holders using FAA TSO'ed equipment. [E]
3. Demonstration jumps into Level 2 areas require a D license with a USPA PRO Rating for all jumpers, including both tandem jump participants. [E]
4. Contact canopy formation activity is prohibited on tandem jumps. [E]
5. Tandem jumps into stadiums are prohibited. [E]
6. Any person performing a wingsuit jump must have at least 200 skydives, and hold a current skydiving license. [E]
7. Freefall within 500 feet vertically or horizontally of any student under parachute, including tandem students, is prohibited. (This requirement excludes scenarios where—during a training jump—a student's instructor(s) and videographer may be within this distance.) Freefall within 500 feet vertically or horizontally of any licensed skydiver under canopy requires prior planning and agreement between the canopy pilot and the skydiver in freefall.

## M. Parachute Equipment

1. FAA regulations [FAR 105.19] require that when performing night jumps, each skydiver must display a light that is visible for at least three statute miles from the time the jumper is under an open parachute until landing.
2. All students are to be equipped with the following equipment until they have obtained a USPA A license:
   a. a rigid helmet (except tandem students)
   b. a piggyback harness-and-container system that includes a single-point riser release and a reserve static line
   c. a visually accessible altimeter (except tandem students)
   d. a functional automatic activation device that meets the manufacturer's recommended service schedule
   e. a ram-air main canopy suitable for student use
   f. a steerable reserve canopy appropriate to the student's weight
   g. for freefall, a ripcord-activated, spring-loaded, pilot-chute-equipped main parachute or a bottom- of-container (BOC) throw-out pilot chute
3. Students must receive additional ground instruction in emergency procedures and deployment-specific information before jumping any unfamiliar system.
4. All instructional rating holders must have a visibly accessible altimeter when conducting student jumps.
5. All skydivers wearing a round main or reserve canopy and all solo students must wear flotation gear when the intended exit, opening, or landing point is within one mile of an open body of water (an open body of water is defined as one in which a skydiver could drown). [S]

## N. Special Altitude Equipment and Supplementary Oxygen

Supplementary oxygen available on the aircraft is mandatory on skydives made from higher than 15,000 feet (MSL).

# 2-2: Waivers to the Basic Safety Requirements

## A. Why BSRs May Need to be Waived

The Basic Safety Requirements represent commonly accepted standards necessary to promote safety in average conditions. Since these standards may be an unnecessary burden in some individual circumstances, USPA provides procedures to document exceptions, known as waivers to the BSRs. These waivers also provide for the responsible research and development of improved techniques and methods.

## B. Classification of Waivers

Waivers to the Basic Safety Requirements are filed at three levels:

1. the USPA S&TA or USPA Examiner
2. the Executive Committee of USPA
3. full Board of Directors of USPA

Neither USPA Headquarters nor any other person or group of persons except those here stated has the authorization to file a waiver to any BSR.

## Requirements and Regulations

Each BSR is waiveable only by the full board, except for those BSRs designated as being waiveable by:

- S&TA or Examiner only [S]
- Executive Committee of the USPA Board only [E]

## C. Procedures for Filing Waivers

Waivers are to be filed only when the person(s) filing the waiver is assured that there will be no compromise of safety.

The person(s) filing the waiver should make periodic inspections to ensure that safety is not being compromised and to determine whether the waiver should be rescinded. In the case of waivers by the Executive Committee, the Regional Director will perform these inspections and make recommendations to the Board.

Any waiver filed by an S&TA or Examiner except for the deployment altitude exception in 2-1 I.4. will be in writing on the waiver form available for download at uspa.org/downloads. A copy of the waiver will be sent to both the USPA Regional Director and USPA Headquarters. The S&TA may waive the minimum deployment altitude for C- and D-license holders from 2,500 feet down to 2,000 feet for a jump or a series of jumps, if necessary. The deployment-altitude waiver does not require any written notification to USPA Headquarters or the Regional Director, however the S&TA should make a note of the waiver for his own records. Any waivers filed by S&TAs or Examiners must specify a location and provide a copy to USPA Headquarters and the location's USPA Regional Director. The waiver will remain in place permanently unless the drop zone changes ownership or location, or the S&TA or Regional Director rescinds the waiver.

S&TAs are not to file waivers for skydiving activities outside their assigned area. If there is a conflict between an S&TA and an Examiner as to whether a waiver should be filed, the decision of the S&TA will be final.

The Executive Committee or full USPA Board of Directors will not approve a waiver without consulting and notifying the local S&TA or USPA Regional Director.

## D. Filing of Waivers

Persons will permanently maintain a record of any waiver they file. The S&TA and Regional Director will maintain permanent records of all waivers filed for skydiving activities within their area. The records will be kept in such a manner as to indicate those waivers currently in effect and those that have been rescinded. USPA Headquarters will maintain a permanent record of all waivers.

### 2-3: Federal Aviation Regulations

The FAA's main responsibility is to provide for the safety of air traffic, as well as persons and property on the ground. The FAA does this by certificating pilots, mechanics, air traffic controllers and parachute riggers and by requiring approval data for aircraft and parachutes. The agency has the authority to impose fines and suspend or revoke certificates it has issued. In the case of a skydiving violation, the FAA can fine the pilot, rigger, and the jumpers, as well as suspend or revoke the certificates of pilots and riggers. The FAA relies upon self-policing from within the skydiving community for most training and operational requirements.

### Important Reference Numbers

- FAR Part 61 (excerpts), pilot certification
- FAR Part 65 (excerpts), parachute riggers
- FAR 91 (excerpts), general flight rules pertaining to skydiving operations
- FAR Part 105 (all), skydiving
- FAR Part 119 (excerpts), limits of jump flights
- AC 90-66, multi-users at uncontrolled airports
- AC 105-2E, sport parachuting
- FAA Air Traffic Bulletins, information for air traffic controllers

### PART 61—Certification: Pilots, Flight Instructors, and Ground Instructors

Found in SUBCHAPTER D—AIRMEN

Important sections to note:

**Sec. 61.1:** Applicability and definitions
**Sec. 61.3:** Requirement for certificates, ratings, and authorizations
**Sec. 61.23:** Medical certificates: Requirement and duration
**Sec. 61.51:** Pilot logbooks
**Sec. 61.56:** Flight review
**Sec. 61.57:** Recent flight experience: Pilot in command
**Sec. 61.133:** Commercial pilot privileges and limitations

uspa.org/far/61

### PART 65—Certification: Airmen Other Than Flight Crewmembers

Found in SUBCHAPTER D—AIRMEN

Important sections to note:

**Sec. 65.1:** Applicability
**Sec. 65.11:** Application and issue
**Sec. 65.12:** Offenses involving alcohol or drugs

uspa.org/far/65

**Sec. 65.15:** Duration of certificates
**Sec. 65.16:** Change of name: Replacement of lost or destroyed certificate
**Sec. 65.17:** Tests: General procedure
**Sec. 65.18:** Written tests: Cheating or other unauthorized conduct
**Sec. 65.19:** Retesting after failure
**Sec. 65.20:** Applications, certificates, logbooks, reports, and records: Falsification, reproduction, or alteration
**Sec. 65.21:** Change of address
**Sec. 65.111:** Certificate required
**Sec. 65.113:** Eligibility requirements: General
**Sec. 65.115:** Senior parachute rigger certificate: Experience, knowledge, and skill requirements
**Sec. 65.117:** Military riggers or former military riggers: Special certification rule
**Sec. 65.119:** Master parachute rigger certificate: Experience, knowledge, and skill requirements
**Sec. 65.121:** Type ratings

Sec. 65.123: Additional type ratings: Requirements
Sec. 65.125: Certificates: Privileges (uspa.org/far/65/125)
Sec. 65.127: Facilities and equipment
Sec. 65.129: Performance standards (uspa.org/far/65/129)
Sec. 65.131: Records
Sec. 65.133: Seal

## PART 91—General Operating and Flight Rules

Found in SUBCHAPTER F—Air Traffic and General Operating Rules

Important sections to note:

Sec. 91.1: Applicability
Sec. 91.3: Responsibility and authority of the pilot in command (uspa.org/far/91/3)
Sec. 91.5: Pilot in command of aircraft requiring more than one required pilot
Sec. 91.7: Civil aircraft airworthiness
Sec. 91.11: Prohibition on interference with crewmembers
Sec. 91.13: Careless or reckless operation
Sec. 91.15: Dropping objects (uspa.org/far/91/15)
Sec. 91.17: Alcohol or drugs (uspa.org/far/91/17)
Sec. 91.19: Carriage of narcotic drugs, marihuana, and depressant or stimulant drugs or substances
Sec. 91.101: Applicability
Sec. 91.103: Preflight action
Sec. 91.107: Use of safety belts, shoulder harnesses, and child restraint systems (uspa.org/far/91/107)
Sec. 91.111: Operating near other aircraft
Sec. 91.113: Right-of-way rules: Except water operations
Sec. 91.119: Minimum safe altitudes: General
Sec. 91.126: Operating on or in the vicinity of an airport in Class G airspace
Sec. 91.127: Operating on or in the vicinity of an airport in Class E airspace
Sec. 91.151: Fuel requirements for flight in VFR conditions (uspa.org/far/91/151)
Sec. 91.155: Basic VFR weather minimums (uspa.org/far/91/155)
Sec. 91.211: Supplemental oxygen (uspa.org/far/91/211)
Sec. 91.215: ATC transponder and altitude reporting equipment and use.
Sec. 91.223: Terrain awareness and warning system
Sec. 91.225: Automatic Dependent Surveillance-Broadcast (ADS-B) Out equipment and use
Sec. 91.307: Parachutes and parachuting
Sec. 91.403: General
Sec. 91.409: Inspections (uspa.org/far/91/409)

## PART 105—Parachute Operations

Found in SUBCHAPTER F—Air Traffic and General Operating Rules

Important sections to note:

Sec. 105.1: Applicability
Sec. 105.3: Definitions (uspa.org/far/105/3)
Sec. 105.5: General

uspa.org/far/105

Sec. 105.7: Use of alcohol and drugs (uspa.org/far/105/7)
Sec. 105.9: Inspections
Sec. 105.13: Radio equipment and use requirements (uspa.org/far/105/13)
Sec. 105.15: Information required and notice of cancellation or postponement of a parachute operation (uspa.org/far/105/15)
Sec. 105.17: Flight visibility and clearance from cloud requirements (uspa.org/far/105/17)
Sec. 105.19: Parachute operations between sunset and sunrise (uspa.org/far/105/19)
Sec. 105.21: Parachute operations over or into a congested area or an open-air assembly of persons (uspa.org/far/105/21)
Sec. 105.23: Parachute operations over or onto airports (uspa.org/far/105/23)
Sec. 105.25: Parachute operations in designated airspace (uspa.org/far/105/25)
Sec. 105.41: Applicability
Sec. 105.43: Use of single-harness, dual-parachute systems (uspa.org/far/105/43)
Sec. 105.45: Use of tandem parachute systems (uspa.org/far/105/45)
Sec. 105.47: Use of static lines (uspa.org/far/105/47)
Sec. 105.49: Foreign parachutists and equipment

uspa.org/far/91

## PART 119—Certification: Air Carriers and Commercial Operators

Found in SUBCHAPTER G—Air Carriers and Operators for Compensation or Hire: Certification and Operations

uspa.org/far/119

## 2-4: Other FAA Guidance

### Advisory Circulars

| | |
|---|---|
|  uspa.org/far/AC90-66B |  uspa.org/far/AC105-2E |
| AC 90-66B—Recommended Standard Traffic Patterns and Practices for Aeronautical Operations at Airports without Operating Control Towers | AC 105-2E— Sport Parachuting <br><br> Contains information about TSO for parachutes, deployment-assisted devices for static line, parachute operations onto and over airports, aircraft inspections, jump pilot responsibilities, exhibition jumping, parachute packing, repairs and alterations, door removal, and field approval process. |

### Seats and Restraint Systems

uspa.org/far/seatbelts

### Air Traffic Bulletins

uspa.org/far/ATB

# Chapter 3: Licenses, Ratings, and Awards

Skydivers can qualify for and receive a variety of licenses and ratings according to their experience, skill, and knowledge level.

USPA **Licenses** are documents of proficiency, divided into four classes from the lowest to highest levels: A, B, C, and D.

USPA **Ratings** are credentials earned through experience and expertise in one of three areas: student instruction, professional demonstration jumping, and competition judging. For more details on the USPA instructional ratings, see the USPA Instructional Rating Manual (IRM). For the USPA PRO Exhibition rating, see SIM Chapter 6, "Exhibition Jumping and PRO Rating." For information on competition judging, see the USPA Skydiver's Competition Manual (SCM).

USPA also presents **Awards** to members in recognition of their accomplishments in skydiving. USPA established these awards programs, representing significant achievement, to provide goals and promote recognition in a variety of fields.

The Federal Aviation Administration (FAA), not USPA, issues certificates for riggers, pilots, and aircraft mechanics. For more information on FAA credentials, refer to the FAA website at faa.gov.

## 3-1: Licenses

USPA intends for its license requirements to encourage skydivers to develop knowledge and skills as they gain experience. All Fédération Aéronautique Internationale (FAI; aka the World Air Sports Federation)-member countries recognize USPA licenses, which serve as official documentation that the holder has attained the stated experience and skills. Licenses are valuable instructional tools, serving both as goals and as guidelines for acquiring the skills and knowledge necessary for a reasonable level of safety and enjoyment.

### USPA License Authority

The National Aeronautic Association and the Fédération Aéronautique Internationale authorize the United States Parachute Association to issue internationally recognized Parachutist Certificates of Proficiency. USPA issues these as A, B, C, and D licenses, ranked according to level of accomplishment, based on demonstrated skill, knowledge, and experience.

### Validity of Licenses and Ratings

USPA licenses and ratings are valid only while the holder is a current USPA member.

USPA licenses are valid in all FAI-member countries and, while valid, entitle the holder to participate in open skydiving events organized in FAI-member countries. USPA issues licenses only to USPA members who meet the conditions set forth for that license.

Applicants may use student-training and military-training jumps toward total jump requirements for licenses and ratings if the appropriate USPA official verifies them.

USPA defines "total freefall time" to include both freefall and droguefall time. The required number of jumps for licenses and ratings can include static-line and IAD jumps.

USPA may suspend, revoke, or refuse to issue a license or rating acting in compliance with existing USPA Board directives.

### Logging Jumps for Licenses and Ratings

Applicants must make skydives offered as evidence of qualification in accordance with USPA requirements in effect at the time of the jump. This evidence must be legibly recorded in chronological order in an appropriate log that contains the following information:

- jump number
- date
- location
- exit altitude
- freefall length (time)
- type of jump (formation skydiving, freeflying, canopy formation, etc.)

# Licenses, Ratings, and Awards

- landing distance from the target
- equipment used
- verifying signature to include a legible USPA membership number, skydiving license number, or pilot certificate number

A witness of the jump—who may be another licensed skydiver, pilot, or USPA Instructor, Examiner, S&TA, or board member—must sign off on jumps submitted to meet **the number-of-jumps requirements** for USPA licenses and ratings.

A USPA Coach, Instructor, Examiner, S&TA, or board member must sign off on jumps to meet **skill requirements**. A USPA Examiner must sign off on special requirements and additional qualifying items such as first-jump courses, air evaluations, ground evaluations, and teaching requirements needed for examiner ratings.

A USPA Instructor, Examiner, S&TA, or board member must sign off on all jumps needed to meet **requirements for licenses or ratings**, except for jumps to meet the number-of-jumps requirements.

Applicants who use **digital devices** instead of traditional paper logbooks to record jumps must ensure that the digital device contains the required information, including a signature verification from a licensed skydiver, the pilot, or a USPA National or FAI Judge who witnessed the skydive. Each instructor, S&TA, examiner, or board member who verifies license requirements for a USPA license must review and verify the jumps logged in a digital device. Skydivers pursuing licenses and ratings must clearly log their first 500 jumps so officials can easily verify them.

## Logging Freefall Time

The following table provides the estimated freefall time from a given altitude. Many factors affect the actual terminal velocity in freefall, including the total weight of the jumper (including equipment), the surface-area-to-weight ratio, jumpsuit, altitude, and skydiving discipline. You should log every jump made, including the amount of freefall time experienced in actual time.

### Freefall-Time Table

| Length of Freefall (feet) | Time at 120 mph (seconds) | Time at 160 mph (seconds) | Time at 50 mph (seconds) |
|---|---|---|---|
| 500 | 2.84 | 2.13 | 6.82 |
| 1,000 | 5.68 | 4.26 | 13.64 |
| 1,500 | 8.52 | 6.40 | 20.45 |
| 2,000 | 11.36 | 8.53 | 27.27 |
| 2,500 | 14.20 | 10.67 | 34.09 |
| 3,000 | 17.05 | 12.80 | 40.91 |
| 3,500 | 19.89 | 14.94 | 47.73 |
| 4,000 | 22.73 | 17.07 | 54.55 |
| 4,500 | 25.57 | 19.21 | 61.36 |
| 5,000 | 28.41 | 21.34 | 68.18 |
| 5,500 | 31.25 | 23.48 | 75.00 |
| 6,000 | 34.09 | 25.61 | 81.82 |
| 6,500 | 36.93 | 27.75 | 88.64 |
| 7,000 | 39.77 | 29.88 | 95.45 |
| 7,500 | 42.61 | 32.02 | 102.27 |
| 8,000 | 45.45 | 34.15 | 109.09 |
| 8,500 | 48.30 | 36.29 | 115.91 |
| 9,000 | 51.14 | 38.42 | 122.73 |
| 9,500 | 53.98 | 40.56 | 129.55 |
| 10,000 | 56.82 | 42.69 | 136.36 |
| 10,500 | 59.66 | 44.83 | 143.18 |
| 11,000 | 62.50 | 46.96 | 150.00 |
| 11,500 | 65.34 | 49.10 | 156.82 |
| 12,000 | 68.18 | 51.23 | 163.64 |
| 12,500 | 71.02 | 53.37 | 170.45 |
| 13,000 | 73.86 | 55.50 | 177.27 |
| 13,500 | 76.70 | 57.64 | 184.09 |
| 14,000 | 79.55 | 59.77 | 190.91 |
| 14,500 | 82.39 | 61.91 | 197.73 |
| 15,000 | 85.23 | 64.04 | 204.55 |
| 15,500 | 88.07 | 66.18 | 211.36 |

## License Exams

### The A-License Written, Oral, and Practical Exams

The examining USPA Instructor will supervise a 40-question **written** USPA A-License Exam (available online). The applicant must score at least 75% on this written exam. See the next section for more details on written exams for all licenses.

The examining USPA Instructor will also conduct an **oral quiz** of at least 20 questions taken from the USPA Integrated Student Program syllabus, with emphasis on the following:

- cloud-clearance and visibility requirements
- equipment operation and maintenance
    - » wing loading and its effects
    - » closing loop
    - » touch fastener (aka Velcro) and tuck flaps
    - » packing and authorization to pack
- canopy flight
    - » traffic patterns and collision avoidance
    - » braked turns and obstacle avoidance
    - » low-turn avoidance and recovery
    - » downwind landing procedures
    - » obstacle landing emergency and recovery procedures
- aircraft procedures
    - » during jump run and exit to observe balance limits
    - » distance between groups to maintain separation
    - » aircraft-emergency procedures
- group breakoff recommendations
- parachute-emergency procedures
    - » deployment malfunctions
    - » cutaway decide-and-act altitude
    - » two-canopies-deployed scenarios
- accountability for FAR compliance

The applicant must score 100% on this oral exam. If the student fails to answer all questions in the oral quiz correctly, the examining instructor will conduct or arrange appropriate review training until passing.

The examining instructor will also conduct a **practical exam** by making a skydive (also referred to as the "A-license check dive") with the applicant to verify practical capabilities in the following areas:

- choosing the spot and selecting and guiding the pilot to the correct exit and opening point in routine conditions
- pre-jump equipment checks for self and others
- planning an effective group breakoff
- right 360-degree turn, left 360-degree turn, and a back loop (back loop to be completed within 60 degrees of the original heading)
- docking from 20 feet (evaluator flies into position)
- breakoff altitude recognition and tracking for a minimum of 100 feet
- signal before deployment and overall awareness during and after deployment
- planning and flying a logical landing pattern that promotes a smooth traffic flow and avoids other jumpers
- packing and preparing equipment for the next jump

The applicant must score satisfactorily on this practical exam. If the student fails to demonstrate practical capabilities in any area, the examining instructor will conduct or arrange appropriate review training and re-jumps until the student passes.

### A-, B-, C-, and D-License Written Exams

An appropriate examining official must supervise license exams. Applicants may not use references or other assistance during the exam and must pass with a score of 75% or more. The official will record any passing score on the license application and in the applicant's logbook.

# Licenses, Ratings, and Awards

When giving written exams on **paper**, the examining official gives the license applicant a blank answer sheet and the questions to the exam. After the test, the examining official collects the materials and grades the exam. An applicant who does not pass will be eligible to retake this exam after seven days.

For written exams taken using USPA's **online** license-testing program, applicants who do not pass may immediately retest using the same method for a total of three attempts per day.

To qualify for a higher license, the applicant must possess a USPA license, meet all qualifications for lower licenses, and have passed all lower-class license exams.

## License Applications

Students can apply for their **A License** using a completed A-License Progression Card either online or paper. If they use the online progression card, they can purchase and receive their A License instantly. A properly completed paper progression card serves as a valid A License for up to 60 days from the date on which it was signed by the certifying instructor. However, the student should send the paper application and the associated fee to USPA Headquarters within 60 days.

Applicants for **all license levels** must submit the appropriate fee and the completed application to USPA through any of the following methods:

- Have requirements verified online and purchase the license **online**.
- Scan and **email** a copy of the card to membership@uspa.org and call USPA Headquarters with credit card payment.
- Copy both sides of the completed license application and **mail** it with payment.
- **Fax** both sides of the completed license application to USPA and call USPA Headquarters with credit card payment.

Once USPA issues a license, it will update the applicant's membership card to include the new license number, which *Parachutist* magazine will publish if the member opts into sharing through their privacy settings in their uspa.org profile. USPA will mail a new physical membership card if the member opts into that mailing preference.

For **paper license applications for B, C, and D licenses**, the verifying official signing the license application should check that each of these items has been completed:

- applicant's personal information
- experience verification (number of jumps and freefall time, if applicable)
- skill verification

The official verifies either that the jump number, date, or score for each requirement is correct and can be found in the applicant's logbook; or, if applicable, the applicant included their appropriate license number with the application. For **experience verification**, the certifying official should verify that the number of jumps and total freefall time are correct and meet the listed requirements for the license sought. For **skill verification**, a current USPA Instructor, S&TA, Examiner, or board member must initial the jump numbers, scores, or date(s) of completion.

You may not sign for your own license application or initial any of the verification blocks of your own license application. An appropriate official (as listed in this chapter) must sign paper applications for all licenses before the application is forwarded to USPA Headquarters. Instructors may verify A, B, and C licenses. USPA S&TAs, Examiners, and board members may verify any license application.

Every USPA B-license application must also include a completed copy of the **B-License Canopy Proficiency Card** signed by a current USPA S&TA, Examiner, or board member. The S&TA must ensure that the person who conducts the training is qualified. In some situations, the best candidate to teach this material may not hold any USPA ratings but may have extensive knowledge about canopy control and landings. The signature of the appropriate official on the proficiency card verifies that the candidate has satisfactorily completed the training.

USPA will charge a separate license fee for each license number issued.

## License Privileges and Requirements

### A License

Persons holding a USPA A License may jump without supervision, pack their own main parachute, engage in formation skydives, perform water jumps, and must have—

- completed 25 freefall jumps
- completed all requirements listed on the USPA A-License Progression Card
- passed the USPA-developed written, oral, and practical USPA A-License Exams conducted by a current USPA Instructor, S&TA, Examiner, Judge or board member

# Licenses, Ratings, and Awards

## B License

Persons holding a USPA B License may exercise all privileges of an A-license holder and perform night jumps, and are eligible for the USPA Coach Rating after making 100 jumps, and must have—

- met all current requirements for or hold a USPA A License
- completed 50 jumps including:
    » accumulated at least 30 minutes of controlled freefall time
    » landed within 33 feet (10 meters) of target center on 10 jumps
- successful completion of the planned formation(s) on 10 formation skydives, or 10 formation freefly skydives, at least five of which, in either discipline, must involve at least three participants
- documentation of live water-landing training with full equipment in accordance with the procedures in the Skydiver's Information Manual
- complete all the requirements listed on the B-License Canopy Proficiency Card available at uspa.org/downloads
- passed the written USPA B-License Exam conducted by a current USPA Instructor, S&TA, Examiner, Judge or board member

## C License

Persons holding a USPA C license may exercise all privileges of a B-license holder, are eligible for USPA Instructor ratings except USPA Tandem Instructor, may participate in certain demonstration jumps, may ride as passenger during USPA Tandem Instructor training and rating-renewal jumps, and must have—

- met all current requirements for or hold a USPA B License
- completed 200 jumps, including accumulating at least 60 minutes of controlled freefall time
- landed within 7 feet (2 meters) of target center on 25 jumps
- successful completed 50 formation skydives, or 50 formation freefly skydives, at least 10 of which, in either discipline, must involve at least four participants
- passed the written USPA C-License Exam conducted by a current USPA Instructor, S&TA, Examiner, Judge or board member

## D License

Persons holding a USPA D License may exercise all privileges of a C-license holder, are eligible for all USPA ratings, and must have—

- met all current requirements for or hold a USPA C License
- completed 500 jumps, including accumulating at least three hours of controlled freefall time
- completed at least two of the following skills requirements (a requirement may be repeated):
    » night jump (following the SIM recommendations)
    » landed within seven feet (2 meters) of the target center on 100 jumps
    » participated in a canopy formation of a 3-stack or larger, completing a full rotation
    » completed an intentional water jump
    » successful completion of 100 formation skydives, at least 25 of which must involve at least eight participants
- passed the written USPA D-License Exam conducted by a current USPA S&TA, Examiner, Judge Examiner or board member

The USPA D-License represents the highest level of licensing within the USPA system, requiring advanced skills and a comprehensive understanding of parachuting safety and procedures. The FAA uses the term '**Master Parachute License**' in its regulations to describe a level of parachuting proficiency required for certain privileges. In alignment with FAA terminology, a holder of a valid USPA D-License satisfies the requirements of the term 'Master Parachute License.'

## Restricted USPA Licenses

In limited circumstances, USPA may issue USPA Restricted Licenses to applicants who have disabilities that make them unable to meet all of the specific license requirements. A person may be qualified for a restricted license if the applicant has met all the requirements for the license desired except for those listed in a waiver they submit to the Safety & Training Committee, containing:

- type of license requested
- specific license requirement(s) that cannot be met
- circumstances that prevent compliance with license requirements
- license application completed, except for the restricted activities

The committee will consider each waiver individually on its own merit. If the board of directors approves the waiver, USPA will issue the license with the word "restricted."

## 3-2: Ratings

## Instructional Ratings

USPA issues instructional ratings, attesting that the holder has not only achieved skydiving skills but has also demonstrated the techniques needed to teach these skills to others.

From lowest to highest, these ratings are:

1. Coach
2. Instructor
3. Examiner

USPA Instructors may be qualified to conduct initial skydiving training in one or more instructional methods:

- harness hold (accelerated freefall or AFF)
- instructor-assisted deployment (IAD)
- static line (SL)
- tandem (TAN)

A USPA Coach may act as a supervised assistant to the USPA Instructor to teach specified portions of the first-jump course. Any instructional rating holder may perform the duties of the coach or of any lower rating holder in their method. Coaches and instructors who have just completed a rating course in any new method should pair with more-seasoned staff as they begin to work with students.

Examiners appoint qualified instructional rating holders as course evaluators in accordance with the requirements outlined in the USPA Instructional Rating Manual (IRM). The IRM contains all policies, procedures, new rating and renewal requirements, and rating-course outlines, support materials and examinations.

## PRO Professional Exhibition Rating

The FAA and USPA cooperate on the means for skydivers to demonstrate competence to perform skydiving shows before the public via the PRO exhibition rating. Chapter 6, Exhibition Jumping and PRO Rating, describes the program. The FAA may ask jumpers who do not hold a PRO rating to demonstrate competence prior to issuing a Certificate of Authorization to conduct a parachute exhibition jump.

## Judge Rating

The purpose of the judging program is to ensure the highest possible standards for judging competitions and records at the local, national, and international levels. USPA issues discipline-specific Regional and National Judge ratings. The FAI, not USPA, rates International Judges. The USPA Skydiver's Competition Manual (SCM) contains details on the judge rating program and judge training courses.

## 3-3: Awards

USPA presents awards to members in recognition of their accomplishments in skydiving.

## Service Awards

USPA reserves its service awards for special USPA members whose contributions to the organization and the sport meet the awards' criteria. These awards include the Gold Medal for Meritorious Service, the Lifetime Achievement Award, the Regional Achievement Award and the Chesley H. Judy Safety Award. The committee also selects nominees for several international skydiving awards, including those for awards given by the Fédération Aéronautique Internationale and National Aeronautic Association.

Service awards recognize excellence in areas such as safety, innovation, instruction, and community involvement. Member participation is essential in identifying individuals who deserve these honors. By nominating fellow skydivers, you can help ensure that their contributions and dedication are recognized and preserved in USPA history. USPA accepts nominations annually at uspa.org/awards.

**The USPA Lifetime Achievement Award** is perhaps the most respected honor offered by the United States Parachute Association. It was originally conceived and created in 1970 as a result of an initial gift of $3,000 from an anonymous donor. The sum was eventually enlarged to a total of $30,000 over a period of years and the funds were placed on deposit with the National Aeronautic Association, which agreed to administer them on behalf of the United States Parachute Association for the purpose of underwriting the cost of a variety of perpetual competition trophies, as well as the Lifetime Achievement Award. The fund ceased to exist in 1982 when the final money available was used to construct the floor-to ceiling display cases at USPA's Headquarters in Alexandria, Virginia. The agreement signed on May 13, 1970, between Attorney John Kerr Wilson, acting for the anonymous donor; National Aeronautic Association Executive Director General Brooke E. Allen, acting for the National Aeronautic Association; and Dr. Edward A. Fitch, president of the United States Parachute Association, acting for USPA, stipulates (among other things) that at any time on or after May 13, 1975, the anonymous donor may identify himself and direct that any and all awards created through his gift carry his name. To date the anonymous donor has not seen fit to exercise this privilege.

The May 13, 1970, agreement, as accepted by USPA, describes the award itself and the qualifications required of recipients, using this language:

> "To provide a bowl or other suitable trophy to be known initially as 'The United States Parachute Association Achievement Award' [renamed 'USPA Lifetime Achievement Award' in July, 2004], which shall be perpetual and will be awarded annually to an expert active or retired sport parachute jumper in recognition of outstanding sportsmanship, skill, or personal contribution to the sport of parachuting and the United States Parachute Association, its goals and purposes. The recipient of such award will be selected by the board of directors by a majority vote during a closed regular or special meeting. In the event a majority of the board of directors cannot agree upon a recipient of such award on account of a lack of preeminence of the sport parachutist in any one year, the award will be made at least once each two years. Such trophy will be kept permanently in an appropriate location to be determined by the board of directors."

The trophy itself is a sterling silver bowl, 15 inches in diameter, seated on an octagonal teakwood base which bears carved wooden replicas of the USPA emblem on four faces and sterling silver plates listing the names and qualifications of recipients of the award on the other four faces. Traditionally, each year the recipient receives a smaller, eight-inch diameter replica sterling-silver bowl as his or her personal possession.

Traditionally, the award is made for the year prior to the year in which it is presented. While the deed of gift requires that the award be given only to an individual, in 1974, the presentation was made to the United States Army Parachute Team and in 2024 to Arizona Airspeed, which suggests that the language in the deed is usable more as a guideline than as a strict requirement.

The Membership Services Committee and the board has usually regarded the statement, "In recognition of personal contribution to the United States Parachute Association, its goals and purposes" as an overriding requirement (i.e., achievements in sport parachuting unrelated to the United States Parachute Association would normally not be considered sufficient to qualify a recipient, lacking specific contributions to USPA).

While the deed of gift states that the award must be made at least once every two years, neither in 1991 nor in 1992 was a recipient named, thereby again suggesting that this particular language serves more as a guideline than as a requirement.

No current member of the USPA Board of Directors may be recommended for the USPA Lifetime Achievement Award during his or her term as a member of the board. In practice, this requirement has been extended to forbid a nomination for at least two full years after the end of board service. It is enlarged to include as ineligible current or former USPA employees, also until at least two years after their employment ends.

**The USPA Gold Medal for Meritorious Service** was established on July 13, 1997, by the USPA Board of Directors. The award is given to no more than three recipients per year, in the form of a struck-brass medal that measures three inches in diameter, weighs approximately five ounces and is slotted at the top for attachment of a 30-inch gold fabric ribbon. On permanent display at USPA Headquarters is a large wooden plaque measuring two feet by six feet and adorned with an exact replica of the medal along with brass metal strips bearing the name of each recipient and the year awarded.

The USPA Gold Medal for Meritorious Service honors outstanding USPA members who, by their efforts over a period of years, have made significant contributions to the skydiving community. Each recipient must be or have been a USPA member and been active in sport parachuting for at least 20 years in the areas of, but not limited to judging, instruction, jumpmastering, photography (still and video), competition, and safety.

No current member of the USPA Board of Directors may be considered for the award and no past member of the board of directors of USPA may be considered for the award until at least two years after retiring from the board. No current employee of USPA may be considered for the award and no past employee of USPA may be considered for the award until at least two years after leaving USPA employment.

**The USPA Regional Achievement Award** honors an outstanding member of a USPA region who, by their efforts over a period of time or one outstanding act, has made a significant contribution to that region's skydiving community. The award is presented in the form of a certificate to a total of no more than five recipients per year.

No current member of the USPA Board of Directors may be considered for the award and no past member of the USPA Board of Directors may be considered for the award until they have been off the board for at least two years. No current employee of USPA may be considered for the award and no past employee of USPA may be considered for the award until at least two years after leaving USPA employment.

**The USPA Chesley H. Judy Safety Award** was created in 2004 to honor members who had promoted skydiving safety. The USPA Board determined that the award was consistent with the original intent of the Ches Judy Safety Fund established in 1997 to honor the memory of Ches Judy, former USPA Director of Safety and Training, who was killed in a skydiving plane crash two years earlier. Distribution of the fund was in abeyance pending the development of a suitable safety-related program.

# Licenses, Ratings, and Awards

USPA Headquarters developed the certificate, which is available at no charge to each drop zone to honor the local USPA member who is most deserving of the award. The award is to be presented on USPA Safety Day in conjunction with the other planned activities for the annual event.

The selection for the award recipient should be based on the previous year's actions or accomplishments of any current USPA member who, through example, deed, training, or innovation, had promoted safe skydiving in a substantive way. The USPA S&TA in consultation with the drop zone owner selects one individual from the drop zone to which the award is appointed based on the above criteria.

The S&TA should request a certificate from headquarters either online or by email to safety@uspa.org. The request should include the correctly spelled name of the recipient and the name of the drop zone. USPA will provide the completed certificate to the requesting S&TA for presentation during that year's Safety Day activities.

## Achievement Awards

USPA members earn achievement awards by accumulating significant levels of experience. For number of freefall jumps, USPA issues Jump Wings in 1,000-jump increments and, for amount of freefall time, Freefall Badges in 12-hour increments.

## Performance Awards

USPA issues canopy performance awards for accomplishments in canopy formation skydiving. These include the 4-Stack Award, CCR (Canopy Crest Recipient) or 8-Stack Award, and CCS (Canopy Crest Soloist) Award, and include night versions of each.

## Tenure Certificates

Upon request, USPA issues tenure certificates to acknowledge membership in USPA for significant periods of time, beginning at 10 years of USPA membership and for each five-year increment thereafter.

## Sportsmanship Award

USPA established the **Ted Strong Award for Extraordinary Sportsmanship** in 2012 to honor extraordinary sportsmanship displayed by teams or individuals at a USPA National Championships. For further information, see USPA National Skydiving Championships General Competition Rules in the Skydiver's Competition Manual.

For more details on these awards, visit uspa.org/awards.

USPA Awards

uspa.org/awards

## FAI and NAA Awards

Nominations for Fédération Aéronautique Internationale and National Aeronautic Association awards go through the Membership Services and Competition Committees of the USPA Board of Directors for endorsement, then to USPA Headquarters for submission to the NAA.

## Fédération Aéronautique Internationale General Awards

**The Paul Tissandier Diploma** is awarded to those who have served the cause of aviation in general and sporting aviation in particular, by their work, initiative, devotion, or in other ways. Each year, the United States may submit the names of up to three candidates.

**The FAI Honorary Group Diploma**, as its name implies, may be awarded to groups of people (design offices, scientific bodies, aeronautical publications, etc.) that have contributed significantly to the progress of aeronautics or astronautics during the previous year or years. Each year, an FAI member may submit the names of two candidates, one for aeronautics and one for astronautics.

**The FAI Gold Parachuting Medal** may be awarded annually for an outstanding accomplishment in connection with parachuting, in the realm of sport, safety, or an invention. The medal was created by an endowment fund provided by Mr. J.A. Istel, President of Honour of the FAI Parachuting Commission.

**The Leonardo da Vinci Diploma** is awarded to a parachutist who has any one of the following:

- been at least twice an individual champion or a member of a champion team at a first-category event
- established at least three world parachuting records
- have been at least three times an FAI/IPC official at a first-category event (Chief Judge, FAI Parachuting Judge, FAI Controller, International Jury Member or any combination thereof)
- have been at least three times a competition director at a first-category event
- have been for at least six years the chair of an IPC Committee (IPC Internal Regulations 6.7) or an IPC Bureau Member or any combination thereof

**The Faust Vrančić Medal** was established in memory of the first person to construct a functioning parachute and is awarded annually for technical innovation or achievement in parachuting. It cannot be awarded to delegates to the FAI Parachuting Commission.

**The Sabiha Gökçen Medal** is awarded to the woman who performs the most outstanding achievement in any air sport in the previous year. It was created in 2002 upon a proposal from Turk Hava Kurumu, and is supplied by the Turkish NAC. Sabiha Gökçen, winner of the FAI Gold Air Medal, was Turkey's first woman pilot and, in 1937, became the world's first female military pilot. She was an inspiration to women pilots.

Refer to **www.fai.org/page/civa-awards** and **naa.aero/awards** for the most up-to-date information. FAI parachuting awards are subject to approval by the FAI Parachuting Commission.

## National Aeronautic Association Service Awards

**The Frank G. Brewer Trophy**, awarded annually, is given to an individual, group or organization for significant contributions of enduring value to aerospace education in the United States. The nomination period is open from May 1 through August 31 every year.

**The Wesley L. McDonald Distinguished Statesman and Stateswoman of Aviation Awards** honor outstanding Americans who, by their efforts over a period of years, have made contributions of significant value to aeronautics and have reflected credit upon America and themselves. The nomination period is open from May 1 through August 31 every year. A nominee must:

- be a living citizen of the U.S who has for at least 25 years been actively identified with aeronautics and has made contributions of significant value to aeronautics;
- have exhibited qualities of patriotism, integrity, and moral courage worthy of emulation;
- be well and favorably known as a person of ability and character.

Refer to **naa.aero/awards** for the most up-to-date information.

# Licenses, Ratings, and Awards

# Chapter 4: Recommendations for Everyone

This section provides USPA's recommendations for skydiving that apply to all jumpers, regardless of discipline or experience. USPA updates them as equipment and techniques change.

## 4-1: Skydiving Emergencies

### A. Types of Emergencies
Types of skydiving emergencies include those occurring in aircraft, during freefall, on deployment, during canopy flight, and on landing.

### B. Prevention and Preparation
Regular, periodic review, analysis, and practice of emergency procedures prepares you to act correctly in response to problems that arise while skydiving:

**Annually**, review all aircraft-, deployment-, and landing-emergency procedures using appropriate training aids.

**Monthly**, dedicate a clear-and-pull or high-pull jump to practicing canopy-flight-emergency-procedure skills.

**Before each jump**, review the procedures for both avoiding and responding to emergency situations. Long periods between jumps not only dull skills but heighten apprehensions.

**At every reserve repack**, practice your reserve emergency procedures on the ground. Simulate some type of main malfunction, then cut away and deploy the reserve. This practice will provide you with first-hand knowledge about the potential pull forces and direction of pull on your gear.

Proper preparation and responsible judgment greatly reduce the probability of encountering an emergency, but even with the greatest care, they may occasionally occur. Anticipating and being prepared to respond to various emergencies makes skydiving safer. One of the greatest causes of fatal incidents in skydiving is failure to effectively deal with an emergency situation.

Doing the following reduces risk:

- Acquiring accurate knowledge
- Jumping only in suitable conditions
- Evaluating the risk factors
- Knowing your personal limitations
- Keeping your options open
- Respecting your decision altitude
- Adhering to the 1,000-foot cutaway hard deck

### Survival Skills

**Altitude Awareness:** Check your altimeter every 5 seconds (approximately 1,000 feet of freefall), every time you complete a maneuver, anytime you encounter difficulty, and if you simply do not know your altitude.

**Pull Priorities:** The number-one priority on any skydive is to pull. You can pull at any time during the skydive when encountering difficulty. The second priority is to pull at the assigned altitude, and the third priority is to preferably pull in a stable body position. A stable, face-to-earth body position improves opening reliability but is secondary to opening at the assigned altitude. Always prioritize altitude over stability.

**Canopy Right-of-Way Rules:** Look before you turn. Turn right to avoid other jumpers. The lower jumper has the right-of-way.

**Landing Priorities:** The number-one landing priority is to land with the wing level while flying in a straight line. The second landing priority is to land in a clear and open area, avoiding obstacles. The third landing priority is to flare, always being prepared to PLF. Remember: Landing with a level wing is a higher priority than landing in a clear and open area.

# Recommendations for Everyone

Land with a level wing, even if you need to make a flat turn to avoid an obstacle. Land in a clear and open area, even if it is farther from the drop zone. To avoid injury, always flare the parachute before touchdown with your feet and knees together, prepared for a PLF.

## C. Aircraft Emergencies

Each skydiving center should establish and review procedures for all possible aircraft emergencies. Every pilot and non-student jumper should thoroughly understand these procedures. All students should take direction from their instructor(s). All licensed jumpers should take direction from the pilot.

## D. Freefall Collisions

Jumpers face danger of collision when exiting in a group or when they lose track of each other when exiting on the same pass. Taking into account horizontal and vertical movement, the difference in speed between jumpers may reach upward of 150 mph. You must take precautions to prevent a collision with freefalling jumpers during and after opening.

## E. Deployment Emergencies

### Parachute Malfunctions (General)

Most malfunctions trace to three causes:

1. poor or unstable body position during parachute deployment
2. equipment failure
3. improper or careless packing

Refer to Category A of the Integrated Student Program for specific, basic procedures for dealing with parachute malfunctions. Licensed jumpers may need to adjust procedures to accommodate different techniques, equipment, and personal preferences. Using safety devices, such as a reserve static line (RSL), preferably with a main-assisted-reserve-deployment (MARD) system; and an automatic activation device (AAD) can significantly reduce risk when encountering malfunctions.

You can prepare for emergencies by thinking through possible scenarios, having a plan in mind, and practicing reacting correctly. You should decide upon and take the appropriate actions by a predetermined altitude that should be no lower than 2,500 feet for students and A-license holders and no lower than 2,000 feet for B- and C-license holders. D-license holders should establish their **decision altitude** for themselves based on their experience and equipment.

### Reserve Activation

Reserve pilot chutes contain a metal spring in the center, which adds to their weight. During a stable, belly-to-earth reserve deployment, the reserve pilot chute can remain in the jumper's burble for several seconds, delaying reserve deployment. Immediately after pulling the reserve handle, look over your right shoulder while twisting your upper body upward to the right or sit up in a slightly head-high orientation to change the airflow behind your container to help the reserve pilot chute launch into clean air.

Most harness-and-container manufacturers secure the steering toggles to reserve risers using touch fasteners (e.g., Velcro), which will firmly hold the toggles in place. Be sure to peel the Velcro before attempting to pull the toggles free from the risers to unstow the brakes.

There are two categories of malfunctions:

1. total malfunction: the main pin is not out; parachute is not activated or is activated but not deploying; the container is closed
2. partial malfunction: the main pin is out; parachute is deployed but is not landable; the container is open

### Total Malfunction

A total malfunction includes deployment-handle problems such as being unable to locate the main handle, a hard pull, a container lock, and a pilot chute in tow. You should attempt to solve the problem only when altitude permits and should make no more than two attempts or take no more than five additional seconds to solve the problem.

### Procedures:

- When no main pilot chute deploys (e.g., cannot find handle or hard pull), deploy the reserve.
- For a pilot-chute-in-tow malfunction, there are currently two common and acceptable procedures, both of which have pros and cons. Seek guidance from an instructor to plan your training and ensure you're prepared before you jump.
  - **Pilot-chute-in-tow procedure 1:** Pull the reserve immediately. A pilot-chute-in-tow malfunction is associated with a high descent rate and requires immediate action. The chance of a main-reserve entanglement is slim, and you could lose valuable time and altitude by initiating a cutaway before deploying your reserve. Be prepared to cut away. The main may deploy after the reserve is open, so be prepared for a two-out scenario.

- **Pilot-chute-in-tow procedure 2:** Cut away, then immediately deploy the reserve. Because there is a chance the main parachute could deploy during or as a result of the reserve activation, a cutaway might be the best response in some situations.

## Partial Malfunction

Deployment or partial deployment of the main parachute characterizes a partial malfunction. This includes pilot-chute entanglement, premature deployment, bag-lock, streamer, line-over, tension knots, major or unlandable canopy damage, and other open-canopy malfunctions

## Emergency Procedures

The recommended procedure for responding to partial malfunctions is to **cut away the main parachute before deploying** the reserve. However, if you are below your cutaway hard deck of 1,000 feet, where it's too low for a safe cutaway, you must **deploy the reserve and land both parachutes**. Also, consider the operating range of the AAD when determining your personal malfunction-response altitudes.

## Premature Main-Container Opening

A premature main-container opening happens when the main pin is dislodged, allowing the container to open and the bag to come out, but the main pilot chute is still stowed.

You can **prevent** a premature main-container opening by inspecting your closing loop regularly and asking for a pin check before exit. Move carefully in the aircraft and avoid your rig contacting the door frame during the climb-out and exit.

The recommended **procedure** is to first attempt to throw the main pilot chute; however, finding the pilot chute may be difficult after the bag is out of the container. Attempt to find the pilot chute twice or for 5 seconds. If that fails, cut away and deploy the reserve. If you are able to deploy the pilot chute, be prepared to execute emergency procedures as the main may not come out of the bag.

## Two Canopies Out

*Note: The following recommendations are drawn from experience with larger canopies during tests conducted in the mid-1990s. Smaller canopies may react differently and require a different response.*

Various scenarios can result in having both parachutes deploy with one of the following outcomes:

- One canopy inflated, another deploying
    - Attempt to contain the deploying canopy by stuffing it between your legs. If the second canopy's deployment is inevitable, disconnect the RSL if possible, wait for inflation, and evaluate the result.
- Stable biplane
    - Land both parachutes. Disconnect the reserve static line if altitude permits. If all toggles are stowed, leave them stowed. If any toggle is unstowed, unstow all of them. Steer using the rear risers of the front canopy only as necessary to maneuver for a safe landing. Land without flaring and perform a PLF.
- Stable side-by-side (choose one procedure):
    - **Side-by-side procedure 1:** Land both parachutes. Disconnect the reserve static line if altitude permits. If all toggles are stowed, leave them stowed. If any toggle is unstowed, unstow all of them. Steer using the rear risers of the dominant canopy (more overhead) only as necessary to maneuver for a safe landing. Land without flaring and perform a PLF.
    - **Side-by-side procedure 2:** If both canopies are flying without interference and altitude permits, disconnect the reserve static line. Confirm the parachutes are completely separated from each other then cut away the main and steer the reserve to a normal landing.
- Downplane or pinwheel (canopies spinning around each other)
    - Disconnect the reserve static line if altitude permits. Cut away the main canopy and steer the reserve to a normal landing.
- Main-reserve entanglement
    - Although rare, main-reserve entanglements can occur in multiple configurations, making a single solution impractical. Land both parachutes. Never give up trying to clear the entanglement or inflate the parachutes. Recommended techniques include pulling in the less-inflated canopy, hand over hand, to contain it, or pumping the brakes or rear risers of both parachutes to increase their inflation. Try to make the parachutes fly straight for landing. Prepare for and execute a PLF on landing.

# F. Canopy-Flight Emergencies

A **canopy-flight emergency** is any canopy emergency that happens under a fully inflated parachute, anytime during the canopy descent or landing. **Canopy-flight emergency procedures (CEPs)** are a set of five skills used in response to a canopy emergency during a canopy descent or landing. Be prepared for unexpected situations with regular practice of these skills. (Stay alive, practice five.)

## Canopy Collisions

The best way to avoid a collision is **prevention**. You should know where other canopies are at all times. Most canopy collisions occur soon after deployment when two jumpers open too close to each other, or below 1,000 feet while in the landing pattern. Higher break-off altitudes, better planning and tracking farther can help ensure clear airspace during deployment. Every time you deploy your canopy, keep your eyes forward, looking for any jumpers deploying nearby who may open coming straight toward you. Steer with rear risers as soon as inflation allows. Fly perpendicularly to the aircraft line of flight until you have identified jumpers exiting after you. Remaining vigilant throughout the canopy descent and always looking in the direction of the turn before initiating it can help you identify and avoid other canopies during the descent. Canopy collisions are more likely to occur in the base leg of the landing pattern. Planning for a longer base leg promotes more predictability and visibility for everyone under canopy. **Practicing the CEP drills of rear-riser turns and turn reversals** monthly during a dedicated clear-and-pull or high-pull jump above decision altitude can build the proficiency needed to avoid a canopy collision.

Canopy collisions and the events leading up to them can be complex, making it impossible to offer just one solution for every situation. The following are accepted **procedures** for the most common scenarios:

**If the canopies are approaching each other head on**, both canopy pilots should steer to the right unless it is obvious that steering left is necessary to avoid the collision (both jumpers are more offset toward the left).

If a **collision is inevitable**, place your left arm across your handles, turn your face away from impact, and spread your legs as wide as possible. If the upper jumper is lower than the bottom skin of the other canopy, that jumper should clear lines and fabric away from their body, harness and three-ring system, cross their legs and be the first to cut away if altitude permits.

## Entanglements after a Collision

If a **collision with the other jumper's suspension lines** is unavoidable, try to capture as many suspension lines as possible to keep from passing through them during the collision. A high-speed collision with suspension lines can lead to severe cuts and burns. Check your altitude with respect to the minimum cutaway decision and execution altitude recommended for your experience.

**Communicate before taking action**. During a cutaway following a collision, the jumper above can strike the jumper below unless one or both are clear or ready to fend off. The lower jumper can worsen the situation for the jumper above by cutting away before they are clear of lines or are ready. Remember, communication may be difficult if one or both jumpers are wearing full-face helmets.

If **both jumpers are cutting away** and altitude permits, the second jumper should wait at least 5 seconds until the first jumper clears the area below. The first jumper should fly from underneath in a straight line after opening.

If the upper jumper is **engulfed in the fabric** of the other jumper's canopy, the lower jumper should be the first to cut away if altitude permits. The upper jumper should clear the cutaway canopy from their face and their canopy's controls. Fly slowly to reduce inflation of the cutaway canopy. It is usually safer to keep the fabric on your body rather than risk having it inflate and downplane if all lines do not clear.

At some point **below a safe cutaway altitude** (1,000 feet), it may become necessary for one or both jumpers to deploy their reserves (may not be a safe option with a single-operation system, aka SOS system). The lower jumper's reserve will usually deploy faster due to more airspeed and being clear of lines or fabric. If both reserves deploy, it may be necessary for the lower jumper to release the entanglement by cutting away after ensuring that both jumpers have a canopy to land. This is called a canopy transfer and can be successfully executed as low as 200 feet to save both jumpers from striking the ground in a downplane. If both jumpers are suspended under one flying canopy at a low altitude, it may become necessary to land with only that canopy. In this case, the upper jumper should attempt to fly level and slowly.

## Low Turns

Low turns under canopy are one of the biggest causes of serious injury and death in skydiving. A low turn can be premeditated, result from an error in judgment, or result from a lack of experience with a situation.

You can avoid low turns by flying to a large, uncrowded landing area free of obstacles and flying a planned landing pattern that promotes a cooperative traffic flow. If landing off, choose a landing area by 2,000 feet and plan a landing pattern with an obstacle-free final approach.

If you choose to turn at a low altitude to avoid an obstacle, use a **braked turn** and be prepared to flare from a braked position. Monthly practice of **half-braked turns** and **half-braked flares** CEPs during a dedicated clear-and-pull or high-pull jump can build the skills needed to avoid injury during landing emergencies.

# 4 Recommendations for Everyone

If you make a turn at an unsafe altitude, where the parachute will not recover to level flight before touchdown without immediate input, a **low-turn recovery**, one of the CEPs, is necessary. As soon as you realize that you've made a turn at an unsafe altitude, use the toggles to get the canopy back overhead, stop the turn and dive, and slow the forward speed. Neutralize the turn by pulling down the toggle opposite the turn, resulting in a braked toggle position. Flare from the braked position and prepare for a hard landing (PLF). Manage the speed induced by the turn. Expect more-responsive flare control with the toggles due to the increased airspeed and expect a longer, flatter flare. In case of premature contact with the ground, no matter how hard the impact, keep flying the canopy to reduce further injury.

Monthly practice of the low-turn recovery CEP on a dedicated clear-and-pull or high-pull jump above decision altitude can build the proficiency needed to avoid injury or fatality due to a low turn near the ground.

## G. Landing Emergencies

Monthly practice of the CEP drills of **half-braked turns and flares** on a dedicated clear-and-pull or high-pull jump can build the skills needed to avoid injury during landing emergencies.

Potential obstacles during landing include water, trees, buildings, power lines, fences and similar hazards. You can usually avoid these obstacles by properly preparing for your canopy flight by observing the winds and planning an appropriate landing pattern. Also, choosing an alternate landing area by 2,000 feet allows you to assess potential obstacles and plan your new pattern. Follow your landing priorities. The following are best practices or actions you can take when landing in or on common obstacles.

### Water Landings

Procedures for an unintentional water landing focus on actions you can take prior to entering the water (time permitting), while landing in the water, and after entering the water.

**Prior to entering the water:** If possible, continue to steer to avoid the water hazard. Time permitting, loosen the chest strap to facilitate getting out of the harness once you're in the water. If applicable, open your helmet's face shield, activate your flotation device and disconnect your RSL to reduce complications in case you need to cut away after splashing down.

**While landing in the water:** Flare to half brakes at 10 feet above the surface, understanding that poor depth perception over water may make this difficult to judge. Prepare for a PLF in case the water is shallow. Take a deep breath a few seconds before entry so that you enter the water with your lungs filled with air. Remain in the harness and attached to the canopy until you are actually in the water. Once you are, cut away the main canopy, throw your arms back and swim forward out of the harness.

**After landing in the water:** In the absence of flotation gear, separating from your equipment is essential. The container can serve as a flotation device if the reserve canopy is packed in the container. Use caution to avoid the main canopy suspension lines if using the reserve container for flotation. Tests have shown that a container with a packed reserve will remain buoyant for up to 45 minutes or longer. If time permits, use your jumpsuit or clothing to make a temporary floatation device by tying knots at the end of the openings and scooping air into it.

If the collapsed canopy covers you, dive deep and swim out from under it. Follow one seam to the edge of the canopy until clear. If under the main canopy in swift or shallow water, pull one toggle in or cut away. Refill your lungs at every opportunity. Swim upwind or upstream and use care to avoid entangling in the suspension lines. Remove any full-coverage helmets in the event of breathing difficulties. Do not attempt to recover your gear.

Air Force-type (LPU) underarm flotation equipment have bladders that inflate outside the harness although they are worn underneath. Consequently, you must first deflate the bladders before removing the harness and then reinflate them orally one at a time.

Wearing weights to increase your fall rate or using additional equipment such as wingsuits, cameras or skysurfing gear increases your risk during a water landing, and you need to plan your procedures accordingly.

Water temperature below 70 degrees Fahrenheit severely limits the amount of time a person can survive while trying to tread water or remain afloat. Treading water or swimming causes the body to lose heat rapidly, because blood moves to the extremities where it cools quickly. Depending on the situation, it may be better to float than swim or tread water while waiting for help to arrive.

You can find more details on water landings in SIM Chapter 2-1, USPA Basic Safety Requirements on water jumping equipment, and SIM Chapter 5-5, Water Landing Recommendations (unintentional and intentional).

### Power Lines

Power lines present a serious hazard to all aviators; know where they are near your DZ. To **prevent** landing in power lines, identify where they are in the landing area as early as possible and steer to avoid them. If you need to make a low turn to avoid a power line, make the minimum, flat, braked turn necessary to miss it, execute a braked landing, flare, and PLF.

If you cannot avoid a power-line landing, drop handles or other objects, bring the canopy to slow flight, prepare for a PLF with your feet and knees tightly together, and turn your head to the side to protect your chin. Land parallel to the power lines so that you do not touch more than one wire at a time.

# Recommendations for Everyone

If suspended in the wires, do not let anyone touch you. Wait for help from the drop zone and power company personnel. Nylon conducts electricity at higher voltages. Verify only with the power company that electrical power is off and will stay off. If the computer controlling the power distribution senses a fault in the line, computer-controlled resets may attempt to turn the power back on without warning.

If your feet are on the ground, disconnect the RSL and cut away, leaving your main behind.

## Trees

**Prevent** landing in trees by spotting carefully and making a good approach-pattern plan for the conditions. The dangers of landing in a tree extend until you are rescued and safely on the ground. A low-altitude diving turn from full flight is just as dangerous as a tree landing. Make any low-altitude avoidance turns from braked flight.

If you can't avoid landing in a tree under a ram-air canopy, hold the toggles at half brakes until tree contact. Prepare for a PLF; often the jumper passes through the tree and lands on the ground. Protect your body by keeping your feet and knees tightly together, but do not cross your feet or legs. Cover your face with your hands while holding your elbows tightly against your chest. Different trees require different procedures, so, consult with your local S&TA for a briefing appropriate for your drop zone. If the trees are very tall, steer to the middle of the tree, then hold on to the trunk or main branch to avoid falling through to the ground.

If suspended above the ground, wait for help from drop zone personnel to get down. Don't attempt to climb down from a tree without competent assistance such as rescue personnel or properly trained drop zone staff.

## Buildings and Other Objects

To **prevent** landing on or into buildings or other objects, plan your landing approach to be well clear of them. Focus on clear, open landing areas and steer there. Use braked turns to maintain a level wing when turning at a low altitude to avoid obstacles.

If you can't avoid landing on a building or object, prepare for a PLF and flare 10 feet above the first point of contact to slow your forward speed. After landing on top of an object in windy conditions, disconnect the RSL if possible, and cut away. If landing under your reserve, retrieve and contain the canopy until removing the harness and wait for competent help.

When approaching the side of a building, perform a flat turn to avoid hitting it head-on. If a collision is unavoidable, prepare to PLF, flare to slow down, and attempt to strike a glancing blow. Change the canopy's direction to avoid a direct impact.

## Landing Out

Jumpers prefer to land in the planned area, which is usually familiar and free of obstacles. However, circumstances such as a spotting error, unexpected wind conditions, inadvertent high opening in strong upper winds, and low opening (especially under a reserve canopy) may make that difficult or impossible.

Students and experienced jumpers have been injured or killed due to problems resulting from less-than-ideal opening positions over the ground, including:

- intentional low turn into an unfamiliar landing area
- unplanned low turn to avoid obstacles
- landing into or on an obstacle or uneven terrain
- errors made after trying to return to the planned landing area or returning lower than planned, when a better choice was available

**Avoid landing out** by knowing the correct exit point for the current conditions. Once at the door of the aircraft, check the spot before exiting and request a go-around if necessary. In freefall, check the spot soon after exiting and adjust opening altitude if necessary and safe to do so, considering other groups or individuals in freefall nearby or jumpers from other planes in multiple-plane operations.

If you **cannot avoid landing out**, decide on a viable alternate landing area by 2,000 feet, based on your current location, the wind speed, and wind direction. Plan a descent strategy and landing pattern for the alternate landing area. Check the alternate landing area carefully for hazards while still high enough to adjust the landing pattern to avoid them. For example, when checking for power lines, it is easier to see the poles and towers than the wires themselves. Determine the wind direction to predict turbulence created by trees or other obstacles and plan a landing spot accordingly. It may be difficult to see hills from higher altitudes. It can also be difficult to see fences, but man-made obstacles often run in straight lines along the ground.

Flying a braked approach or making a braked turn allows a slower forward speed and descent rate but may lengthen the approach glide. You may need to use an altitude-conserving braked turn to avoid an obstacle. A low-altitude braked turn may not allow recovery to full flight in time for a landing flare, so you may need to flare from a braked position to avoid a flight cycle. You should frequently practice the CEP drills of **braked turns and approaches** to prepare.

Choose a landing area that gives the longest runway for landing and follow the landing priorities. Landing into the wind is desirable, but not at the risk of a low turn. A PLF is especially important during off-field landings, as the terrain may be uneven.

Respect property when landing off the drop zone. Do not disturb livestock. Leave gates as you found them. Avoid walking on crops or other cultivated vegetation. Report any property damage to the property owner and make arrangements for repairs. Remember, USPA membership includes insurance for such situations.

## 4-2: Currency Training

Currency training and jumps should include confirmation of knowledge and ability for a stable exit and body position, altitude awareness, stable deployment, tracking proficiency, canopy-flight planning and CEPs, execution of the pattern, flare technique, and emergency procedures. **Great care is necessary when choosing canopy size.** Depending on the length of the layoff, returning jumpers may require a larger, more conservative canopy than they were previously jumping until the jumper demonstrates proficiency in their canopy skills.

### A. Students
Students who have not jumped within the preceding 30 days should make at least one jump under the direct supervision of an appropriately rated USPA Instructor.

### B. Licensed Skydivers
Skydivers returning after a long period of inactivity encounter greater risk that requires special consideration. Take care to regain or develop the knowledge, skills, and awareness needed to satisfactorily perform the tasks planned for the jump. Jumps aimed at sharpening survival skills should precede jumps with other goals.

### C. Changes in Procedures
Any time you change deployment or emergency procedures, you should train and practice under supervision in a harness simulator until proficient. Follow up ground training with a solo jump that includes several practice sequences and deploy at a higher-than-normal altitude. Repeat ground practice at short intervals, such as before each weekend's jump activities, and continue to deploy at a higher-than-normal altitude until thoroughly familiar with the new procedures.

### D. Long Layoffs
Jumpers should receive refresher training appropriate for their skydiving history and time since their last skydive. Jumpers who were very experienced and current but became inactive for a year or more should undergo thorough training upon returning to the sport. Skydivers who historically jump infrequently should review training after layoffs of even less than a year.

Skydiving equipment, techniques, and procedures change frequently. During currency training following long periods of inactivity, jumpers may encounter new and unfamiliar equipment and techniques. Procedures change to accommodate developments in equipment, aircraft, flying styles, FAA rules, and local drop zone requirements.

Returning skydivers require thorough practical training in the following areas:

- aircraft procedures
- equipment
- exit and freefall procedures
- canopy control and landings
- emergency procedures for aircraft, freefall, deployment, canopy-flight, and landing, as described in Chapter 4-1

### A License
USPA A-license holders who have not made a freefall skydive within the preceding 60 days should make at least one jump under the supervision of a currently rated USPA instructional rating holder until demonstrating altitude awareness, freefall control on all axes, tracking, and canopy skills sufficient for safely jumping in groups.

### B License
USPA B-license holders who have not made a freefall skydive within the preceding 90 days should make at least one jump under the supervision of a USPA instructional rating holder until demonstrating the ability to safely exercise the privileges of that license.

### C and D License
USPA C- and D-license holders who have not made a freefall skydive within the preceding 180 days should make at least one jump under the supervision of a USPA instructional rating holder until demonstrating the ability to safely exercise the privileges of the license.

# 4-3: Equipment

## A. Federal Regulations on Equipment

The Federal Aviation Administration of the U.S. Department of Transportation, which publishes the Federal Aviation Regulations (FARs), regulates the design, maintenance, and alteration of parachute equipment.

All skydivers should be familiar with the following FARs and their applicability to skydiving (see Chapter 2-3 and 2-4 of this manual):

- Part 65—Certification of Parachute Riggers
- Part 91—General Flight Rules
- Part 105—Parachute Operations

Advisory Circular 105-2—explains in detail various areas of parachute equipment, maintenance, and modifications.

The FAA grants **approval of parachutes** to manufacturers in the form of Technical Standard Orders (TSOs). TSO C-23 is issued to parachutes that comply with the current performance standards.

- NAS 804 for TSO C-23b
- AS-8015A for TSO C-23c
- AS-8015B for TSO C-23d

These standards specify the tests that a parachute system and its component parts must pass to receive approval for civilian use. FAR Part 21 contains the procedures for obtaining TSO approval.

Only those with FAA approval may perform **alterations to approved parachutes**. Approval may be obtained by submitting a request and description of the alteration to the manufacturer or to an FAA Flight Standards District Office. An FAA Master Rigger and a manufacturer with an approved quality-assurance program are eligible to receive alteration approval. Alterations may not be performed without full documentation of FAA approval for the specific alteration.

## B. Main Parachute

Jumpers should choose canopies that will provide an acceptable landing in a wide range of circumstances by considering several factors including canopy size, wing loading, planform (shape), skill level, and experience. Owners should verify with a rigger that their gear complies with all applicable updates and bulletins.

Jumpers should observe the canopy manufacturer's recommendations for the correct canopy size, which usually includes maximum recommended weight with respect to the jumper's experience, drop zone elevation, and conditions such as density altitude.

**Wing loading**, measured as exit weight in pounds per square foot of canopy size, provides only one gauge of a canopy's performance characteristics. A smaller canopy loaded equally to a larger one of the same design will exhibit a faster and more radical control response, with more altitude loss in any maneuver. Design, materials, and construction techniques can cause two equally loaded canopies to perform very differently. Different planforms (square vs. elliptical) exhibit very different handling characteristics.

The Minimum Canopy-Size Recommendations chart provides the minimum recommended canopy size by taking exit weight and the number of solo-equipment jumps made with square parachutes into account. A student's canopy size is at the discretion of the instructor. Due to the varied sizes of canopies from different manufacturers, any canopy less than 3% smaller than the listed recommendation is acceptable. Canopy choices for jumpers who have made more than 1,000 jumps is at their own discretion. These minimum-canopy-size recommendations may be too aggressive for some jumpers and, in other cases, too conservative. Instructors, canopy coaches and drop zone leadership should assist skydivers in selecting a canopy appropriate for their ability and progression. The USPA Downsizing Best Practices Card, available at uspa.org/downsize, is a valuable self-assessment tool.

### Minimum-Canopy-Size Recommendations

**EXIT WEIGHT** (Jumper plus all equipment)

| NUMBER OF JUMPS | 100 | 110 | 120 | 130 | 140 | 150 | 160 | 170 | 180 | 190 | 200 | 210 | 220 | 230 | 240 | 250 |
|---|---|---|---|---|---|---|---|---|---|---|---|---|---|---|---|---|
| 0-25 | 190 | 190 | 190 | 190 | 190 | 190 | 200 | 200 | 200 | 220 | 220 | 220 | 220 | 240 | 260 | 280 |
| 26-50 | 170 | 170 | 170 | 170 | 170 | 190 | 190 | 190 | 190 | 190 | 190 | 200 | 200 | 220 | 240 | 260 |
| 51-100 | 170 | 170 | 170 | 170 | 170 | 170 | 170 | 170 | 170 | 190 | 190 | 190 | 200 | 200 | 220 | 240 |
| 101-200 | 150 | 150 | 150 | 170 | 170 | 170 | 170 | 170 | 170 | 170 | 170 | 170 | 190 | 200 | 200 | 220 |
| 201-300 | 150 | 150 | 150 | 150 | 150 | 150 | 150 | 150 | 170 | 170 | 170 | 170 | 190 | 190 | 190 | 200 |
| 301-400 | 135 | 135 | 135 | 150 | 150 | 150 | 150 | 150 | 150 | 150 | 170 | 170 | 170 | 190 | 190 | 190 |
| 401-500 | 135 | 135 | 135 | 135 | 135 | 135 | 135 | 135 | 150 | 150 | 150 | 170 | 170 | 170 | 190 | 190 |
| 501-750 | 120 | 120 | 120 | 135 | 135 | 135 | 135 | 135 | 135 | 135 | 150 | 150 | 170 | 170 | 170 | 170 |
| 750-1000 | 107 | 120 | 120 | 120 | 135 | 135 | 135 | 135 | 135 | 135 | 135 | 150 | 150 | 170 | 170 | 170 |

## C. Reserve Parachute

All skydivers should use a steerable reserve canopy. The FAA requires that the reserve parachute assembly—including harness, container, canopy, risers, pilot chute, deployment device, and ripcord—are approved.

Jumpers must observe FARs regarding the manufacturer's maximum certificated weights and speeds for parachutes. Parachutes approved under FAA Technical Standard Order C-23b, C-23c, and C-23d are subject to different testing standards and operation limits. The entire parachute system is limited to the maximum certificated load limit of the harness-and-container system or reserve canopy, whichever is less. Load limits are found in the owner's manual, the manufacturer's website, or placarded on the parachute component itself.

For a ram-air reserve, jumpers should not exceed the maximum suspended weight specified by the manufacturer (not necessarily the maximum certificated load limit). A jumper may exceed the rated speeds of a certificated parachute system (harness and/or parachute) by jumping at higher MSL altitudes or falling in vertical freefall orientations.

**A round reserve canopy** should be equipped with a deployment device to reduce the opening force and control deployment, should have a rate of descent that does not exceed 18 feet per second (fps), and must not exceed a rate of descent of 25 fps at sea level conditions (NAS 804). The following scale indicates the minimum size round reserve canopy recommended for use according to the exit weight of the skydiver:

| Total Suspended Weight* | Recommended Equivalent Descent Rate (high-porosity flat circular) |
|---|---|
| Up to 149 pounds | 24-foot |
| 150 to 199 pounds | 26-foot |
| 200 pounds and over | 28-foot |

*The use of lower-porosity materials can reduce the rate of descent.

## D. Harness-and-Container System

The FAA requires the harness of a dual parachute assembly to be approved. All harness ends should be folded over and sewn down or wrapped and sewn down to prevent the harness from unthreading through the hardware during parachute deployment.

Canopy-release systems should be maintained according to the schedule and procedures in the owner's manual. The location of operational handles should align with the manufacturing industry's standardized locations. The harness should be equipped with single-point riser releases (one handle releases both risers) for easy and rapid disengagement from the main canopy.

Loop-type reserve handles should be made of metal. Plastic and composite reserve handles are not recommended. Jumpers should practice peeling and pulling pillow-type reserve handles until certain they can operate them easily in an emergency.

All ripcord-housing ends should be secured. Ripcord pins, when seated, should either be started inside the housing or clear the closing loop before entering the housing. A ripcord-cable stop should not be used; fatal accidents caused by reserve entanglements with ripcords secured in this manner have been documented.

The reserve system is usually designed to use a specific type of pilot chute. The reserve pilot chute should be properly seated in the container and repacked if it has shifted.

Deployment brake systems should provide secure stowage of the steering toggles and slack brake line to prevent brake-line entanglements and premature brake release.

## E. Main Pilot Chute

The main pilot chute is part of the main parachute system. Pilot chute size can affect the opening characteristics of the main canopy.

Spring-loaded and hand-deployed pilot chutes of both types (throw-out and pull-out) each have strengths and weaknesses that affect the user's emergency procedures and other decisions.

On throw-out hand-deployed systems, the pilot chute and pouch size must be compatible. Collapsible pilot chutes add complexity and have more required maintenance since forgetting to set or cock the pilot chute can cause a high-speed pilot-chute-in-tow malfunction, and the moving parts create additional wear to the system.

## F. Reserve Static Line (RSL) and Main-Assisted-Reserve-Deployment (MARD) Device

With very few exceptions, USPA recommends that jumpers use a reserve static line (RSL), a backup device that automatically initiates reserve deployment when a jumper cuts away. Preferably, the RSL is equipped with a main-assisted-reserve-deployment device (MARD). RSL use is mandatory for students. Though RSLs (with or without MARDs) are proven lifesavers, jumpers should never rely on them to initiate reserve deployment and must manually pull the reserve ripcord immediately after a cutaway.

# Recommendations for Everyone

On an RSL-equipped rig, one end of the RSL lanyard attaches to a main riser, and then the lanyard runs to the reserve ripcord cable, where the other end attaches. When the main risers depart following a cutaway, the RSL lanyard pulls the reserve pin and releases the reserve pilot chute, which deploys the reserve parachute. When the RSL includes a MARD device, the RSL lanyard hooks to the reserve-pilot-chute bridle, which allows the departing main parachute to assist in extracting the reserve, speeding up its deployment. RSLs help to both ensure and speed up reserve deployment when fractions of a second matter; MARDS speed up the deployment even further.

**RSL vs. MARD-Equipped-RSL Reserve Activation:** Reserve activated via a traditional RSL (left) and a MARD-equipped RSL (right). Photo by Niklas Daniel of AXIS Flight School.

An RSL, with or without a MARD, may also incorporate a **Collins lanyard**. This lanyard attaches to the reserve static line and is designed to release the non-RSL-side riser in the event the RSL-side riser breaks or disconnects prematurely. Consult a rigger for more information.

USPA recommends an RSL, preferably with a MARD, for all experienced jumpers with the possible exception of those attempting linked canopy formations. If temporarily disconnecting an RSL, take care to ensure it doesn't interfere with the operation of the parachute system; consult a rigger.

When misrouted or attached incorrectly, these safety devices may not function and can even complicate or prevent a cutaway. Unless the manufacturer's instructions state otherwise, do not use a connector device between the left and right main risers.

## G. Automatic Activation Device (AAD)

USPA encourages **all licensed skydivers** to use an AAD—a device that initiates reserve deployment when the jumper reaches a preset altitude and descent rate—and requires its use for student skydivers. An AAD is only a backup device, and **no jumper should rely on it to deploy a parachute**. Those who use one and are educated on its function are significantly more likely to survive loss of altitude awareness or consciousness during a skydive.

The FAA requires those who use an AAD to maintain it in accordance with the manufacturer's instructions (FAR 105.43.c). Each jumper should read and understand the owner's manual for the AAD.

An AAD may complicate certain situations, particularly if the jumper deploys the main parachute low enough for the AAD to activate. Understanding and reviewing the emergency procedures for two canopies out (SIM Chapter 4-1) is essential.

*Note: AADs may also be used with main parachutes, but this occurs only in specialized circumstances.*

## H. Static Line (Main)

The FAA requires static-line deployment to be either by direct bag or pilot-chute assist. The **direct-bag** method reduces the chance of the student interfering with main-canopy deployment. The **pilot-chute-assist** method must use an assist device according to FAR 105.47. The assist device must attach at one end to the static line so that the container opens before the device is loaded, and at the other end to the pilot chute. The FAA requires the pilot-chute-assist device to have a load strength of at least 28 but not more than 160 pounds.

The static line should attach to an approved structural point of the airframe. A seatbelt attachment point is considered part of the airframe, but the static line should pull on it in a longitudinal direction. Aircraft seats are not considered part of the airframe.

Static-line construction should include:

- a length of at least 8 feet but not more than 15 feet and should never come into contact with the aircraft's tail surfaces
- a locking slide fastener, ID number 43A9502 or MS70120
- webbing of not less than 3,600 pounds tensile strength

## I. Borrowing or Changing Equipment

No one should rent or loan a parachute to persons unqualified to carry out an intended skydive or of unknown ability. The use of unfamiliar (borrowed or new) equipment without sufficient preparation has been a factor in many fatalities. Whenever possible, **avoid or minimize changes in equipment type during student training or when borrowing equipment.** Any jumper who makes equipment changes should receive adequate transition training.

When jumping a new or different main parachute, a jumper should follow the recommendations in Chapter 5-9C: Downsizing Progression.

## J. Use of Altimeters

Skydivers must always know their altitude and may choose to use a combination of altimeter types to maintain altitude awareness during all phases of a skydive. Common altimeter types include digital and analog altimeters that can be worn on the wrist or chest strap, as well as audible altimeters worn in or on a helmet.

### Altimeter Errors

All altimeters use electronic and/or mechanical components that are subject to damage and may fail in use. You can expect minor differences in indicated altitude, so turn on or zero the altimeter at the landing area and do not re-adjust the altimeter after leaving the ground. Altimeters may lag during both ascent and descent; expect inaccuracies of up to 500 feet, plus or minus. The needle of an analog altimeter can also stick during both ascent and descent.

When an altimeter is in a burble (as when the jumper is falling back-to-earth), it may read inaccurately. To prevent damage that can cause accuracy errors, handle altimeters with care and maintain and store them according to the manufacturer's instructions.

## K. Accessories

Weather, drop zone conditions, the proficiency of the skydiver, and the skydiver's experience with the type of jump they will be performing should determine the use of personal equipment. Jumpers should wear adequate protective clothing, including jumpsuit, helmet, gloves, goggles, and footwear for all jumps, with the possible exception of intentional water landings. Gloves are essential when the jump-altitude temperature is lower than 40° F.

A jumper should carry a protected but accessible knife. All skydivers using solo equipment should wear a lightweight, rigid helmet that does not restrict vision or hearing. All jumpers should wear flotation gear when the intended exit, opening, or landing point of a skydive is within one mile of an open body of water (defined as one in which a skydiver could drown).

## L. Main Parachute Packing

The main parachute of a dual assembly may be packed by—

1. an FAA rigger
    a. An FAA rigger may supervise other persons in packing any type of parachute for which that person is rated (FAR 65.125.a and b).
    b. A non-certificated person may pack a main parachute under the direct supervision of an FAA rigger (FAR 105.43.a).
2. the person who intends to use it on the next jump (FAR 105.43.a)

Each individual skydiver should have the written approval of an S&TA, USPA Instructor or Examiner, or an FAA rigger to pack their own parachute. All parachute packers should know and understand the manufacturer's instructions for packing, maintenance, and use.

Tandem main parachutes may be packed by (FAR 105.45.b.1)—

1. an FAA rigger
2. the parachutist in command making the next jump with that parachute
3. a packer under the direct supervision of a rigger

Exercise extreme caution when using temporary packing pins.

## M. Parachute Maintenance

The equipment owner should frequently inspect equipment for any damage and wear. A qualified person should promptly correct any questionable condition. The Equipment Section of Category G of the USPA Integrated Student Program details owner inspection of the parachute.

### Maintenance and Repair of the Reserve

The FAA requires the entire reserve assembly to be maintained as an approved parachute. Only an FAA-certificated parachute rigger may do repairs to the reserve assembly.

### Maintenance and Repair of the Main

An FAA-certificated rigger or the owner (if he or she has adequate knowledge and skill) may perform repairs to the main. The main parachute and its deployment bag and pilot chute need not be maintained as "approved."

Major repairs and alterations may be performed only by or under the supervision of an FAA Master Rigger, the parachute manufacturer, or any other manufacturer the FAA considers competent.

## 4-4: Pre-Jump Safety Checks and Briefings

## A. Equipment Preparation

Preparing all skydiving equipment and procedures prior to each jump is critical to preventing accidents. This information is intended to provide instructional staff and other licensed jumpers with guidance in developing an appropriate personal checklist.

In some cases, others—the pilot, instructor, coach, rigger, ground crew chief, etc.— will have principal responsibility for these checks; however, no one should assume that others have carried out these responsibilities. Initially, the USPA Instructor performs these pre-jump safety checks and briefings for their students. As students progress, they should begin to learn to do them for themselves. Through leadership and attitude, instructional staff can foster a respect for safety that will serve the beginning skydiver well when they assume sole responsibility for their skydiving activities.

USPA highly recommends that every jumper, regardless of experience level, engage in a **mutual gear check** with another licensed jumper. This peer-review process serves as an essential safety verification step to identify and rectify any oversights or errors in equipment preparation. The practice of mutual gear checks cultivates a culture of collective responsibility and vigilance, enhancing safety standards in skydiving activities.

Progressing students and all experienced jumpers should review the items on these lists to familiarize themselves with the wide range of details. This section includes checklists for:

- aircraft preflight
- ground-crew briefing
- pilot briefing
- skydiver briefing
- equipment check
- before-takeoff check
- takeoff
- spotting
- jump run
- descent and landing in aircraft
- post-jump debriefing

## B. Briefings

Aircraft preflight (primarily the responsibility of the pilot, but the supervising instructional rating holder should check):

- placards: in place (as required)
- seats removed (as required)
- door stop (under Cessna wing) removed
- sharp objects taped
- loose objects secured
- steps and handholds secure, clean of oil
- aircraft altimeter set
- filing and activation of notice to airmen (NOTAM)
- aircraft radio serviceable
- static-line attachment secure

- knife in place and accessible
- remote spotting correction and communication signals operational (larger aircraft)
- winds-aloft report or wind-drift indicators available
- seat belts available and serviceable
- passenger hand straps near door removed

A load organizer (a senior jumper or instructional rating holder) should coordinate to ensure that everyone is in agreement by conducting a **ground crew briefing**. This briefing should include communications procedures to meet BSR requirements for ground-to-air communication (smoke, panels, radio, etc.), jump order, distance/time between groups on exit, landing pattern priorities, and control of spectators and vehicles. For student operations, the briefer should be a USPA Instructor and discussion should include:

- wind limitations
- setting up and maintaining a clear target area
- critiques of student landings
- maintenance of master log
- accident and first-aid procedures

The load organizer also **coordinates with the pilot** on jump-run altitudes and direction, communications (ground to air, jump-master to pilot, air traffic control), aircraft attitudes during corrections on jump run, and jump-run speed and cut. If applicable, the briefing should include locking the wheel brake (the parking brake is not to be used). In addition, the briefing should address the gross weight and center of gravity requirements and limitations, procedures for aircraft emergencies, and procedures for equipment emergencies in the aircraft.

The load organizer also **briefs the skydivers**, discussing items such as seat-belt-off altitude (1,500 feet AGL or designated by DZ policy); movement in the aircraft, especially during jump run; aircraft emergency procedures, including communication procedures; and parachute-equipment-emergency procedures.

A USPA instructor **briefs students** after reviewing the student log or record. The jump plan includes exit and freefall, including jump commands, emergency procedure training or review, canopy control and landing pattern, and drop zone appearance and hazards using an aerial photo or map. The discussion should also include conduct in the aircraft such as protection of operation handles and pins, movement, and mental preparation before the jump.

## C. Equipment Checklist

Each individual skydiver should ensure that their own equipment is inspected four times prior to each jump:

1. before putting it on
2. immediately after putting it on
3. prior to boarding
4. prior to exit

Utilizing a gear-check routine that you perform in the same order each time is both efficient and helps prevent inadvertently missing an item. The following list of items, used in any logical order, is an example of a pre-flight checklist:

- helmet: proper fit and the chin strap threaded correctly
- goggles or glasses: secure and clean
- three-ring release system: properly assembled and periodic maintenance performed
- reserve static line (RSL): hooked up and routed correctly (refer to manufacturer's instructions)
- altimeters: checked and set; visual altimeters do not block operation handles
- main parachute:
    - main canopy properly sized
    - container properly closed, pull-up cord removed, and closing loop in good condition
    - pilot chute: secure in the pouch, bridle routed correctly and secure, pin secure on the bridle and seated in the closing loop, slack above the pin (if applicable), and color in the kill-line window (if applicable); if using a pull-out pilot chute (not approved for student use): handle secure, pin seated, free movement of the handle through pin extraction (see manufacturer's instructions)
    - practice-main-deployment-handle secure (student)
- harness:
    - straps routed correctly and not twisted
        - chest strap
        - leg straps
        - belly band, if applicable
    - snaps secured and closed and/or friction adapters properly threaded

# Recommendations for Everyone

- adjusted for proper fit
- running ends turned back and sewn
- loose ends tucked into keepers
- belly band (if used):
  - correctly routed
  - adjusted
  - friction adapter properly threaded
- reserve:
  - proper size for jumper
  - pin condition: seated, not bent, and closing loop(s) in good condition
  - pilot chute seated
  - packing data card in date and seal in place
  - reserve-handle pocket condition
  - pin-cover flap closed
  - overall appearance
- risers: not twisted and toggles secure
- suspension and control lines: not exposed
- personal accessories:
  - footwear: proper type and fit, no open hooks or buckles
  - protective clothing
    - jumpsuit pockets closed
    - other outerwear compatible with jumping
    - gloves as needed
  - empty pockets
  - earplugs (if desired)
- automatic activation device (AAD):
  - serviced according to manufacturer's schedule
  - in the correct mode for the jump (changeable-mode AADs)
  - proper routing of cable(s)
  - control unit secured in proper location
  - turned on and calibrated (offset for altitude if needed)
- condition of all touch fastener (aka Velcro) and tuck tabs
- overall fit and appearance

## 4-5: Weather

### A. Determining Winds

According to the BSRs, jumpers must determine the appropriate altitude and surface winds prior to conducting any skydive. You should measure surface winds at the actual landing area. Winds-aloft reports from the FAA flight service are only forecasts. You can make observations while in flight using navigation systems such as global positioning satellite systems (GPS). Winds can change at any time, so the jumper should check all available information before and during the jump.

### B. Hazardous Weather

Fronts approach with much warning but can catch the unaware off guard. A gust front (a line of sudden and severe weather) precedes some fronts. Rapid and significant changes in the strength and direction of the winds aloft and on the surface may accompany frontal approach and passage.

Gusty winds, thermals, abrupt changes in temperature, and even terrain can create turbulence in canopy flight at all altitudes, including near the ground. **Turbulent or gusty winds on landing can also initiate a flight cycle**, causing your parachute to dive toward the ground. Canopies with lighter wing loadings are less predictable in turbulence. When flying in turbulence regardless of your altitude, maintain the desired heading using smooth but effective toggle input. Fly in full flight unless directed otherwise in the canopy owner's manual. If turbulence exists near the ground, prepare for a quick and forceful flare and a PLF.

On calm, hot, humid days, thunderstorms can spontaneously generate and move in unpredictable patterns.

**Dust devils** are strong, well-formed, and relatively short-lived whirlwinds (mini-tornadoes). They usually form on days with significant thermal activity, (i.e., hot days with clear skies and strong sunshine). Dust devils may or may not be visible when they form. You should avoid flying in or near dust devils as they may cause sudden and unpredictable changes in your altitude and direction of flight and may even cause your canopy to collapse. If you do encounter a dust devil while in flight, continue to actively pilot your canopy toward a safe landing area and be prepared to PLF.

Cold weather can also be hazardous. Having cold hands or wearing gloves can change how the pilot chute and emergency handles feel, and Velcro becomes much stiffer during cold temperatures. This may make operating the handles more difficult.

Weather websites, weather apps, TV forecasts, continuous observation by you and your pilot (who is legally responsible to know the weather conditions before flight) can provide practical information.

## C. Density Altitude

Parachute performance is measured at sea level in moderate temperatures and humidity. Altitude, heat, and humidity influence the density of air. Density altitude is a measure of air density that is calculated according to the temperature and altitude.

As density altitude increases, airspeed increases by almost 5% per 3,000 feet up to 12,000 feet MSL, and more than 5% per 3,000 feet above 12,000 feet MSL. As density altitude increases, a ram-air canopy pilot can expect the following:

- a higher stall speed
- a faster forward speed
- a faster descent rate
- higher opening forces

Additionally, higher density altitude affects aircraft in the following ways:

- longer distances required for takeoff and landing
- reduced propeller effectiveness
- poorer turbine and piston-engine performance
- slower and flatter rate of climb
- less useful load given the aircraft's maximum allowable gross weight

The pilot is responsible for knowing the density altitude prior to takeoff, and skydivers should consider the effects of density altitude on canopy performance.

## 4-6: Aircraft

Skydivers play a more integral role in aircraft operations than ordinary passengers, because their procedures can dramatically affect the controllability of the aircraft, particularly during exit.

Parasitic drag reduces airspeed necessary for flight and reduces the effectiveness of control surfaces. Excess weight in the rear of the aircraft can cause the pilot to lose control of the aircraft and cause it to stall. A jump pilot should brief all jumpers on the topics outlined in Aircraft Briefing from Category E of the USPA Integrated Student Program. The smallest aircraft used for student jumping should be able to carry the pilot and at least three jumpers.

Those planning to open their parachute above the normal opening altitude (generally 5,000 feet AGL and lower) should inform the pilot and all jumpers on board, as well as any other jump in flight at the time.

**Aircraft fueling operations** should occur away from skydiver landing and loading areas, and no person, except the pilot and necessary fueling crew, should be aboard the aircraft during fueling. USPA accepts the practice of rapid refueling (fueling an aircraft while an engine is running) for certain turbine-powered aircraft when performed in accordance with the guidelines of Parachute Industry Association Technical Standard TS-122. Piston-powered aircraft should never be rapid-refueled.

Students should never **approach an aircraft**, whether the engine is running or not, unless they are under the direct supervision of a USPA instructional rating holder. Everyone should always approach a fixed-wing aircraft from behind the wing and always approach a helicopter from the front or the side, only after making eye contact with the pilot. Everyone should always protect their handles while entering the aircraft and follow procedures to avoid the accidental activation of any equipment.

On the **ride to altitude**, everyone on board the aircraft is subject to the seating requirements found in FAR 91.107 and the parachute requirements found in FAR 91.307. Everyone should have a thorough understanding and be prepared to take the appropriate actions in the event of an accidental activation of parachute equipment in the aircraft. Seatbelts should remain fastened and all hard helmets and other potential projectiles secured until the pilot notifies the jumpers that they may unfasten them. Students should sit still and move only when their instructor(s) or coach specifically directs them to do so. Jumpers should determine seating arrangements—which will vary according to the particular aircraft and the size and type of the load—in advance.

Failure to maintain proper **weight and balance** throughout the flight may result in loss of control of the aircraft. This means the load must be properly distributed in the aircraft to maintain balance in relation to the center of gravity, which is necessary for the aircraft to fly safely. The jumpers must cooperate fully with the pilot to keep the aircraft within its safe performance envelope throughout the entire flight. The aircraft must not carry more weight than the maximum allowed in the manufacturer's operating manual.

# Recommendations for Everyone

Seatbelts/restraints should be stowed out of the way but never fastened together unless being worn. All pilots and other occupants of a jump aircraft must wear parachutes when required by the FAA.

## 4-7: Spotting

### A. Why Spotting is Important

Choosing the correct exit point and guiding the pilot to it (spotting) helps fulfill each skydiver's responsibility to land in an appropriate clear area. Jumpers must demonstrate basic spotting abilities prior to obtaining the USPA A license. Spotting in more difficult circumstances requires continued practice and study. In addition to considerations for getting one jumper or group out of the aircraft at the correct point, spotters must consider the correct exit points for multiple individuals or groups on the same pass from a larger aircraft.

### B. Priorities

Be familiar with the DZ and surrounding area, including exit and opening points. Jumpers should observe and talk to those on previous jumps to help determine the correct jump-run direction and exit and opening point. The Standard Operating Procedure sections of Categories D, E, and F of the Integrated Student Program explain the methods for estimating the exit and opening point based on winds-aloft forecasts.

Calculation of the spot using the winds-aloft report has replaced the use of **wind-drift indicators** (WDI) for most routine drop zone operations. However, use of WDIs can also be effective for determining drift under canopy. Jumpers aboard the aircraft observe the drift of a piece of weighted crepe paper released at canopy opening altitude over an observed position (or at half of the opening altitude with ground travel doubled for the jump) to determine the distance and direction of the best opening point upwind of the target. Jumpers are responsible for wind drift indicators after they land.

To spot, look out the open door of the aircraft for traffic and clouds below, and identify the DZ, the climb-out point, and the exit point. Category D of the ISP discusses techniques for determining the point straight below the aircraft.

Jumpers can use the mnemonic **SPACE** to quickly remember the items they need to check while spotting:

- **S**kydivers
- **P**lanes
- **A**irport
- **C**louds
- **E**xit light

Make sure you have enough separation between the skydivers in front of you and your group. According to FAR 105.5, the jumper and the pilot are jointly responsible for making sure plane traffic is clear before jumping. You should be at a distance and direction from the airport that allows you to make it back to the drop zone given the winds for that day. According to FAR 105.17, the jumper and pilot are jointly responsible for staying the appropriate distance clear of clouds. The pilot communicates the final OK for exit either with a light system or verbally.

### C. Exit Separation on Jump Run

Slower-falling jumpers and groups have a longer exposure to upper headwinds, which blow them farther downwind than faster-falling jumpers and groups. Slower-falling groups should exit before faster-falling groups when jump run is into the wind.

On days with strong upper headwinds, allow more time between groups on the same pass to get sufficient horizontal separation over the ground. Provide at least 1,000 feet of ground separation between individuals jumping solo. Provide at least 1,500 feet of ground separation between small groups, adding more as the size of the groups increase.

Once your parachute opens, delay flying up or down the line of flight until any jumpers in a slower-falling group that exited **before** you have opened their parachutes and turned toward the landing area, and members of the group exiting **after** have completed their freefall and opened.

Flying jump run across the upper winds (crosswind) helps achieve separation between groups. Whether flying one or more aircraft, each pass should allow enough time for jumpers on a previous pass to descend to a safe altitude before dropping jumpers from the next pass.

## D. Exit and Flight-Plan Considerations for Different Disciplines

Larger jump aircraft may include several different groups of skydivers performing different disciplines, some of which use more airspace than others. The following exit order is a general guide, but drop zones may adjust the order based on local considerations such as prevailing upper winds, the terrain, other disciplines on the load, weather conditions, and skill level of jumpers or group leaders.

1. Movement group 1 (angle, tracking, etc.)
2. Formation skydivers falling in a belly-to-earth orientation (largest to smallest)
3. Freefly groups falling in head-down, standing or sitting positions (largest to smallest)
4. Movement group 2 (angle, tracking, etc.)
5. Freefall students with instructors
6. Tandem students and instructors
7. High-pulls
8. Wingsuit flyers

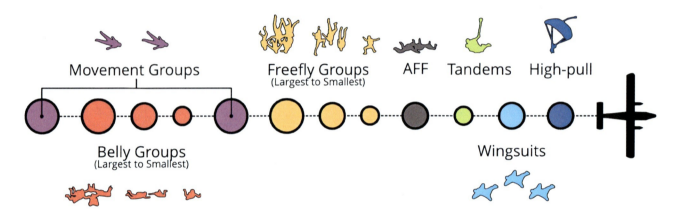

**Group Separation Exit Order**

Some of these groups—**formation skydivers, freeflyers, solo students and tandem students**—tend to fall straight down after exit, drifting horizontally with the effects of wind but otherwise not moving much in the airspace. They gain adequate separation from one another by exiting in groups largest to smallest per discipline and waiting the appropriate length of time between groups before exiting the airplane.

Other Groups—**movement groups (angle, tracking, etc.), canopy formation jumpers, and wingsuit flyers**—cover large horizontal distances that you must take into account when planning a descent strategy. These groups must fly a specific flight path that they plan before boarding the aircraft. The jumper leading this type of group must keep the group flying the planned path the entire freefall. This plan may include turning downwind after sufficient lateral distance and flying parallel to groups that exited earlier. The breakoff point must be far enough laterally to allow for the jumpers to gain horizontal separation from each other, as well as any of the groups that exited the airplane earlier.

**Wingsuit flyers** should exit last, as they typically follow the plane along jump run after exit, while **high pullers** tend to fly back through the jump-run path. There are possible exceptions to this generalization, such as a canopy formation team exiting with a major offset, e.g. greater than one mile past the last wingsuit flyer exiting. Airplane loads that include more than one wingsuit group add complexity to determining the airspace necessary to allow each group to open in a clear area.

Loads that include more than two **movement groups** require greater planning to determine exit order. Generally, no movement group should exit immediately after another. Immediately after exit, a movement group must fly perpendicular to jump run to provide lateral separation from the other groups that have exited or will exit the aircraft. After gaining sufficient lateral distance, the group may then turn downwind, flying parallel to groups that exited earlier. A second movement group on the same load should fly the opposite direction of the first, while still flying perpendicular to jump run, to allow for greater separation.

Depending on the situation, it may be safer to restrict each airplane load to no more than two movement groups and one wingsuit group.

# 4-8: Incident Reports

## A. Incidents

Reporting incidents helps USPA track current trends in the field and gives direction to USPA staff and board members addressing equipment issues, training methods, and safety procedures. It is particularly important to report any event that requires a jumper to receive medical attention or raises a safety concern, but jumpers should also report noteworthy malfunctions, unsafe procedures, unusual or ethically unacceptable skydives, or other extraordinary occurrences concerning skydiving operations. USPA rating holders and S&TAs, the leaders in the field, are the key to encouraging skydivers to file incident reports.

Incident reports are warranted for (but not limited to):

- Fatalities
- Injuries requiring medical attention (anything more than local first aid)
- Any injury to a student (including tandem students)
- Reserve deployments (intentional or unintentional)
- AAD activations
- Off-field landing or obstacle landings (buildings and other objects, water, power lines, trees)
- Emergency exits from an aircraft
- Freefall or canopy collisions
- Premature deployments in aircraft or freefall
- Harness or canopy damaged during jump
- The unplanned dropping of equipment during jump
- Anything filed on an insurance claim

## B. Investigation and Reporting of Incidents

Fatalities and other significant incidents are an unfortunate part of skydiving. To help skydivers learn essential lessons from the mistakes of others and reduce the number and severity of incidents, USPA members should fill out an incident report when it meets any of the conditions in the list above. When appropriate, an S&TA can act as an impartial investigator. Jumpers should coordinate efforts through the local S&TA when an event requires several reports, witness accounts or personal observations of the investigator. Incidents can be reported online at uspa.org/ir.

USPA keeps reports confidential by following the procedures included in this section. The integrity and effectiveness of the reporting system rely on each USPA official following USPA's procedures precisely as outlined.

## C. Submission and Disposal of Incident Reports

USPA follows strict operating procedures to maintain the confidentiality of reports and protect the integrity of the incident-reporting system. If possible, the reporting party should use the online submission form at uspa.org/ir, but may also print or type the report and send it to USPA Headquarters.

USPA maintains only the information that identifies trends for USPA and the skydiving industry. USPA removes dates, locations and names of involved parties and enters the remaining information into a database, then destroys the submitted reports.

USPA may publish a brief synopsis of the report in *Parachutist*, excluding the date, specific location and names of anyone involved.

## D. The Incident Reporting Form

You can ensure that USPA receives the most accurate and useful data by providing detailed information in your incident report and by specifying the type of injury (if one) that occurred. Completing the narrative area, including all factors that led to the incident, helps USPA produce an accurate summary. If filing a report of a non-fatal incident that caused injury, include the prognosis for the jumper's recovery.

## E. USPA Policy Regarding Privileged Information

The success of USPA's safety-reporting program depends upon the free exchange of information between field reporters and USPA Headquarters. If reporting officials believe that the information will be used only for statistical and educational purposes and that the reports themselves will not be released to third parties, the reporting system will continue to serve the best interests of the membership. If, on the other hand, this privileged information is released to third parties for whatever reason, USPA will lose the trust of the field reporters and, with it, valuable safety-generating data.

USPA's policy includes:

- Documents for use only by the reporting party and USPA officials as necessary to enhance safety through education and training.
- All requests by third parties to access such information or documents will be referred to the USPA Executive Director, who, in consultation with the USPA President, will determine the need to refer to counsel.
- Failure to adhere to these procedures will subject the violating USPA member to disciplinary action per Section 1-6 of the USPA Governance Manual.

# Chapter 5:
# Discipline-Specific Recommendations

This chapter provides guidance for various disciplines in skydiving: formation skydiving; freeflying, freestyle and skysurfing; night jumping; water landings; canopy formations; high-altitude jumping; camera flying; wingsuit flying; canopy piloting; movement jumps; and speed skydiving. These guidelines will also assist you in meeting your skill and knowledge requirements for the USPA B, C, and D Licenses and USPA ratings.

## 5-1: Formation Skydiving

### A. Introduction and Definition
Formation skydiving, traditionally called "relative work" or "group freefall," is the intentional maneuvering of two or more skydivers in proximity to one another in freefall.

### B. Training and Procedures
Before training for formation skydiving, each student should complete all the training and advancement criteria through Category F of the USPA Integrated Student Program.

Students should begin training for group freefall skills as soon as they complete Category F of the ISP. This encourages them to maintain their interest in skydiving, fosters relaxation in the air, develops coordination, establishes participation in group activities, and develops safe attitudes and procedures. Initial training should begin with no more than two jumpers—the trainee and a current USPA Coach or Instructor. Categories G and H of the ISP contain a recommended training outline for beginning group freefall skills.

### C. Hazards Associated with Formation Skydiving
Mid-air collisions and funneled formations are not only undesirable but can be dangerous. Two bodies colliding in flight can cause severe injuries or death. The greatest danger exists when jumpers lose sight of each other and open their canopies independently, which may set the stage for a jumper in freefall to collide with an open canopy. Even after opening, if the jumpers do not follow proper safety procedures, they risk a canopy collision.

### D. Breakoff Procedures
The minimum breakoff altitude **for groups of five or fewer** should be at least 1,500 feet higher than the highest planned deployment altitude in the group (not counting one camera flyer). For **groups of six or more**, minimum breakoff altitude should be at least 2,000 feet higher than the highest planned deployment altitude in the group.

Minimum breakoff altitude should be even higher than these recommendations for the following:

- groups with one or more jumpers of low experience
- jumpers with slower-opening or faster-flying canopies
- jumpers engaging in freefall activities that involve a fall rate faster than belly-to-earth terminal velocity
- jumps involving props, toys, or other special equipment, such as signs, banners, smoke, flags, hoops, tubes, items released in freefall, etc.
- jumps taking place over an unfamiliar landing area or in case of an off-field landing
- any other special consideration

At the breakoff signal or upon reaching the breakoff altitude, whichever comes first, each participant should turn 180 degrees from the center of the formation and flat track away to the planned deployment altitude. Jumpers can achieve a flat track by initiating with their legs, which will result in more horizontal separation than diving.

Before pulling, jumpers should perform a distinct wave-off to signal jumpers who may be above them. During the wave-off, look up, down, and to the sides to ensure that the area is clear. The low person has the right-of-way, both in freefall and under canopy.

Discipline-Specific Recommendations

## 5-2: Freeflying, Freestyle, and Skysurfing

### A. Introduction and Definition

Freeflying refers to all activities that incorporate back, standing, head-down, or sitting freefall positions, including freestyle and skysurfing. These recommendations provide guidance for vertical freefall body positions, which are generally associated with high fall rates and rapid changes in relative speed. The diverse freefall speeds among jumpers engaged in different freefall activities affect separation between groups exiting on the same pass over the drop zone.

### B. Qualifications

Before engaging in freeflying, you should hold a USPA license and have received freeflying instruction from a USPA instructional rating holder with extensive freeflying experience. Before freeflying, you should have demonstrated sufficient air skills, including:

- orienting to the line of flight of jump run
- maintaining consistent altitude awareness
- performing basic formation skydiving skills
- Proficiently performing basic backfly skills such as rotation and moving up, down, forward and backward prior to attempting head-up or head-down maneuvers
- tracking to achieve sufficient horizontal separation

### C. Equipment

Freeflying poses specific potential equipment problems. A **premature opening** at the speeds involved in freeflying could injure you severely or stress your equipment beyond the manufacturer's limits.

To prevent premature deployment of either canopy, **properly secure your gear**. Deployment systems and operation **handles** need to remain secure when you are flying at high speeds and in various orientations. Therefore, equipment for freeflying should include a bottom-of-container mounted, throw-out pilot-chute pouch or pull-out pilot chute with tuck tabs. USPA recommends against using a leg-strap-mounted pilot chute, which is an extreme hazard, as is any exposed pilot-chute bridle. Maintain and properly size your **closing loops** and ensure your **pin protection flap** and **riser covers** are in good shape and stay secure during freefall. Connect **leg straps** with a bungee to keep them from sliding to your knees while in a head-up freefall position or making transitions. Tightly **stow excess** leg and chest strap material.

USPA recommends freeflyers use an **AAD and an RSL with a MARD** due to the increased potential for collisions and loss of altitude awareness.

When using **skysurfing** boards, use a board-release system that you can activate with either hand without bending at the waist.

Personal accessories for freeflying should include:

- audible altimeter (two are recommended)
- visual altimeter
- hard helmet
- clothing or jumpsuit that will remain in place during different orientations of freefall and will not obscure or obstruct deployment or emergency handles or altimeters

### D. Training

Freeflying has many things in common with face-to-earth formation skydiving. A beginner will develop awareness and progress much faster and more proficiently with a coach. Novices should not jump with each other until receiving basic training in freeflying and demonstrating the ability to maintain a vertical axis and control movement up, down, forward and backward in a head-up position.

Prior to jumping with larger groups, progress should follow the same model as for the freefall and canopy formation disciplines: 2-way formations of novice and coach to develop exit, body position, docking, transition, and breakoff skills.

### E. Hazards Associated with Group Freeflying

Inadvertently transitioning from a fast-falling body position to a slower, face-to-earth position is known as "**corking**" and results in **rapid deceleration**, typically from 175 mph to 120 mph. This could potentially lead to a high-speed freefall collision. To freefly safely in a group, you should be able to consistently remain in a vertical position at all times and remain clear of other freeflyers' airspace. During breakoff, clear airspace above, below, and behind.

When learning freeflying from a belly-to-earth background, it can be easy to **lose altitude awareness**. From 13,000 feet, a belly-to-earth jump is approximately 60 seconds while the freefall time of a freefly jump may be as short as 40 seconds. Also, the vertical freefall body positions can make visual altimeters difficult to see. Depending on the helmet used, audible altimeters may also be hard to hear with the increased wind speed of the vertical position. As with any other skydiving discipline, participants must be diligent in maintaining altitude awareness.

Novice freeflyers often **drift in various directions** in freefall. Prior to each jump, freeflyers should note jump run as well as landmarks perpendicular to jump run in order to set up facing off the line of flight (90 degrees to jump run). This is especially important for solo freeflyers. An experienced coach can identify whether a participant is drifting and provide guidance. Experienced freeflyers must be aware of drifting when coaching or performing dives involving horizontal movement (see Chapter 5-10, Movement Jumps).

Freeflyers must consider **wind drift**, as well as their drift from body position, to provide adequate **separation between groups**. As a general rule, faster-falling groups should exit the aircraft after slower-falling groups. Vertical freefall groups should stay upwind to allow clear canopy airspace for groups exiting prior.

Important planning considerations to address these hazards include:

- Get a briefing from an instructor experienced in freeflying.
- Consider getting a coach and mentor early in your progression.
- Ensure your equipment is "freefly friendly."
- Utilize both visual and audible altimeters.
- Keep the size of the groups small until proficient.
- Plan higher breakoffs than usual.
- Gradually transition from a fast fall-rate to tracking position for separation in case a skydiver is above the formation in a vertical position
- Avoid maneuvers near breakoff that increase separation and level changes from the group.
- Not only gain separation from other jumpers, but also slow down after breakoff to ensure normal freefall speeds for deployment.

## 5-3: Night Jumps

### A. Introduction and Definition

Night jumps can be challenging, educational, and fun, but they require greater care on the part of the jumper, pilot, spotter, and ground crew. As with all types of skydiving, night jumping can be safer with special training, suitable equipment, pre-planning, and good judgment.

Every skydiver, regardless of experience, should participate in night-jump training to learn or review:

- techniques for avoiding disorientation
- use of identification light, lighted instruments, and flashlight
- target lighting
- ground-to-air communications
- emergency procedures

Any jumps made between official sunset and official sunrise are considered night jumps. Jumpers must maintain safety and comply with FAA regulations using this definition. However, night jumps to meet license requirements and to establish world records must take place between one hour after official sunset and one hour before official sunrise.

### B. Qualifications

Skydivers participating in night jumping should meet all the requirements for a USPA B or higher license. Participants should complete a comprehensive briefing and drill immediately before the intended night jump. A USPA S&TA, Examiner, or Instructor who has completed at least two night jumps should conduct this training. This official should sign and document the training, including the date and location, in the jumper's logbook.

### C. Hazards Associated with Night Jumps

Night jumps can present new and unusual situations, and jumpers must approach this challenge with caution because darkness greatly impairs vision and depth perception, causing the **opportunity for disorientation**, a different appearance of the earth's surface, and a lack of familiar reference points. You should be thoroughly familiar with the effects of **hypoxia** (oxygen deprivation) on night vision found in the FAA Aeronautical Information Manual (AIM) online at faa.gov. One of the first effects of hypoxia, evident as low as 5,000 feet, is loss of night vision. It takes approximately 30 minutes to recover from the effects of hypoxia. Smokers suffer the effects of hypoxia sooner than non-smokers. Carbon monoxide from exhaust fumes, deficiency of vitamin A in the diet, and prolonged exposure to bright sunlight all degrade night vision.

Night vision requires 30 minutes to fully adjust. A jumper's own **shadow cast by the moon** can resemble another jumper below and cause confusion. Skydivers infrequently make night jumps and are less familiar with and less proficient in handling themselves under the conditions of this new environment. Since the skydiver cannot perceive what is taking place as rapidly and easily as in daylight, it takes more time to react to each situation.

# Discipline-Specific Recommendations

## D. Special Equipment

For protection from aircraft, the FAA requires night jumpers to have a **light visible for at least three statute miles displayed from opening until the jumper is on the ground**. USPA recommends using constant-beam lights rather than strobes, which can interfere with night vision and depth perception. Constant lights are preferable, but jumpers can use flashing lights once they open and are in full control of their canopies. Road flares and other pyrotechnics exude hot melted chemicals while burning and are hazardous when skydivers in freefall use them. In addition, the glare greatly increases the possibility of disorientation.

**Additional equipment** recommendations include a lighted altimeter, clear goggles, and a flashlight or light on a helmet pointing up to facilitate checking the canopy. A bright LED pointed at the canopy during the entire canopy descent illuminates the parachute for other jumpers, greatly decreasing the chance of a canopy collision. Night jumpers often carry a whistle to warn other jumpers under canopy, signal other jumpers after landing, and to aid rescuers in locating a lost or injured jumper.

**Turn your AAD off and back on** before beginning night jumps to ensure it is within the time-frame operational limits for the night jump. Drop zone staff should have and check the manifest after night jumps to ensure all jumpers landed safely.

The landing area should contain **sufficient lighting**—provided by flashlights, electric lights, or similar devices—to illuminate the target. Open flames can be extremely hazardous, so do not use road flares or other pyrotechnics. Car headlights may be used for lighting; however, vehicles clutter the landing area.

## E. Procedures

Skydivers should conduct night jumps in light winds and only in clear atmospheric conditions with minimal clouds. Moonlight greatly increases visibility and night-jump safety. USPA recommends jumping during a full moon when conducting group freefall skydives at night. Skydivers should wear white or light-colored jumpsuits.

The **BSRs require that you consult the local S&TA or a USPA Examiner** for advice for conducting night jumps. Additionally, you may need to notify FAA, state, and local officials as required. Use a topographical map or photo with FAA Flight Service weather information for appropriate altitude and surface winds to compute jump-run compass heading and exit and opening point. One senior member should be designated as jumpmaster for each pass and be responsible for accounting for all members of that pass once everyone has landed. Each jumper performing a night jump who is not familiar with the drop zone should **make at least one jump during daylight hours on the same day** to become familiar with the drop zone and surrounding areas.

To configure your **target for accuracy**, arrange lights in a circle around the target area at a radius of 82 feet (25 meters) from the center. Remove three or four of the lights closest to the wind line on the downwind side of the target and arrange them in a line leading into the target area. This will indicate both wind line and wind direction. By following a flight path over this line of lights, the jumper will be on the wind line and land upwind. Place a red light protected by a plexiglass cover at dead center, flush with the surface. In case of emergency, adverse weather or other hazardous jump conditions, extinguish all lights to indicate "no jump." Ground-to-air radio communications should be available.

Current wind information for both surface and aloft conditions is critical at night to ensure a **proper spot**. Spotters should familiarize themselves with the drop zone and surrounding area in flight during daylight, noting ground points that will display lights at night and their relationship to the drop zone and any hazardous areas. The spotter should plan to use both visual spotting and aircraft instruments to assure accurate positioning of the aircraft. During the climb to altitude, familiarize each jumper with the night landmarks surrounding the drop zone.

## F. Group Jumps: Freefall and Canopy

A person's first night jump should be solo. On subsequent night jumps, they can make group skydives, starting with a 2-way and then gradually progressing to larger formations. Jumpers should consider staggering their deployment altitudes to reduce the risk of a canopy collision both during deployment and during the canopy descent and landing pattern. When staggering deployments, the jumpers with the lowest wing loadings should deploy at the highest altitude and jumpers should continue in order by wing loading until the jumpers with the highest wing loadings deploy at the lowest altitude.

Once under canopy with others in the air, jumpers should fly predictably and avoid spiraling turns. All jumpers on each pass should agree to the same downwind, base, and final approach and the altitudes for turns to each leg of the landing pattern. Jumpers planning canopy formations should practice together during daylight and rehearse before boarding for each night jump. USPA recommends that skydivers participate in night canopy formations during a full moon. All jumpers should wear brightly colored clothing.

# 5-4: Water Landings

## A. Introduction and Purpose

Accidental water landings have caused a number of fatalities, usually because the jumper did not use flotation gear, used incorrect procedures, or landed in extremely cold water. USPA recommends water-landing training to improve chances for survival from both intentional and unintentional water landings.

The purpose of wet training (required for the USPA B license) is to expose the individual to a worst-case scenario in a controlled situation. Proper training should decrease the likelihood of panic, which should decrease the likelihood of drowning since drowning is usually brought on by panic.

Unintentional water entry may occur due to spotting error, radical wind changes, malfunctions, and landing under a reserve rather than a main. Intentional water jumps are preplanned jumps into a body of water.

## B. Training for Unintentional Water Landings

The ISP includes training recommendations for unintentional water landings in the obstacle-landing training of Category A (the first-jump course). Chapter 4-1G contains a more complete and detailed briefing outline.

### Dry (Theoretical Training)

A USPA S&TA, Examiner, or Instructor should sign documentation of this training, including the date and location, in the jumper's logbook and A-license application or on a separate statement.

Theoretical training should include classroom lessons covering:

- techniques for avoiding water hazards
- how to compensate for poor depth perception over water
- preparation for water entry
- additional risks of water landings in cold water temperatures
- recovery after landing

Practice should combine both ground and training-harness drills and should continue until the jumper is able to perform the procedures in a realistic timeframe.

### Wet (Practical Training)

After taking a class on theory, jumpers should undergo practical training in a suitable environment such as a swimming pool, lake, or other body of water at least six feet deep. This training meets the USPA B-License training requirements for intentional water landings and a USPA S&TA, Examiner, or Instructor should sign the documentation of it, including the date and location, in the jumper's logbook.

Those conducting this training need to consider the safety of the participants. Safety personnel should include properly trained and certified **lifeguards**. If suitably qualified skydivers are not available, assistance may normally be solicited from the local American Red Cross or other recognized training organization. Flotation gear and other lifesaving apparatus is recommended for non-swimmers.

Participants may wear swimsuits for initial training but should wear normal jump clothing during final training to simulate water landings. For the **non-swimmers**, training should include basic skills covering breath control, bobbing, and front and back floating. For the **swimmers**, training should include all of the above, plus the breaststroke, sidestroke, backstroke, and treading water.

While wearing a parachute harness-and-container system and all associated equipment, the participant jumps into the water. The USPA Instructor should then cast an open canopy of any type over the jumper before any wave action subsides. The jumper should then perform the steps necessary to escape from the equipment and the water. Repeat this drill until proficient.

## C. Procedures for Intentional Water Landings

Any person making an intentional water landing should hold a USPA A license, have undergone wet training for water landings, and be a swimmer. They should also undergo preparatory training within 60 days of the water jump. A USPA S&TA, Examiner, or Instructor should conduct this training and sign and document the date and location in the jumper's logbook.

Theoretical training should include classroom lessons covering:

- preparations necessary for safe operations
- equipment to be used
- procedures for the actual jump
- recovery of jumpers and equipment
- care of equipment

# Discipline-Specific Recommendations

**In preparation**, the BSRs require jumpers to obtain advice for the water jump from the local USPA S&TA or Examiner. Jumpers should also check the landing site for underwater hazards and use an altimeter for freefalls of 30 seconds or more.

Preparations should include no less than **one recovery boat per jumper**, or, if the aircraft drops one jumper per pass, one boat for every three jumpers. Boat personnel should include at least one qualified skydiver and stand-by swimmer with a face mask, swim fins, and experience in lifesaving techniques, including resuscitation.

Each jumper should receive a thorough briefing concerning the possible emergencies that may occur after water entry and the proper corrective procedures. Jumpers should open no lower than 3,000 feet AGL to provide ample time to prepare for water entry, especially when the landing area is a small body of water and the jumper must concentrate on both accuracy and water entry. A second jump run should not occur until all jumpers from the first pass are safely aboard the pickup boat(s).

In calm conditions with readily accessible pick-up boats, the best procedure is simply to inflate the flotation gear after canopy inflation and concentrate on landing in the proper area. In strong winds, choppy water conditions, in competitive water-jump events, or if the flotation gear cannot be inflated, separation from equipment after water entry is essential.

Water may damage some altimeters and automatic activation devices. When skydivers opt to jump without these standard instruments and AADs, they should use extra care.

## D. Hazards Associated with High-Performance Water Landings

Although making **high-performance landings** over water may reduce injuries in cases of slight misjudgment, larger errors that cause the jumper to hit the water too hard will still cause serious injury or death. Jumpers should obtain coaching from an experienced high-performance canopy pilot familiar with high-performance landings across water prior to attempting them. Raised banks at the approach entry and exit from the body of water present a serious hazard. An injury upon landing in a water hazard can increase the jumper's risk of drowning, so jumpers should approach high-performance landings involving water using the standard water-landing precautions, including the use of a flotation device. The area around the body of water should be clear of hazards and spectators in case high-speed contact with the water causes the jumper to lose control.

## E. Water-Jump Safety Checks and Briefings

Jumpers should perform a complete gear check, paying particular attention to any additional equipment to be used or carried for the water jump (see more in Chapter 4-4).

Boat and ground crew briefings should include:

- communications procedures (smoke, radio, buoys, boats)
- wind limitations
- jump order
- control of spectators and other boats
- setting up the target
- maintenance of master log
- how to approach a jumper and canopy in the water (direction, proximity)

# 5-5: Canopy Formations

## A. Introduction and Definition

Canopy Formation (CF) is the name of the competition discipline for the skydiving activity commonly called canopy relative work (CRW or "crew") Jumpers build canopy formations by intentionally maneuvering two or more open parachute canopies near or in contact with one another during flight. The goal is smooth flow and grace between two or more jumpers and their canopies in flight. The most basic canopy formation is when two canopies are joined vertically during flight. This can be a stack, where the jumper's feet are docked at the top of the lines, or a plane, where the jumper moves down the lines to secure the feet below the slider of the bottom jumper on the cross connectors (see Equipment below).

Canopy formation specialists consider the recommendations in this section to be the safest, most predictable, and most productive procedures. Experienced canopy formation specialists should lead canopy formation jumps, whether they occur during the day or at night.

## B. Qualifications

Before engaging in canopy formations, a jumper should have thorough knowledge of canopy-flight characteristics, to include riser maneuvers and the relative compatibility of various canopies. They should also have demonstrated accuracy capability of consistently landing within 16 feet of a target.

## C. Equipment

The following items are essential for safely building canopy formations:

# 5 Discipline-Specific Recommendations

- hook knife—necessary for resolving entanglements
- ankle protection—adequate socks to prevent abrasion from canopy lines and no boots with hooks
- gloves for hand protection
- self-retracting or removable pilot-chute-bridle systems
- cross connectors— A secure foothold at the top of the risers is essential for building planes, which can develop greater tension as they grow larger. Cross connectors are a length of webbing attached between the front and rear risers only, not from side to side. Side-to-side cross connectors can snag on the reserve container during deployment and cause a dangerous entanglement.

The following items are **strongly recommended** for safely building canopy formations:

- visual altimeter to provide altitude information for dock, abort, and entanglement decisions
- protective headgear that allows adequate hearing of voice commands in addition to collision protection
- long pants and sleeves for protection from line abrasions
- extended or enlarged toggles to make grasping them easier
- cascades removed from the two center A lines, which should be marked in red

## D. Training

Initial training should occur with two jumpers—the beginner and a canopy formation specialist—and include lessons in basic docking, breakoff procedures, and emergency procedures. The first few jumps should include only stacks and planes, as offset formations are less stable.

## E. Procedures

Avoid jumping in turbulent air or gusty wind conditions. In areas subject to thermal turbulence and other unstable air conditions, jump in the early morning and early evening. Avoid passing near clouds, which are associated with unpredictable air conditions. Use caution in flying formations over plowed fields, paved surfaces, or other areas where thermal conditions often exist. When unexpectedly encountering bumpy or turbulent air, fly the formation directly into the wind.

Factors you must consider in every **pre-jump briefing include:**

- exit order
- time between exits
- length of freefall
- designation of base
- canopy wing loading and trim
- order of entry
- direction of flight and techniques of rendezvous
- approach and breakoff traffic patterns
- docking procedures
- formation-flight procedures
- one-word verbal commands
- breakoff and landing procedures
- emergency procedures

**Spotting** should account for upper-wind velocity and direction. Advise the pilot that a canopy formation group is exiting and opening high. Leave a minimum of two seconds of separation between **exits**. With greater experience and the use of staged openings, one-second separation may be possible but drastically increases the chance of collision when an off-heading canopy opening occurs. Any opening delay should be adequate to assure clearance from the aircraft, jumper separation, and stable body position at opening. Each jumper must be prepared to avoid a collision at any time upon leaving the aircraft.

When establishing **docking** procedures, identify the jumper who is the base. This position requires the most expertise; however, docking skills are used in all slots. All jumpers should discuss docking methods before boarding the aircraft.

During **formation flight**, it is important that the formation pilot maintain a constant direction of flight along a predetermined course and establish an orderly flight pattern for canopies attempting to dock, which will enable interference-free approaches and lessen the possibility of canopy collisions. No canopies should ever pass in front of a formation; the wake turbulence created will disturb the formation's stability and could lead to a very dangerous situation.

For smoothness and safety when **approaching** the formation, approach on level with the dock and slightly behind by only a couple of feet. This also avoids imparting vertical energy into the formation, which can cause the wings on the other side to come around into the center of the formation. This type of approach is recommended for vertical formations, as well. Approaching from below is not recommended.

When **docking**, grasp only the center section of a docking canopy when the canopy closes third or later in a stack formation. To complete the stack dock, the top jumper should place both feet between both A lines of the center cell of the lower jumper and hook one by each instep. A center-cell dock is preferable for beginners.

## Discipline-Specific Recommendations

Improper docks are the most common cause of **collapsed** canopies. You should release a collapsed canopy to allow reinflation only if it will not make the situation worse. To prevent dropping an entangled jumper into a potential collision, make sure the area behind and below is clear. Experienced participants may be able to reinflate a collapsed canopy by continuing to plane down the lines. The jumper with the collapsed canopy can try using brakes or rear risers to back the canopy off and reinflate it. A jumper wishing to be released from the formation should use the term "drop me." This command is to be obeyed immediately, unless it will drop the jumper into a worse situation. The jumper issuing the command should be sure to check behind for other canopies on approach before asking to be dropped.

When in **formation flight**, verbal commands should be concise and direct, omitting non-essential conversation. The pilot should fly the formation with limited control movements to minimize oscillations and facilitate docking. The formation pilot should never use deep brakes in the formation. If a lower canopy is collapsing in a vertical formation, the jumper should slide his feet back up to the canopy for re-inflation or follow the agreed emergency procedures for the planned formation. Continuing to plane down the lines may end with the canopy completely collapsing and potentially causing entanglement.

**Oscillations** are a primary concern in canopy formations, because they can result in collapsed canopies and entanglements. To reduce their effect and frequency, jumpers in the formation can—

- maintain an arch for speed and stability especially for offset and diamond formations
- when on the bottom of the formation, sit still in the harness and cross their legs
- when on the bottom, apply the appropriate control to reduce or increase tension
- manipulate a lower jumper's lines to dampen the oscillation
- drop the bottom jumper before the oscillation develops into something worse

**Diamonds and offsets** require different flying techniques than vertical formations. It is imperative to receive proper training before attempting them.

For **breakoff and landing** procedures, approaches and docking should stop no lower than 2,500 feet AGL. Formation pilots should avoid all obstacles, including suspected areas of thermal activity, such as paved surfaces, plowed fields, buildings, etc. Only those with a high level of CF proficiency should attempt to land canopy formations. Breakoff for landing should take place no lower than 2,500 feet AGL because of the danger of entanglement at breakoff time. Jumpers should not attempt to land formations in high or gusty winds, high density altitudes, or high field elevations. CF groups landing off the airport should try to land together.

For guidance on **night canopy formations**, see Chapter 5-3 Night Jumps.

## F. Hazards and Emergency Procedures

Jumper-to-jumper collisions or hard docks that result in deflated canopies or entanglements can result in serious injury or death. **Entanglements** are the greatest hazards when building canopy formations. Jumpers should know their altitude at all times, because altitude will often dictate the course of action.

**If a collision is imminent**, you should not take canopy formation grips with any small diameter lines unless you are extremely knowledgeable and proficient on those particular canopies. Beside the danger of slicing into muscles and cutting through harness components, those lines and attachment points are not usually strong enough to withstand the loads that can occur in a docked formation. They are more susceptible to failure, possibly long after the dock has been dropped, potentially much lower than 2,500 feet. Avoid body-to-body contact at all cost, and hit lines or fabric instead. Attempt to clear the entanglement by following the risers out, peeling away fabric and lines while protecting your handles.

If the upper jumper is engulfed **in the fabric** of the lower jumper's canopy and is unable to disengage, the lower jumper should be instructed to cut away first. The upper jumper should then clear their face and their controls from the canopy that was cut away and take control of their own canopy. It is safer to fly slowly and keep the cutaway canopy's fabric on you than it is to try to clear it and risk having a line or lines snag on you, causing the other canopy to inflate and downplane or spin into your canopy.

If the upper jumper **is entangled in the suspension lines** of the lower jumper's canopy, under the bottom skin of that canopy, the upper jumper in the lines should cut away first. That jumper should clear lines and fabric from their body and three-rings to create a path down and out. The upper jumper should also disconnect the RSL (if worn and if time and altitude permits) in case the jumper does not clear the other lines immediately upon initiating cutaway procedures. Crossing your legs prior to cutting away can also prevent straddling cascaded lines or risers. Once clear of the entanglement, the jumper should pull the reserve immediately and not wait to gain stability, as it can take up to 1,000 feet to stop tumbling after a cutaway. If you cannot untangle, make only two attempts to clear the entangled canopy before deploying the reserve. The sooner the reserve is deployed, the more time and altitude you have available to prevent the cutaway canopy from interfering with control of the reserve.

**Why upper jumper first?** The entangled jumper needs the lower jumper to stay attached to that canopy to provide tension on the lines to allow the upper jumper to slide out of them. If the lower jumper performs cutaway procedures first, the upper jumper becomes hopelessly entangled in the lower jumper's suspension lines while that canopy is temporarily released and re-inflates into a downplane.

If the cutaway canopy does not clear the lower jumper's canopy, the lower jumper needs to wait at least 5 seconds before performing cutaway procedures. Once reserves are deployed, steer clear of the other jumper and the cutaway canopies.

Jumpers should try to land together following a canopy formation emergency.

## 5-6: High-Altitude Jumps

### A. Introduction and Definition

A high-altitude skydive is a jump made at or above 15,000 feet mean sea level (MSL), but lower than 18,000 feet MSL. MSL is not to be confused with AGL (above ground level) or the drop zone's elevation.

USPA does not provide recommendations for skydiving at and above 18,000 feet MSL since it is outside of sport-parachuting altitudes. Those who do opt to skydive at or above these altitudes should seek outside expertise and use specialized oxygen equipment. The jumpers must develop procedures for the specific jump or event, as well as procure specialized equipment and support.

Skydives from altitudes higher than 15,000 feet MSL present participants with a range of important considerations, since reduced atmospheric pressure, decreased partial pressure of oxygen, environmental factors including temperature, and higher winds greatly increase the level of risk.

### B. Hazards and Hypoxia

**According to FAR 91.211, each occupant of the aircraft must be provided with supplemental oxygen at cabin pressure altitudes at or above 15,000 feet MSL.** Hypoxia is a medical condition that develops when there is not enough oxygen in the body's tissues and is the most immediate concern between 15,000 feet MSL and 18,000 feet MSL. Hypoxia can result in impaired judgment and motor function and eventually cause unconsciousness or even death. All participants involved in the jump will benefit from familiarization training that covers the oxygen equipment being used, aircraft drills, and information about the physiological conditions encountered when exposed to reduced atmospheric pressures. Undergoing hypoxia-recognition training that allows the simulation of objective and subjective signs and symptoms of hypoxia is also extremely beneficial.

### C. Equipment

In the event of a malfunction in the primary oxygen system, a backup oxygen system should be available on board the aircraft. Each aircrew member and skydiver will have access to their own oxygen mask or nasal cannula, although a common central oxygen bottle and regulator system may be used as a supply.

### D. Oxygen-Use Procedures

Warning: Oxygen explosively accelerates burning! To prevent damage to aircraft and equipment and injury to persons from oxygen-fed flash fires, the aircraft should be electrically grounded during all ground practice. No smoking should be permitted in the vicinity of the aircraft, either on the ground or aloft, while oxygen equipment is on board.

Oxygen-use procedures will vary with the equipment used, but the following are basic:

- All participants should don masks or nasal cannulas with a positive flow of oxygen prior to exceeding 15,000 feet MSL. Oxygen flow should be continuous throughout the remainder of the climb and jump run and should be monitored continuously via gauges or visual flow indicators. The aircraft operator should ensure sufficient oxygen supply for all exposures above 15,000 feet MSL, including supply for extended delays at altitude.
- Prior to exit, jumpers should stay on oxygen for as long as possible, removing their masks or cannulas at the "climb out" or "exit" signal. Participants should rehearse these procedures on the ground in order to ensure a safe climb to altitude and aircraft exit.
- In the event of an aborted jump run, all participants will ensure the re-donning of their own oxygen equipment, assist others and await further instructions from the aircrew.

## 5-7: Camera Flying

### A. Introduction

Skydiving provides a wealth of visual inspiration that can be readily captured through still and video photography. Smaller and lighter cameras have made it easier and less expensive to take cameras on a jump, but jumpers still need to exercise caution with their camera equipment and its interaction with the parachute system throughout all activities on the jump, paying close attention to breakoff procedures and special emergency procedures for camera flyers. Only after a camera flyer has become completely familiar with the equipment and procedures of the discipline should they experiment and be creative.

**USPA recommends that jumpers be licensed and have completed 200 jumps before jumping with a camera.**

## B. Background

Early pioneer camera flyers had to solve the obvious problems presented by big, cumbersome camera equipment and parachutes. Only the most experienced jumpers and photographers would brave the activity of filming others. More recently, miniature digital still and video cameras present less of a challenge, encouraging more jumpers to use cameras on their jumps. Skydivers have become less concerned about the skill of a camera flyer jumping with their group.

## C. Purpose

Jumpers should realize that flying a camera—even a small one—requires additional effort and attention on each jump and should not take the decision to begin flying camera lightly. To support education for new camera flyers, the USPA Library offers an online course, Camera Flying Recommendations, at uspa.org/library.

## D. Equipment

A camera flyer should consult another experienced camera flyer and a rigger before using any new or modified piece of equipment on a camera jump, including:

- helmet
- parachute
- deployment-device modification
- camera
- camera mount
- flash
- switch and mounting
- camera suit
- emergency release
- other items such as sky surfboard or skis, tubes or other freefall toys, wingsuit

Prior to filming other skydivers, a camera flyer should jump with each new or additional piece of equipment until they are completely familiar with it and have adjusted any procedures accordingly.

### Camera Equipment

Small cameras are not necessarily safer to jump than larger ones. Regardless of the location of the camera mount, users should place and rig them with respect to deploying parachutes. Camera flyers should cover, tape, or protect by other means all edges and potential snag areas. Snag points that cannot be mitigated on helmet-mounted cameras should at least face away from the deploying parachute. A pyramid shape of the entire camera-mounting system may deflect lines better than an egg shape. Deflectors can help protect areas that cannot otherwise be modified to reduce problems. All gaps between the helmet and equipment, including mounting plates, should be taped or filled. Protrusions, such as camera sights, should be engineered to present the least potential for snags. Test for these potential problems on the ground by dragging a suspension line over the camera assembly to reveal snag points.

Sharp edges and protrusions can injure other jumpers during a collision or emergency aircraft landing. During deployment, jumpers should make sure that any cameras mounted on their extremities are kept clear of the deploying canopy, lines, etc. Camera-operation devices such as switches and cables need to be simple and secure. Analyze each piece of added equipment for its potential interaction with the overall camera system and parachutes.

### Helmets and Camera Mounts

A rigger or an experienced camera flyer should evaluate all camera platforms, whether custom or off the shelf, for safety and suitability to your purpose. The helmet should provide full visibility for the camera flyer in freefall and under canopy, but especially during emergency procedures. Cover and tape empty camera mounts to prevent snags.

Any camera helmet should have an emergency release that is easy to operate with either hand in case of entanglement. Use a reliable helmet closure or clasp that also functions as an emergency release.

### Parachute

Camera flyers should use a reliable parachute that opens slowly and on heading. Those who use a camera suit need to ensure it is compatible with their deployment system. Camera-suit wings and lower connections must not interfere with the camera flyer's parachute-operation handles or main-bridle routing in any freefall orientation. If using a camera suit, the pilot chute and bridle length must be sufficient to overcome the additional burble the suit creates. If the camera flyer generally opens higher than the other jumpers on the load, they may wish to use a slower descending canopy to help reduce traffic conflicts. As always, proper attention to packing and maintenance, especially line stows, helps prevent hard openings and malfunctions.

Recommended **accessory equipment** includes an audible altimeter, a visual altimeter that can be seen while filming, and a hook knife. USPA recommends camera flyers use an **AAD and an RSL with a MARD**.

## E. Procedures

Prior to jumping with a camera, a skydiver should have enough general jump experience to be able to handle any skydiving emergency or minor problem easily. A camera flyer should possess well-above-average skills that are applicable to the discipline or activity planned for the jump.

USPA recommends that jumpers be licensed and have **completed 200 jumps before jumping with a camera**. The jumper should have made **at least 50 recent** jumps on the same parachute equipment to be used for camera flying and should know the experience and skills of all the jumpers in the group.

The **deployment altitude** should allow time to deal with the additional equipment and its associated problems. The camera flyer must remain aware of other jumpers during deployment.

Each camera flyer should conduct a complete camera- and parachute-equipment check before rigging up, after rigging up, before boarding the plane, and again prior to exit. They should approach camera jumps procedurally, following the same routine on every jump. The priorities on the jump should be the parachute equipment and procedures first, then the camera equipment and procedures. Introduce only one new variable—either procedure or equipment—at a time. A camera jump requires additional planning, and jumpers should never consider it to be just another skydive.

### Aircraft

Camera flyers should wear or secure any camera during takeoff and landing to prevent it from becoming a projectile in the event of sudden movement. Be aware of the additional space a camera takes up, and practice climb-out procedures in each aircraft to prevent injury resulting from catching the camera on the door or other part of the aircraft. To prevent injury and damage to the aircraft, the camera flyer should coordinate with the pilot before attempting any new climb-out position.

### Exit

Unless the plan calls for the camera flyer to be part of the exit, they should remain clear of the group, being mindful of the airspace opposite the exiting jumpers' relative wind. Be aware that:

- Wearing a camera helmet can make collisions with other jumpers more serious.
- Student jumpers can become disoriented when unexpectedly encountering a camera flyer.
- A tandem parachutist in command requires clear airspace to deploy a drogue.
- Skydivers occasionally experience inadvertent openings on exit.

### Freefall

Jumpers should prepare a freefall plan with the camera flyer to include the camera flyer's position in relation to the group and any planned camera-flyer interaction with the group. The jumpers and the camera flyer should follow the plan.

All jumpers on the load should understand the camera flyer's breakoff and deployment plan. Two or more camera flyers must coordinate the breakoff and deployment more carefully than when only one camera flyer is involved. Filming other jumpers through deployment should be planned in consideration of the opening altitudes of all the jumpers involved and with their cooperation. The camera flyer should maintain awareness of his or her position over the ground and deploy high enough to reach a safe landing area.

### Deployment

The camera flyer must exercise increased caution during deployment to prevent malfunctions, assure an on-heading deployment, reduce the likelihood of line twists, and avoid neck injury. New camera flyers should consult with experienced camera flyers for specific techniques to prevent accidents during deployment and inflation. Malfunction, serious injury, or death can occur if the lines of a deploying parachute become snagged on camera equipment.

### Parachute Emergencies

The additional equipment worn for filming can complicate emergency procedures. Each camera flyer should regularly practice all parachute emergency procedures under canopy or in a training harness while fully rigged for a camera jump and should practice routine emergency procedures before every jump. Emergency-procedure practice should include removing the helmet with either hand in response to certain malfunctions. A camera flyer should release their helmet during equipment entanglements, obstacle landings (water, trees, building, power lines), and whenever a dangerous situation presents itself.

## F. Considerations for Videoing Students

Refer to the Instructional Rating Manual for additional guidelines for flying camera for student training jumps. A skydiver should have extensive camera-flying experience with experienced jumpers prior to photographing or videoing student jumps, including at least **300 group freefall skydives and at least 50 jumps flying camera** with experienced jumpers.

The USPA Instructor supervising the jump should conduct a thorough briefing with the camera flyer prior to boarding. The USPA Coach or Instructor, the camera flyer, and the student making the jump should all be aware of the procedures and the camera plan. The instructors' full attention is supposed to be on the student, and the student is incapable of considering the movements and needs of the camera flyer.

The camera flyer should avoid the area directly above or below a student or instructor(s), because students may deploy without warning and because disturbing the student's or instructors' air could compromise their performance and the safety of the jumpers.

The camera flyer should plan an exit position that avoids contact with the student or the instructor(s). **During the exit**, students often give erratic exit counts, making exit timing difficult for the camera flyer. The camera flyer may leave slightly before the student exits when the count is reliable. The camera flyer should follow slightly after the student's exit whenever the student's exit timing is uncertain. When filming tandem jumpers, the camera flyer must remain clear of the deploying drogue

The camera flyer needs to maintain independent altitude awareness and never rely on the student or instructor(s). The camera flyer is responsible for opening separation from the student and the instructor(s). Although the footage may be dramatic, aggressive filming of openings compromises the safety of the student, the instructor(s), and the camera flyer.

When using larger aircraft, student groups typically exit farther upwind, which may require a higher opening for the camera flyer to safely return to the landing area.

When using a hand-mounted camera to video students, the tandem instructor should review the information contained in the Instructional Rating Manual Tandem Section regarding hand-cam training.

## 5-8: Wingsuit Flying

### A. Introduction and Definitions

A **wingsuit** is a specialized suit designed with arm wings and a leg wing intended to increase the total surface area of the skydiver, which decreases vertical (downward) speed and increases horizontal (forward) speed. A wingsuit will decrease the skydiver's full range of motion, whereas baggy jumpsuits and tracking suits still allow for a full range of motion. A **wingsuit pilot** is a skydiver who wears a wingsuit.

These recommendations provide guidance for a skydive that entails wearing a wingsuit, along with parameters for wingsuit progression and more advanced wingsuit-flying jumps.

### B. Qualifications

The **BSRs** require any person performing a wingsuit jump to have at least 200 skydives and hold a current skydiving license. USPA also recommends the participating skydiver become a well-rounded, multi-discipline skydiver and canopy pilot. A wingsuit pilot should possess situational awareness regarding loading the plane, aircraft climb pattern and location, jump-run direction, exit order, exit separation, parachute opening, canopy flight, and landing pattern.

Before engaging in wingsuit jumps, a participating skydiver should take a **first-flight course (FFC)** with an experienced wingsuit coach. While USPA does not have a specific rating for wingsuit coaches, wingsuit manufacturers often offer instructional ratings for their products and provide contact details for endorsed wingsuit coaches. Regardless of manufacturer endorsement, a wingsuit coach should have a current USPA Coach rating and be a highly experienced wingsuit pilot. The drop zone where the FFC is held determines who can conduct it.

### C. Equipment

Wingsuit pilots should use non-elliptical **canopies** with reliable, on-heading openings. A beginner wingsuit pilot should limit their wing loading to no more than 1.3:1. An experienced wingsuit pilot should limit their wing loading to no more than 1.5:1.

Wingsuits create a large burble above and behind a skydiver and may not provide the **pilot chute** enough air for clean inflation and extraction of the deployment bag from the pack tray. USPA recommends a pilot chute with a diameter of at least 26 inches. Wingsuit pilots should use a pilot chute handle that is as light as possible, and USPA strongly recommends a bridle length of at least 7 feet from pin to pilot chute. The bottom-of-container throw-out pilot chute is the only **deployment system** that wingsuit pilots should use.

USPA recommends wingsuit pilots use an **AAD and an RSL with a MARD**. Jumpers should consult their drop zone about its rules regarding AAD use for wingsuit pilots. Wingsuit pilots should wear **helmets**, especially when flying in groups, and use an audible **altimeter** and a visual altimeter mounted on the chest strap or mud flap. Wingsuit pilots should wait to wear any **camera** until their exits, flights and deployments are consistent, stable, and routine.

### D. Training

Regardless of experience in other disciplines, jumpers should seek thorough training with an experienced wingsuit coach before engaging in wingsuit flying. Before flying wingsuits in larger groups, **novice wingsuit pilots** should fly formations with a coach to develop exit, body position, docking, transition, breakoff, and deployment skills, following the same model as for the freefall and canopy-formation disciplines.

Regardless of wingsuit experience, jumpers should **learn new wingsuit skills** in groups no larger than a 3-way. This includes acrobatic maneuvers such as barrel rolls and docked transitions, XRW (mixed canopy and wingsuit jumps), performance flying, and dynamic flying. Before flying in a group larger than three wingsuit pilots, each participant should be able to make a stable and controlled exit. They each should be able to approach other wingsuit pilots in a gradual and controlled manner, checking their airspace and remaining aware of all other wingsuit pilots in their group. They should also each be able to break off and create a safe distance from other wingsuit pilots for deployment.

**Wingsuit size progression** should follow the manufacturer guidelines regarding minimum jump numbers. Larger wingsuit sizes require more skill. A wingsuit pilot wishing to advance into the next suit size should seek guidance from an experienced wingsuit coach. Just as it is important to have solid skill sets on a current canopy before downsizing, it is also important to have solid skill sets on a current wingsuit before upsizing.

## E. Procedures

Group wingsuit flights should have planned **breakoff and deployment altitudes**. Wingsuit groups should have a planned breakoff signal to communicate that the group flight is over. The beginner wingsuit pilot—as well as wingsuit pilots who do not have consistent, stable deployments—should deploy at a minimum of 5,000 feet AGL.

Wingsuit deployments require active management of forward speed and body symmetry. Arm wings of the suit may fully obstruct the jumper's ability to quickly deploy their main parachute without a specialized deployment technique. Wingsuit pilots should become proficient at the deployment technique before advancing in their progression of suit size.

Wingsuit pilots have additional steps to their **post-deployment procedures** following normal canopy inflation:

1. clear airspace
2. unzip arm wings first
3. perform canopy housekeeping
4. stow the tail wing (This depends on the personal preference of each wingsuit pilot and should not take priority over flying the canopy predictably and safely.)

Wingsuit pilots often **share canopy airspace** with tandems and jumpers still on student status, as well as other jumpers who may have deployed higher than 6,000 feet AGL. Wingsuit pilots should exercise awareness around these other canopies to avoid canopy collisions.

**Emergency Procedures:** Arm wings may restrict movement and inhibit the wingsuit pilot from grabbing their risers until the arm wings are unzipped. Any wingsuit, regardless of the model, should allow enough range of motion for the wingsuit pilot to pull the main cutaway and reserve handles without unzipping the arm wings.

During a **high-speed canopy malfunction**, the jumper should immediately execute emergency procedures without wasting time unzipping the arm wings first. In the event of a **low-speed canopy malfunction**, it may be necessary to unzip the arm wings in order to reach the risers. Wingsuit pilots should demonstrate the ability to unzip the arm wings all the way in a smooth and controlled fashion while practicing low-speed-canopy-malfunction drills. Unzipping the tail wing is not crucial for canopy flight, and an unzipped tail wing can potentially entangle with the main or reserve.

There are many facets to **advanced wingsuit flying**. Due to the increased risks involved, only experienced wingsuit flyers with the assistance of a coach following the prescribed outline under Section D—Training of this chapter should attempt any of the following disciplines:

- **XRW** – a discipline in which a wingsuit pilot flies in close proximity to and/or completes docks with a canopy pilot flying a high-performance parachute at a high wing loading.
- **Performance** – a competitive discipline that involves a wingsuit pilot flying for maximum performance in three separate tasks: speed, distance, and time.
- **Acrobatic** – a competitive discipline that consists of docking with other wingsuit pilots and performing acrobatic maneuvers.
- **Mixed** – any wingsuit flight that occurs with other skydivers in freefall, such as rodeo, angles, and carving around freefall groups.
- **Large Formations** – as a record category, wingsuits can fly in large formations to achieve state, national and world records.
- **Dynamic Flocking** – a type of wingsuit flying that consists of group members flying together in a steep angle, such as layouts, flares, and carving.
- **Accessories** – jumping with accessories to wingsuit gear such as brackets, streamers and/or harnesses with ropes or handles. Wingsuit pilots should exercise great care, be cautious about entanglement issues, and plan cutaway procedures for everyone on the jump, whether they are in wingsuits or not.

Discipline-Specific Recommendations

# F. Hazards Associated with Wingsuit Jumps

**Restricted Movement:** Arm movements are more restricted during a wingsuit skydive, although the amount of restriction is model-specific. Arm wings of the suit may fully obstruct the jumper's ability to quickly deploy their main parachute without a specialized deployment technique.

**Limited Visibility:** The wingsuit pilot should follow the wingsuit manufacturer's guidelines when attaching a wingsuit to the harness-and-container system and use special care to ensure that the wingsuit does not obstruct the cutaway and reserve handles. Since harness leg straps are not visible when the wingsuit is fully zipped up, jumpers should take great care to ensure the leg straps are fully tightened while gearing up and during the pre-jump gear check.

**Tail Strikes:** During exit, wingsuit pilots must be especially careful to avoid colliding with the tail of the aircraft. A wingsuit flyer must direct their head into the relative wind, avoid jumping up while exiting, and refrain from fully opening leg and arm wings until they have passed below the tail of the aircraft. Wingsuiters should ask the pilot whether an engine cut is possible for their exit, since a solid engine cut helps wingsuiters avoid colliding with the tail during the exit, particularly in low-tail aircraft.

**Out-of-Control Flight:** Due to the responsiveness of pressurized wingsuits, stable and controlled flight requires subtle and relaxed movements. If a wingsuit pilot cannot control the heading of their flight, they may tumble and become disoriented in what is known as out-of-control flight (OCF). Wingsuit pilots should seek out coaching early in their progression to learn the skills necessary to control their wingsuit flight and avoid OCF. USPA strongly advises wingsuit pilots to adhere to the manufacturer's recommendations for the minimum number of jumps required to fly a certain size or style of wingsuit. If OCF occurs above deployment altitude and controlled flight cannot be regained within 5 seconds or within 5,000 feet of altitude loss, deploy the main parachute. If unable to locate the bottom-of-container deployment handle, pull the reserve immediately. If OCF occurs below a wingsuit pilot's planned deployment altitude, they should deploy regardless of their body position, which follows the pull priorities for any skydive. The inability to fly and deploy in a stable and controlled orientation will increase the likelihood of needing to execute emergency procedures. Wingsuit pilots should frequently practice their emergency procedures while visualizing the various scenarios where OCF occurred.

**Coordination with Other Groups:** Wingsuiters should be aware of other groups' deployment altitudes and types of skydiving activities on their loads. Wingsuiters should be especially aware of any other movement groups and any skydivers on the load intending to deploy above 6,000 feet. If multiple groups of wingsuiters plan to exit on the same load, the groups should coordinate their flight patterns to allow separate airspace per the drop zone's policies.

**Navigation and Weather:** Wingsuiters can travel for miles between exiting the aircraft and the deployment point. Thus, navigation—plotting a route, maneuvering to follow that route, and adapting when conditions change—is a critically important skill. Wingsuit pilots should determine winds aloft prior to jumping by consulting the pilot or winds-aloft forecasts. Wingsuit pilots must meet the cloud-clearance and visibility requirements of FAR 105.17, and the margin needed for their horizontal flight may exceed what other freefall groups need. If the wingsuit flight occurs near a coastline or other large body of water, the wingsuit flight pattern should remain close enough to the shoreline to ensure that each wingsuit pilot can make it to the designated landing area or another suitable landing area. Wingsuit pilots should consider wearing flotation gear on these types of jumps.

Wingsuit pilots generally fly a planned **flight pattern**, which may vary due to drop-zone and air-traffic concerns. The wingsuit flight pattern should avoid crossing jump run and should consider canopy traffic, particularly tandem and AFF students. The BSRs require at least 500 feet of vertical and horizontal separation from tandem pairs and students, and a safe distance from any other canopy.

**Landing Out:** If improper navigation occurs, a wingsuit pilot may land off. Wingsuit pilots should be familiar with the off-landing procedures of the drop zone. If landing in water is unavoidable, the jumper must fully unzip the arm and leg wings before landing in the water to allow as much freedom of movement as possible after entering the water.

## G. Pre-Flight Checklist

This pre-flight checklist can help you determine the specifics of your jump. Draw your flight plan on the map of your drop zone and confirm it with the drop zone staff, load organizer, pilot, and S&TA.

- ☐ What is jump run for your load?
- ☐ What are the forecasted winds at these points during your jump?
    - ☐ Exit altitude
    - ☐ Flight
    - ☐ Deployment
    - ☐ Landing Pattern
    - ☐ Current Ground Conditions
- ☐ How many groups and other jumpers are on your load?
- ☐ What is your exit order?
- ☐ Are there any other wingsuit or movement jumps on your load?
    - ☐ Have you discussed and coordinated deployment areas with these groups?
- ☐ What are the terrain factors to consider in navigation?
- ☐ What is the intended landing pattern and holding area for the jump?
- ☐ Have you ensured that your flight path does not interfere with jump run?
- ☐ Is your flight plan appropriate for the skill level and wingsuit size for other jumpers in your group?

# 5-9: Canopy Piloting

## A. Introduction and Purpose

USPA pursues a canopy education strategy in coordination with drop zone instructional staff, expert canopy pilots, advanced canopy training schools, and canopy manufacturers. Basic but comprehensive canopy-flight training starts in the USPA Integrated Student Program leading to the A license. Yet, the canopy designs and flying techniques that jumpers often choose to use as they progress in the sport require training beyond what skydiving students receive. This section serves as a bridge between your basic license training and your future goals, whatever they may be.

Analysis of incident reports indicates that jumpers are at risk without continued canopy training at each license level and throughout their skydiving careers. Even canopies considered lightly loaded can be dangerous if jumpers are not properly trained to fly them. Jumpers who have progressed without continued training are largely unprepared for how to handle their canopy in difficult canopy flight and landing situations. Preparation for unusual canopy flight and landing emergencies is key to reducing canopy-piloting mistakes, injuries, and fatalities.

USPA encourages all jumpers to take canopy-piloting training courses to refine canopy skills, especially as they downsize to smaller canopies with increased wing loadings and performance characteristics.

## B. Hazards Associated with Canopy Piloting

Some of the maneuvers described to develop understanding of canopy flight involve a greater risk of injury, even serious injury or death, than a routine parachute landing using a straight-in approach flown at the canopy's natural speed until flaring. Any pilot who manipulates the canopy controls to induce additional speed prior to landing presents a greater hazard to themselves and others. Before jumping begins, the canopy coach, instructor or course director should require each participant to complete an assumption-of-risk agreement in conjunction with a comprehensive liability-risk-management program applied in accordance with applicable local and state laws.

## C. Definitions and Procedures

A jumper chooses the correct canopy for their experience level based on canopy performance, which is significantly influenced by wing loading and design. A canopy designed for more performance may exhibit relatively docile characteristics when it's loaded lightly and flown conservatively. A canopy designed for docile performance that is flown aggressively at a higher wing loading can exhibit high-performance characteristics.

Novice canopy flyers can make errors on larger, docile canopies without getting hurt that on smaller, more heavily loaded canopies could have serious consequences. All canopies can be deemed high performance depending on the wing loading. High performance generally refers to canopies loaded as follows:

- above 230 square feet, 1.1 pounds or more per square foot
- from 190 to 229 square feet, 1.0 pound or more per square foot
- from 150 to 189 square feet, .9 pound or more per square foot
- canopies smaller than 150 square feet at any wing loading

# Discipline-Specific Recommendations

## Canopy Design

Typical characteristics of elliptical canopies compared to rectangular canopies of the same size and material:

- flatter glide for same airspeed
- faster turns
- greater loss of altitude in a turn
- may continue to dive after stopping control input following a turn
- slower, less predictable opening (some models)
- shorter toggle stroke for flare (some models)
- quicker, more abrupt stall (some models)

The **stall speed** of any wing increases as the wing loading increases due to more suspended weight. Sudden maneuvers, such as flaring hard after a dive, can increase the stall speed, as well.

Jumpers should approach changing their **canopy's design** with as much caution as downsizing. They should learn whether the canopy's design elements match their overall expectations, goals and experience level. Many design elements drastically change the flight characteristics, stability, and overall level of performance of a parachute.

Jumpers should explore only one new **design element** at a time and separate it from downsizing; that is, change only one design characteristic while staying at the same square footage. These elements include tapered or elliptical planform (degree of taper or ellipse varies according to design), cross-bracing or other airfoil-flattening or stiffening design modifications, and anything requiring additional in-flight procedures (for example, a removable pilot chute, deployment bag, or slider).

## Downsizing Progression

Each progressive step in downsizing, technique, and canopy design should be a conscious decision based on common sense, experience level, and demonstrated ability, rather than considered a routine part of a skydiver's progression. Downsizing decisions must be based on each individual jumper's readiness; however, the following are downsizing increments that are generally acceptable on the same canopy design.

1. above 230 square feet, 20 to 30 square feet
2. from 229 to 150 square feet, 20 square feet or less
3. from 149 to 120 square feet, 15 square feet or less
4. below 120 square feet, in smaller increments

### Considerations *Before* Changing or Downsizing Canopies

How do you know whether you are ready to downsize? Consider the following:

- Change planform (type of canopy) or size, not both
- Downsize one size at a time
- Take a canopy class to master your current parachute
- Consider competency and currency rather than only jump numbers

**Proficiency Exercises**
On your current canopy, can you reliably perform the following exercises to the satisfaction of the S&TA or DZO?

**In-Air Exercises – Perform Above 2,000 Feet**
Guidance for these canopy drills can be found in Chapter 1, Category E, and in the USPA Library online modules.

- Rear-riser turns and slow flight
- 90-degree braked turns with braked flares
- Toggle and rear-riser stalls and recovery
- Flight cycle and how to prevent one
- Harness turns and flare turns
- Low-turn recovery with braked flares

**Landing Exercises – (Practice in a Canopy Course)**
- Reliable stand-up landings in no wind and crosswind.
- Reliable stand-up landings within 30 feet of a target in different wind conditions.
- Full-glide landing approach.
- Flare turns on final (no more than 45 degrees).

**Other Considerations Before Downsizing**
Have you been jumping your current canopy recently or have you had a layoff? Do you feel you have mastered your parachute? Do you feel confident landing off? If you have any doubt, make 50 to 100 more jumps on your current canopy before downsizing. There is no penalty for waiting!

# Discipline-Specific Recommendations

## Considerations *When* Changing or Downsizing Canopies

You have your new-to-you canopy and are ready to make your first jump. Items to consider when learning about your new canopy include:

- Inspect used canopy for wear
- Are steering lines the correct length?
- Does the canopy require a staged or a continuous flare?
- Read the owner's manual.
- Flight characteristics and landing techniques will be different. Plan on dedicating several hop-and-pops to learning about your canopy and practicing canopy-flight emergency procedures (CEPs).

**In-Air Exercises – Perform Above 2,000 Feet**
First Jump:

- Find stall point with toggles.
- If stall point is above a full flare, focus on practice flares to find stall point to avoid a stall on landing

Subsequent Jumps:

- Find the sweet spot for the best flare
- Maximum glide/minimum descent
- Canopy-flight emergency procedures
    - Rear-Riser Turns
    - 90-Degree Braked Turns
    - Half-Braked Flares
    - Turn Reversals—Max Rate of Turn
    - Low-Turn Recovery

**Landing Exercises**
- Full-glide landing pattern and approach
- Braked pattern and full-glide final approach
- Accuracy practice

## Considerations *After* Changing or Downsizing for Long-Term Proficiency

Staying proficient on your canopy is your best defense against injury when forced to deal with a canopy-flight emergency. You should practice the following five canopy-flight emergency procedures at least once a month on hop-and-pop or high-pull jumps so you can use them quickly and correctly when needed. **Stay alive, practice five!**

1. Rear-Riser Turns
2. 90-Degree Braked Turns
3. Half-Braked Flares
4. Turn Reversals—Max Rate of Turn
5. Low-Turn Recovery

uspa.org/downsize

Practicing canopy-flight emergency procedures (CEPs) is just as important as practicing malfunction emergency procedures, and you should practice them regularly. Maintain traffic, altitude, and position awareness under canopy while practicing so a simulated emergency does not turn into a real emergency.

The **USPA Downsizing Best Practices** printable checklist is available at uspa.org/downsize or with this QR code. It includes all the information discussed in this section and provides a valuable guide for S&TAs, canopy coaches and jumpers themselves to prepare for and assess readiness to downsize or change canopy designs.

## High-Performance Maneuvers

High-performance maneuvers occur when jumpers use control manipulation during descent and on the final landing approach to induce speeds greater than stabilized full flight, i.e., their natural speed and glide angle. This activity is commonly known as **swooping**. These types of landings are demanding and unforgiving and require careful supervision, practice, and planning.

A jumper's experience, canopy size and canopy design determine which **techniques** might be considered conservative or high performance. Canopy-flight characteristics and control become more challenging as field elevation, temperature, and humidity increase. For safety, jumpers should receive specialized information and training to fly canopies at wing loadings approaching 1.5 pounds per square foot and beyond or canopies approaching 120 square feet or smaller. The decision to progress to high-performance canopy maneuvers and parachutes should include **focused canopy coaching** and continued consultation with a canopy coach to help the jumper assess readiness and skill level. Neglecting to undertake such training greatly increases the canopy pilot's risk of serious injury or death. Most successful high-performance canopy pilots have practiced extensively and taken multiple canopy courses with larger canopies before experimenting with higher wing loadings and high-performance maneuvers.

## Discipline-Specific Recommendations

### High-Performance Landing Areas

Jumpers must perform high-performance landings using strategies to avoid collisions with other jumpers who are on a standard approach and be prepared to abort a high-performance landing maneuver if traffic exists. According to the **USPA Group Member Pledge**, drop zones must establish landing procedures that will include separation of high-performance and normal landing areas; such separation may be by location or time. Jumpers can achieve separation from others in the following ways:

1. **Make a high-pull jump:** Canopy pilots must consider other high-opening jumpers (students, tandems, and others) and look for traffic during the descent.
2. **Perform a hop-and-pop:** Canopy pilots exiting on a lower pass must fly to the holding area to clear the airspace for jumpers going to full altitude.
3. **Use a separate landing area:** High-performance and standard landing procedures should be prominently displayed and communicated to all jumpers.

You must never attempt a high-performance landing with a **turn of more than 90 degrees** when other jumpers are landing using a standard landing pattern in the same area.

Canopy pilots should be completely familiar with all techniques and characteristics of advanced landings in a variety of weather conditions and using a variety of approaches before landing in the vicinity of any hazard, including water, as well as before attempting flight into a competition-style course.

## D. B-License Canopy Proficiency Card

To get the most from the topics presented in this outline, a jumper should have completed all the exercises listed under "Canopy" in SIM Chapter 1, Categories A-H of the ISP, and hold a USPA A license. Jumpers who complete a course of instruction covering the topics listed here, including evaluation jumps and continued practice, should be better prepared to make choices regarding parachute size, design and maneuvers.

### Instructor or Course Director Qualifications

USPA does not issue instructional ratings specifically for canopy coaching. Ideally, those who intend to teach a canopy-piloting course should hold a USPA Instructor rating; however, in some situations the person most qualified to teach this material may not hold any USPA instructional ratings but may have extensive knowledge about canopy control and landings. Regardless, for **USPA B-License requirements**, an S&TA must approve the instructor or course director and sign the **B-License Canopy Proficiency Card** once the jumper completes the course.

Instructors who intend to teach this material must realistically assess their level of knowledge regarding canopy flight and instruction. Before teaching this course, instructors must work through the outlined canopy skills using a variety of canopy designs and wing loadings. Attending any one of several commercially available canopy-flight schools as a student is highly recommended before teaching this course.

### B-License Requirements

Every USPA B-License Application, paper or online, must also include a completed, verified B-License Canopy Proficiency Card. The B-license canopy training requires a **minimum of five training jumps** that may be completed in a structured course with all jumps completed in succession or individually, working one-on-one with an approved canopy coach. Some skills may require more than one jump to gain proficiency. The instructor or course director responsible for supervision, training and evaluation of the jump must sign each of the training jumps listed on the B-License Canopy Proficiency Card. A current S&TA, Examiner, or board member must verify the completed card to confirm that the candidate has satisfactorily completed the training.

### Evaluation

The course director or instructor will evaluate each candidate's participation, understanding, and demonstrated ability during the ground school and training jumps. The instructor or course director will debrief each skill, approach and landing. Attendees should be better able to self-assess their canopy aptitude and proficiency during future practice based on their experience with the supervised training maneuvers. The course director should sign and date the entries on the B-License Canopy Proficiency Card as jumpers successfully complete the required skills.

### B-License Canopy Ground School Outline

#### Part 1: Equipment

**A. Equipment choice considerations**

Studies of USPA's serious-injury and fatality summaries reveal that jumpers under canopies popularly considered "average sized" or "conservatively loaded" frequently mishandle them in non-routine landing situations.

Jumpers should:

# Discipline-Specific Recommendations

1. select equipment based on their goals and abilities, understanding that smaller canopies offer some advantages but also pose greater risks.
2. should follow the guidance of the **Downsizing Best Practices** form to assess skill and readiness to change canopies.
3. seek out reliable information and advice before changing to smaller canopies.

The sport of skydiving includes a series of specialized activities that require exclusive equipment, for example:

- classic accuracy
- canopy formation
- wingsuit flying
- camera flying
- high-performance landings
- competition canopy piloting

All jumpers should set goals in the sport, choose the best equipment to meet their needs, learn how to use that equipment, and skydive within the limits of their equipment and capabilities.

## B. Basic aerodynamics
- Lift
    - Air passing over an airfoil creates a force called lift.
    - Lift is always perpendicular to the velocity.
    - A ram-air parachute is trimmed nose-down by cutting the A lines shorter and each group behind them a little longer.
- Drag
    - The resistance created by air as an object moves is called drag.
    - Drag is always parallel to the velocity.
    - The lines, pilot chute, slider, jumper's body, and even the surface of the canopy itself produce drag (parasitic drag).
- Gravity
    - Gravity is a constant in the equation of forces acting on the jumper and canopy.
    - Using the force created by gravity, the airfoil deflects the air to make the canopy glide.
- Momentum (force)
    - Mass: Doubling the mass of a moving object gives it twice as much energy.
    - Speed
        - The term "speed" refers to the magnitude of velocity.
        - Energy increases as the square of the speed. (Doubling the speed produces four times the energy. Tripling the speed produces nine times the energy.)
        - Inertia: The term "inertia" means that an object in motion will stay in motion until resisted.

## C. Wing loading
Wing loading is the jumper's exit weight divided by the area of the parachute canopy, expressed in the U.S. in pounds per square foot. The higher the wing loading, the faster and higher performance the canopy will be. However, even if the wing loading is the same between two otherwise identical parachutes, the size of the canopies affects the performance characteristics. A 150-square-foot parachute at a one-pound-per-square-foot wing loading will have a steeper glide ratio, faster turns, and be more high performance than a 190-square-foot parachute at the same wing loading. This means that, **regardless of the wing loading, all small canopies (150 square feet or less) are high performance.**

- Smaller canopies with shorter lines will respond differently than larger canopies of the same design and equal wing loading.
- Compared to a canopy with longer lines, a shorter-lined canopy will have quicker turns, quicker flare response, and quicker pendulum action (quicker to dive after an early flare).
- Lighter jumpers will remain on larger parachutes at lower wing loadings for a longer period of time.
- Most jumpers can get a lot more performance from their canopies without needing to increase their wing loading with a downsize.

## D. Performance-enhancing designs
- Tapered shape (planform)
    - more dimensional stability (less distortion)
    - faster forward speed due to decreased drag
    - faster turns and less flight stability
- High aspect ratio
    - flat glide
    - easier flare
        - lighter toggle pressure
        - shorter toggle stroke (some models)

# Discipline-Specific Recommendations

- quicker flare response
- Higher rib frequency to reduce billowing between ribs
  - seven-cell vs. nine-cell
  - cross bracing
- Thickness (after inflation)
  - thicker: slow speed, more predictable and gentler stall
  - thinner: faster speed, more abrupt stalls at a higher speed

### E. Drag reduction
- Zero-porosity fabric
- Small-diameter lines
- Collapsible pilot chute
- Collapsible slider:
  - cloth or metal links with covers
  - larger vs. smaller slider grommets
- Risers
- Outerwear
- Removable deployment systems
- Body position

### F. Controls: toggles and beyond
- Brakes
  - toggle types for ease of handling
  - steering-line length to allow front-riser maneuvers (toggles in hand)
- Front risers and control-enhancement discussion (loops, blocks, etc.)
- Back risers and how they work
- Front risers and how they work
- Harness turns

### G. Accessories
- Jumpsuit (reinforced butt and knees)
- Hard helmet
- Gloves, pros and cons
- Altimeter
  - altimeter use under canopy
  - digital vs. analog
- Weights

### H. Speed
- The pilot perceives the forward speed more than the downward speed, so a faster canopy can seem a lot scarier to fly.
- The faster the canopy goes, the more effect adding drag (by using a control) will have on the flight path.

### I. Glide
- Skydiving canopies: approximately 2.5:1 in natural flight
- Changing the glide
  - using brakes or rear risers
  - using induced speed to temporarily add lift

## Part 2: Maintenance

### A. Environment
- Dirt degrades fabric, lines, and slider.
- Ultraviolet degrades nylon.
  - sunlight
  - fluorescent lighting (50% of the strength of sunlight)
- Water distorts reinforcement tapes.

### B. Collapsible pilot chute and slider
- Wear results from friction as the line moves through its channel.
- Pilot chute centerlines shrink with use.

### C. Suspension lines
- Spectra can't stretch, and it shrinks with a lot of use.
- Vectran is stable in both directions but abrades.

# 5 Discipline-Specific Recommendations

- HMA is stable but can break when it still looks new.
- Dacron stretches on opening, is stable and durable, but larger.

### D. Brake lines
- Wear
- Shrinkage
- Dangers of a broken line
  - upon flaring
  - of landing a smaller canopy using risers

### E. Packing
- On-heading opening
- Even risers
- Symmetrical bag
- Line-stow placement and tension
- 24 inches of unstowed line to allow the bag to lift out of the burble over the jumpers back

### F. Equipment inspection
- Pre-jump
- During packing (various times throughout the course)

## Part 3: Breakoff, Opening, Separation, and Canopy Traffic

### A. Breakoff
- Breakoff altitude should allow enough time to open clear of others and handle both routine and abnormal circumstances.
- Tracking review
  - conserving altitude during turning and tracking
  - body position and flat-track technique
  - opening when clear at the optimum altitude
- Flying through and managing the opening
  - shoulders level (use this time to look at the horizon)
  - allow legs to move forward during opening, like sitting in a chair, keeping hips level to avoid harness inputs during opening.
  - knees-up position helps to stop the swing going to the hips and absorbs the shock in the event of a hard opening.
  - If turning occurs during opening, use the harness to stop the turn.
  - Keep your head looking forward at the horizon to avoid accidental harness input during the opening.
  - Have your hands on your rear risers as soon as they are available immediately after deployment to steer for collision avoidance, even if you believe you have jumped alone.
  - Look forward for any jumpers opening nearby who may be coming toward you. Be prepared to turn right, unless you obviously need to turn left, with rear risers to avoid a collision.
- Once confirming that you're clear of other jumpers, continue using the rear risers with the brakes set (if responding correctly) to orient toward the drop zone or holding area prior to releasing brakes and completing the canopy-controllability check. Dealing with a standard problem is more difficult as canopy performance increases.
  - Discuss the following from the perspective of higher-performance canopies:
  - line twists
  - premature brake release
  - locked brake(s)
  - slider/brake system fouling
  - Spinning under a smaller canopy results in rapid altitude loss. Check altitude and if above the 1,000-foot cutaway hard deck, **don't delay, cut away!**

### B. Traffic
- As canopies fly faster, jumpers must pay better attention to other canopy traffic on descent.
- Altitude managementuse of brakes to stay aloft
  - relative wing loading
    - self-assessment

## Discipline-Specific Recommendations

- knowing the wing loading of others
  - placement in the aircraft
  - a dive plan, such as stacked approaches, to promote vertical separation under canopy
- Awareness of others
  - Know or judge others' canopies, wing loading, and habits.
  - Fly the landing pattern or land elsewhere.
  - Fly a straight final approach avoiding S-turns.
  - Dealing with others' errors:
    - In the event of a traffic issue, discuss the problem with the canopy pilots who were involved.
    - canopy wake turbulence, which is behind and above the canopy in flight (yours and others')
    - only need to miss by a little—no low turns necessary
- Off-wind landings (technique)
  - crosswind
  - downwind
- Landing away from the crowd
  - less pressure; room to practice
  - familiarity and consistency with using the same landing area every time
- Situations that pop up:
  - Crowded landing area: Follow someone you trust closely and let them know you're there.
  - Cutaways disrupt the plan for a normal main-canopy descent and landing
  - Landing accidents on the ground can lead to confusion and chaos.
  - Off-field landing
    - Plan and follow a sensible pattern.
    - Keep your eyes open.
    - Follow the landing priorities and perform a PLF.

**Having your hands on your rear risers** immediately after opening has two important purposes:

- It keeps your body in line with the canopy so you can turn with the canopy if it is turning.
- It prepares you for immediate action if you are close to another canopy.

**USING BRAKES TO STAY ALOFT:** Think of brakes as a vertical-braking tool, not only a forward-movement braking tool. Brakes affect vertical speed by a greater margin than horizontal speed. Anytime you do not like the traffic or anything else happening during the flight, add brakes to buy time and vertical distance from other jumpers who may create a conflict.

## B-License Canopy Proficiency Card Exercises

### A. Flight Plan

The course director should assist the class with an aircraft, canopy flight, and landing plan prior to each jump included in the course. The plan should include an individualized progression plan for each student according to experience and goals. The plan should consider wind conditions, DZ layout and target areas, traffic management to keep clear of other jumpers not participating, and landing separation between canopy students. The course director should videotape landings for debriefing. The first jump in the course should follow the presentation and discussion of the ground-school topics.

### B. Canopy Skill Practice Jumps

**JUMP 1—BRAKED TURNS, ACCURACY, AND FLARE EVALUATION**
**Classroom Briefing**
- Discuss collapsing slider and loosening chest strap
- Inspecting the canopy's steering lines while in full flight with the brakes released.
  - steering lines on most canopies should bow slightly behind the back of the canopy
  - check with the manufacturer for recommendations for adjustments
  - steering lines should have enough slack so that the jumper can pull the front risers with the toggles in hand and still not deflect the tail of the canopy.
  - A parachute rigger should adjust the length of the steering lines, if necessary, before the next jump.
- Reasons for flying in brakes
  - vertical separation from canopy traffic
  - slow forward speed and descent rate to conserve altitude
  - returning from a long spot
  - flat turn as a **Canopy-Flight Emergency Procedure** at low altitudes
- Avoid stalling the canopy.
  - effect of brakes on glide

# Discipline-Specific Recommendations

- slower forward speed
- lower descent rate
- Change in glide angle:
  - Experiment to determine the change in glide path at different degrees of braked flight.
  - Most modern nine-cell canopies fly flatter when a slight amount of brakes are applied.
- Methods for initiating braked turns
  - Pull both toggles to the quarter-braked position (ears).
  - Pull one toggle down to turn.
  - Pull both toggles to half-braked position (mid chest).
  - Pull one toggle down slightly to initiate a turn in the same direction.
- Flaring Techniques
  - On final approach in natural flight, your body is below the center of the canopy.
  - During initial flare using toggles or rear risers, the canopy rocks slightly behind the jumper, raising the nose in relation to the tail and temporarily increasing lift.
  - Gradually pulling the toggles farther down adds drag on the tail, keeping the canopy at the correct angle and providing the most lift for the remainder of the flare.
  - The most effective flare technique varies by canopy type.
  - Practice an effective flaring technique, focusing on a smooth finish.
    - Make a straight-in approach facing into the wind, with minimal input for the last 10 seconds before the landing flare.
    - Focus on flying your canopy as long as possible before allowing your feet to touch the ground and finish the flare completely even after your feet first touch the ground.
    - Finish the flare and hold hands down for a few steps after touch down.

**TWO COMMON FLARE TECHNIQUES FOR DIFFERENT CANOPIES**

**The Continuous Flare** is one smooth motion that should take about the same time that it takes to count slowly to five. You may count slower or faster depending on wind conditions or your sight picture. Regardless of the speed of your flare, you should time it to be smooth and consistent overall, responding to how your canopy is performing.

**Two-Stage Flare:** The first stage is flaring to the sweet spot, where you pause during the flare stroke. Flare with the stroke rate and depth that causes the canopy to remain flying flat for as long as possible. In the second stage, time the stroke rate to finish the flare just before touching down.

## Under Canopy
- Collapse slider and loosen chest strap.
- Inspect the canopy's steering lines while in full flight, with the brakes released.
- Practice flare technique based on the canopy type.
- Braked turns
  - Practice braked turns using all the methods discussed.
- Pattern and landing
  - Choose a target for landing. A safe, soft landing from a straight-in approach is the priority regardless of accuracy.
  - Perform a straight-in approach in full flight, with minimal input for the last 10 seconds before starting your normal flare technique.

## JUMP 2— FLIGHT CYCLE AND CROSSWIND LANDINGS
### Classroom Briefing
- Flight Cycle
  - A flight cycle occurs after any input as the canopy responds and then returns to stabilized full flight.
  - More drastic input equals a bigger flight cycle or surge, where the canopy picks up speed and is moving faster than when in full flight.
  - While turning or flaring your parachute, your body's location in relation to the canopy changes, creating a flight cycle.
  - In a turn, momentum swings your body out from under the canopy.
  - During the flight cycle, your body begins to swing back under the canopy.
  - Recovery from a flight cycle should take 4 to 8 seconds, depending on the canopy.
  - Prevent a flight cycle by raising the toggles slowly, preventing the nose from pitching forward, surging and picking up speed.
  - Flaring from a braked position
  - Expect a different glide on a braked final approach.
  - Expect a shorter and quicker stroke needed for an effective flare.
  - Prepare for a PLF due to potentially harder landing.
- Crosswind landings
  - Fly a landing pattern that allows for a crosswind final approach and landing.

## Discipline-Specific Recommendations

- For training and familiarization, perform the crosswind landing only in winds up to 5 miles per hour.
- All jumpers on the same pass must use the same landing pattern to promote a smooth flow of traffic.
- On final approach, focus on crosswind correction necessary to prevent crabbing.
- A crosswind landing may require pulling the upwind toggle deeper than the downwind toggle to keep going in the same direction and reduce the ground speed upon landing. Performing an uneven flare in this manner increases the stall speed of the canopy. A PLF is recommended for any unusual landing.

**Under Canopy**
- Flight Cycle—Do all flight-cycle exercises above your decision altitude.
    - Flare the canopy to three-quarter brakes and hold for 5 seconds. Let the toggles up quickly to induce the flight cycle.
    - Repeat the exercise and count the number of seconds to recover to full flight.
    - Repeat the exercise but slowly raise the toggles over 3 to 4 seconds to prevent the flight cycle.
- Braked Flares
    - Practice flaring several times from the quarter and half-braked positions, focusing on an effective flare from each position.
- Crosswind landing
    - Choose a target for landing and execute a crosswind-oriented downwind, base, and final approach.

## JUMP 3—STALLS
### Classroom Briefing
- Stalls
    - A stall is an aerodynamic event where a wing loses its ability to produce lift. When a ram-air parachute stalls, it will lose lift and pressurization and will no longer support the weight of the jumper. For this reason, perform stalls carefully and always above decision altitude.
    - A stall can occur as the result of either too much or too abrupt input with the toggles or the rear risers. Applying too much input is associated with a slow-speed stall, where the canopy loses airspeed and will eventually stall. Applying input too abruptly is associated with a higher-speed stall, where the stall will occur more suddenly and at a higher airspeed.
- Toggle stalls
    - Intentionally stalling with toggles begins with straight-and-level flight. Slowly pull the toggles down to full arm extension until you feel the stall onset, a feeling like rocking back in a chair and falling backward.
    - The ideal stall point using toggles is down at full arm extension, with the stall occurring after holding the toggles there for 5 to 6 seconds. The exact toggle position will differ from canopy to canopy and from jumper to jumper based on the length of the steering lines.
    - You must find the stall point on any canopy that you are jumping for the first time. If the steering lines were adjusted for a person with shorter arms, you may be able to stall the canopy at something less than full arm extension, which risks a stall close to the ground during a normal landing flare.
    - Once you feel the onset of the stall, you can hold the toggles and allow the stall to fully develop. The air will leave the canopy, it will fold into the shape of a bow tie, and you will begin descending at a high rate of speed.
    - Use the same procedure whether recovering from the onset of a stall or a fully developed stall: slowly raise the toggles back up to a position where the canopy inflates and returns to normal flight.
    - Avoid raising the toggles too quickly to recover, which can cause the canopy to surge, dive, or spin into line twists. A forward surge can be severe enough that the jumper gets tangled in the suspension lines, and some line twists can be severe and unrecoverable. Practice stalls carefully and always above your decision altitude.
- Rear-riser stalls
    - The same concepts and guidelines as stalling with toggles apply to rear-riser stalls, but rear-riser stalls change the shape of the parachute by affecting the C and D lines (the back half of your canopy).
    - When stalling using rear risers, the stroke is only 5-6 inches as compared to the long control stroke when stalling with toggles. The shorter stroke makes it more difficult to gently approach the stall point and easier to over-control the rear risers, potentially stalling your parachute accidentally.
    - Rear-riser stalls commence more suddenly than toggle stalls but recovering from them is easier and smoother.
    - Once you feel the stall's onset, hold the risers and let it fully develop. The back of the parachute will distort, taking the shape of a hot dog bun.
    - Slowly let your rear risers up to recover from the stall.
- High-speed stalls
    - Stalls can occur at higher airspeeds, such as when the canopy is in a turn or a dive.
    - At higher airspeeds, adding too much input with risers or toggles or adding input too abruptly can cause the canopy to stall. These high-speed stalls will happen quickly and less predictably than the low-speed stalls, making them much more dangerous. You should avoid doing them intentionally.

# 5  Discipline-Specific Recommendations

- o The best way to avoid high-speed stalls is to understand the limits of your canopy when flying at higher airspeeds. Practice the input limits of your canopy above your decision altitude.

**Under Canopy**
- Stall-practice procedure—perform above decision altitude
  - o Stall using toggles
    - Gently apply brakes to a point where forward flight diminishes and the canopy begins to sink.
    - Hold the brakes down until the canopy is shaped like a bow tie.
    - Slowly raise the toggles 4 to 6 inches at a time until resuming forward flight.
  - o Stall using rear risers
    - Grab high on the riser with full arm extension, keeping toggles in your hands.
    - Slowly pull down the rear risers several inches until forward flight stops.
    - After adding more riser input, the canopy will eventually sink and begin to descend in a backward direction, taking the shape of a hot dog bun.
    - Let the risers up slowly to recover to forward flight.
- Three-quarter-braked turns
  - o Pull both toggles to the three-quarter-braked position (hip bones).
  - o Let one toggle up slightly to initiate a turn in the opposite direction.
- Choose a target for landing and execute a downwind, base, and final approach into the wind.

## JUMP 4— REAR-RISER TURNS AND FLARES
**Classroom Briefing**
- Rear-riser turns and flares
  - o On opening, using rear risers is the quickest way to turn the parachute.
  - o You can use rear-riser turns to turn toward your holding area right after opening or quickly turn away from another jumper to avoid a collision.
  - o Steer with rear risers for flatter turns to conserve altitude.
  - o Pull down one to two inches, smoothly and symmetrically, with both rear risers to flatten the glide when flying in a crosswind or headwind.
  - o Practice with your rear risers to avoid over-controlling (using too great of an input).
  - o Landing using rear risers instead of toggles requires practice to avoid stalling close to the ground.

**Under Canopy**
- Rear-riser turns with brakes stowed:
  - o Grab high on the riser with full arm extension.
  - o Initiate alternating 90-degree turns using rear risers.
- Rear-riser turns with brakes unstowed, keeping toggles in your hands:
  - o Grab high on the riser with full arm extension.
  - o Initiate alternating 90-degree turns using rear risers.
- Rear-riser flares with brakes unstowed, keeping toggles in your hands:
  - o Practice rear-riser flares without stalling the canopy.
  - o Fly the canopy descent using rear risers.
  - o Choose a target for landing and execute the turns onto the downwind, base, and final legs with the rear risers.
  - o Take your hands off the rear risers by 150 feet AGL and land into the wind using your toggles.

## JUMP 5—LONG SPOT
**Classroom Briefing**
- Return from a long spot by projecting the landing point.
  - o Discover how to locate the point on the ground that a parachute in full flight will reach.
- Alter the glide using brakes and rear risers.
  - o Use brakes with a tailwind.
  - o Use rear risers with a crosswind or headwind.
  - o Minimize drag.
  - o Collapse the slider.
  - o Pull legs up, arms in, and arch to reduce air resistance.
  - o Loosen the chest strap to improve glide.
  - o If holding brakes, reduce fatigue by hooking your thumbs in the harness. (Be careful not to hook onto your cutaway or reserve handles.)

# Discipline-Specific Recommendations

- Decide on a new landing area by 2,000 feet.
- Choose an alternate landing area if necessary and follow off-field landing recommendations.
- Allow enough altitude to fly a pattern.
- Expect the winds to weaken as you get lower.

### Under Canopy
- Exit the aircraft at 5,000 feet AGL at least 1.5 miles upwind of the main landing area.
- Determine the glide path of the canopy and the landing point using the projected landing point. Determine the point on the ground that is neither rising nor sinking in your field of vision.
- Alter the glide and compare effectiveness:
  - using brakes
  - using rear risers
- If you cannot reach the intended landing area in time to start a pattern at the planned altitude, choose an alternate by 2,000 feet AGL.
- Choose a target for landing, and execute a downwind, base, and final-approach leg for landing, following the landing priorities.

## 5-10: Movement Jumps

## A. Introduction and Definition
Movement jumps include but are not limited to tracking and angle-flying jumps. These recommendations provide guidance for a non-wingsuit jump on which a skydiver or group intends to move horizontally off the line of flight during freefall.

## B. Qualifications
Before engaging in movement jumps outside of the Integrated Student Program, a **participating skydiver** (not a leader) should hold a USPA A license and demonstrate proficiency at tracking while maintaining situational awareness.

Before engaging in movement jumps as the **leader**, the skydiver should have:

- At a minimum, qualified for the USPA C License.
- The ability to maintain consistent awareness of altitude and location
- Proficiency and experience in the discipline
- Received formal instruction on:
  - DZ terrain (changing ground levels, bodies of water or any other ground obstacles) and alternate landing areas (outs)
  - exit order
  - navigation (ability to move in the correct direction and deploy where planned)
  - communication with drop zone authorities, other jumpers and the pilot (to determine jump run and spot)
  - understanding weather (including reading a winds-aloft forecast, and maintaining awareness of clouds prior to jumping)
  - Making a flight plan (including exit order, breakoff and designated deployment area) and adjusting that flight plan as necessary to accommodate changing conditions to avoid other groups

## Discipline-Specific Recommendations

Jumpers can use the graph below to determine their skill levels:

|  | Beginner | Intermediate | Advanced |
|---|---|---|---|
| Group Size | 1-3 | 4-7 | 8+ |
| Angle of Jump | Flat | Shallow | Steep |
| Transitions | 0 | 1-3 | 4+ |
| Relativity | Can fly in a quadrant, oriented head down (on both back and belly) | Can fly in quadrant or on level, oriented head down (on belly and back), manage speed and pitch | Ability to maintain slot and stability in any orientation and matching speed and pitch |
| Breakoff | Fan out, choose a clear path and airspace | Can accelerate, choose a clear path and airspace to flatten out | Can accelerate, choose a clear path and airspace to flatten out, while mitigating congestion |
| Wind Conditions at Altitude | Calm | Calm to Mild | Calm to Extreme |
| Wind Speed and Weather | No-to-light ground winds | Medium ground winds | High ground winds, wind shear between uppers and canopy winds, clouds, emerging weather |

## C. Equipment

Properly secure your gear to prevent premature deployment of either canopy. A premature opening at the speeds involved in this type of skydiving could result in severe injury to the body or stress to the equipment beyond limits set by the manufacturers. Deployment systems and operation handles should remain secure during inverted and stand-up flight. Therefore, equipment for movement jumps should include either a throw-out pilot chute with a bottom-of-container-mounted pouch, or a pull-out pilot chute. Exposed leg-strap-mounted pilot chutes present an extreme hazard. Also, any exposed pilot-chute bridle presents a hazard. Use a tuck-tab to provide additional security for the pilot chute. Maintain and properly size your closing loops and ensure your pin-protection flaps and riser covers are in good shape.

Connect leg straps with a bungee to keep the leg straps from moving toward your knees. Tightly stow excess leg and chest strap material. USPA recommends participants use an **AAD and an RSL with a MARD** due to the high potential for collisions and loss of altitude awareness associated with movement jumps.

Personal accessories for movement jumps should include:

- audible altimeter (two are recommended)
- visual altimeter
- hard helmet
- clothing or jumpsuit that will remain in place during movement flights and will not obscure or obstruct deployment, emergency handles or altimeters
- GPS

## D. Training

Movement flying has many things in common with belly-to-earth formation skydiving. A beginner will progress more quickly and safely with a coach. Novices should not jump with each other until they have received specific training in movement jumps and have demonstrated the ability to control navigation, pitch, and speed.

Prior to jumping with larger groups, progress should follow the same model as for the freefall and canopy formation disciplines: Novices should begin with coached 2-way formations to develop breakoff skills and exit, body-position, pitch and speed control, and then gradually progress to larger and more complex movement jumps.

## E. Hazards Associated with Movement Jumps

**Navigation** is a critically important skill that entails plotting a route, maneuvering to follow that route, and adapting when conditions change. Jumpers must plan accordingly to:

- Move off the aircraft's line of flight
- Consider other movement groups on the load
- Avoid other groups in freefall and under canopy
- Open where they've pre-determined
- Account for the DZ terrain
- Have a backup plan for landing out

**Weather** is important in the planning phase to determine navigation and exit order and to coordinate with other movement groups. Cloud conditions can change during freefall and canopy flight.

## Discipline-Specific Recommendations

Prior to boarding, it is of the utmost importance to **communicate** your intentions with the drop zone authorities (such as manifest, an S&TA or a load master) and the entire load in order to understand local drop zone restrictions and requirements for movement jumps, share your flight plan, and determine exit order. It is also important that everyone in the group understands the DZ terrain, hazards, and alternate landing areas.

Several factors—such as local DZ rules and terrain, weather and leader experience—influence how many movement groups may safely be on any one aircraft load. However, the general recommendation is to limit movement groups to two per load.

Exit order will depend on weather, freefall drift, DZ terrain, deployment altitudes, other groups, and DZ rules and considerations. The group leader must communicate with the S&TA, drop zone, pilot, and others on the load.

Every jump plan should accommodate the **skill level** of the jumper with the least experience in order to execute the flight plan and open in the determined spot. Opening in the correct, predetermined spot is crucial for safety, so jumpers must be able to demonstrate proficiency on beginner-level movement jumps before progressing to intermediate or advanced jumps. Jumpers who are unable to follow intermediate or advanced movement jumps may cause their groups to conflict with others on the load. Adding speed and pitch changes and transitions greatly increases the difficulty of the jump, requiring an expert leader to consider all the variables of the jump so as to avoid collisions, maintain the flight plan and open in the predetermined spot.

Maintain visual contact with the leader so you can adapt if you are far behind, above, to the side of, or low relative to the group. Even if you are far away from the group, continue moving in the same direction to avoid collisions. Maintain the same heading as the rest of the group. Off-heading collisions are more dangerous than collisions between jumpers heading in the same direction. Never turn 180 degrees from the group's heading, even if you think there is no one behind you. If you have passed the group, slow down and let it catch up. If you are flying to the side of the group and the group starts turning toward you, turn toward the same heading, even if you are far away.

It is crucial to understand the elements of **breakoff** to avoid congestion and collisions. Choose a clear path and fan out from the other jumpers while flattening the pitch to a track. Maintain awareness by looking in all directions. If you are on your back at breakoff, avoid flipping to a belly-to-earth orientation until you are on a clear trajectory with no one above you. Once on your belly, continue to track off until it is time to clear airspace and pull.

## F. Pre-Flight Checklist

This pre-flight checklist can help you determine the specifics of your jump. Draw the flight plan on the map of your drop zone and share it with the drop zone staff, other jumpers on the load, and the pilot to confirm you can perform the skydive safely:

- ☐ What is jump run for your load?
- ☐ What are the forecasted winds aloft at these points during your jump?
    - ☐ exit altitude
    - ☐ freefall
    - ☐ under canopy
    - ☐ in the landing pattern
- ☐ How many groups and other jumpers are on your load?
- ☐ What is your exit order?
    - ☐ Are there any other movement jumps on your load?
- ☐ What are the DZ terrain factors to consider in navigation?
- ☐ What is the intended landing pattern and holding area for the jump?
- ☐ Have you ensured that your flight path does not interfere with jump run?
- ☐ Does your flight plan take into consideration freefall, DZ terrain, canopy flight path and weather?
- ☐ Is your flight plan appropriate for the skill level of all the jumpers?

## 5-11: Speed Skydiving

### A. Introduction

These recommendations guide skydivers who are intentionally attempting to reach their highest terminal velocity in freefall. Although speed skydives incorporate both freeflying and angle-flying elements, the high vertical speeds present several unique considerations. The speeds achieved will vary dramatically based on skill and experience. Only a tiny minority of top competitors surpass 300 mph. Most beginners, especially those without extensive angle-flying and tunnel experience, will likely fly in the low-200-mph range. Jumpers can find competition rules in Chapter 15 of the USPA Skydiver's Competition Manual (SCM).

### B. Qualifications

Before engaging in speed skydives, a skydiver should hold a C license or higher, have made a **minimum of 200 jumps**, and exhibit consistent awareness of altitude and location over the ground.

- To avoid other groups, speed skydivers must make a **flight plan** that includes exit order, freefall, breakoff, and canopy flight path. Speed skydivers should have a qualified person inspect their gear and should consult a local S&TA or drop zone staff on:

- the terrain and alternate landing areas around the drop zone
- communication with drop zone authorities, other jumpers, and the pilot to determine jump run and spot
- Weather, including reading a winds-aloft forecast and maintaining awareness of clouds before jumping
- exit order
- navigation plan determining the correct direction to move and deployment altitude and location

## C. Equipment

Jumpers must adequately secure their gear to prevent premature deployment of the main or reserve parachutes. Because speeds can surpass the maximum deployment speeds of the FAA's Technical Standard Order (TSO) for gear, a premature opening could result in severe injury or death. Deployment systems and operation handles should remain secure during inverted flights. Therefore, equipment for speed skydives should include either a well-maintained bottom-of-container-mounted throw-out-pilot-chute pouch, or a pull-out pilot chute. Exposed leg-strap-mounted pilot chutes are hazardous. Any exposed pilot-chute bridle also presents a danger. Jumpers should use a tuck tab to provide additional security for the pilot chute. Closing loops, pin-protection flaps, and riser covers should be well-maintained and adequately sized. Jumpers must tightly stow excess leg and chest strap material. USPA recommends that **speed skydivers use an AAD** because of the high potential of losing altitude awareness.

**Personal accessories** for speed skydiving should include:

- Two audible altimeters, preferably including flashing visuals inside the helmet, since the wind noise on a speed skydive may drown out the audible beeps. Jumpers must increase the volume of all audible altimeters to maximum.
- Visual altimeter
- Hard helmet. If a jumper uses a full-face helmet, they must ensure that the visor stays shut during the jump, either through its design or by using additional constraints (e.g., tape). The jumper must have a plan in case vision becomes limited by lens fogging. If a jumper uses an open-face helmet, they must ensure that eye protection is secure.
- Appropriate clothing. Most speed skydivers choose to fly with extremely tight clothing or a jumpsuit that helps cut down on drag. Consequently, jumpers need better body-flight skills to maintain control. A jumper's chosen attire should not obscure or obstruct deployment or emergency handles or altimeters.
- Speed measuring device (SMD). This device, mounted on the skydiver's body or equipment, records the real-time, three-dimensional position of the jumper.

While jumpers may experiment and **modify equipment** as the discipline progresses, there are safety considerations. Jumpers can use aero-shaping—the process of aerodynamic shape optimization, i.e., changing the shape of equipment from its original factory design to a discipline-specific intent—during training or experimentation. Competition speed skydivers may use only standard skydiving equipment.

Maximizing freefall performance for speed skydiving involves reducing drag force. Experimental processes to identify variables include but are not limited to fabricating equipment and bolt-on items using special materials and fabrics. Jumpers should use caution when making modifications to helmets, as a shape or weight change may result in severe torques to the neck and spine that could result in severe injury. Competitors may not wear a propulsion system or added weight. If a jumper wishes to train or experiment with such items, an experienced speed skydiver or S&TA should review them before use. Using a tandem rig for speed skydiving is not permitted in competition nor recommended in training.

New speed skydivers, who may not yet have the skills necessary to fly at 200-plus mph in a skin-tight suit, should consider using a suit with some **drag**. Jumpers should use a conservative approach when decreasing drag in the speed discipline, relatable to upsizing a wingsuit or downsizing a canopy.

## D. Training

Speed skydiving is a solo discipline, and participants primarily evaluate their performance by analyzing data from an SMD. Speed skydivers can also employ a coach to help analyze data and film their routines, since the analysis of body-flight performance is just as vital as the recorded data from an SMD. During a jump with a speed skydiver and coach, the jumpers must actively mitigate the risk of collisions at high speeds by closely matching speed and direction.

Speed skydiving requires similar skills and shares elements with freeflying and movement jumps. A beginner will progress faster and safer with a coach. **Novices** should not attempt speed skydiving until they have received training in some combination of tracking, angle flying, tunnel flying, and freeflying, and, if possible, demonstrate the ability to control navigation, body pitch, and speed. Angle flying includes many essential skills for novice speed flyers, such as body positions, freefall awareness and flight planning for freefall and under canopy. Once proficient with those skills, jumpers can begin with solo runs, prioritizing control rather than speed to develop exit, body position, heading control, pitch and speed control, and breakoff skills, then progress gradually to faster terminal velocities. Using a coach can maximize the progression and understanding for jumpers new to speed skydiving.

**A speed skydiver's breakoff altitude should be no lower than 5,600 feet (1,707 meters) AGL.** Competition rules do not include any measurements below the breakoff altitude. Higher breakoffs also ensure the performer has adequate time to slow down before deploying a parachute. The performance window is the scoring part of the speed jump, which starts at the exit. The end of the performance window is either 7,400 feet. (2,256 meters) below the exit or at breakoff altitude, whichever comes first.

# Discipline-Specific Recommendations

No one should attempt a speed run on a low-altitude pass, for example, a hop-and-pop.

## E. Hazards Associated with Speed Skydives

Before boarding, speed skydivers must communicate their intentions with the drop zone manifest, an S&TA, or a load organizer, as well as the entire load.

**Exit order** primarily depends on the speed the jumper consistently attains. Once a speed skydiver can demonstrate that they are consistently exceeding normal maximum freefly speeds (more than approximately 250 mph), they should exit first and turn away from jump run. Speed skydivers who exit after other jumpers create an extreme safety risk. A collision between a speed skydiver traveling at 300 mph and a solo belly jumper in a baggy suit will have a 200-mph closure rate. If more than one speed skydiver is on a load, exit order should be fastest out first, with consideration given to deployment altitudes and parachute type and size. Each jumper should take an opposite direction of flight (e.g., first person turns 90-degrees right off jump run, seconds turns 90-degrees left, and so on). When integrating with other disciplines, speed skydivers should be classified as a movement jump and should not be followed by another movement group.

After exit, the speed skydiver should move off the aircraft's line of flight yet remain on course. Maintaining **stability and orientation in freefall** is important.

Sinus problems and even sinonasal injury can result from uncompensated change in ambient pressures. During a speed dive, sinuses have less time to equalize than during a typical skydive. During a skydive, a jumper can equalize the pressure by swallowing, yawning, or tensing the muscles of the throat. In addition, jumpers can perform the Valsalva maneuver after landing by closing the mouth, pinching the nostrils closed and gently blowing air through the nose. Issues with sinuses can severely hinder spatial awareness and the ability to hear audible altimeters. To prevent issues in case of disorientation, speed skydivers should ensure their flight path does not converge with other groups. If disoriented, a speed skydiver should terminate their run.

**Breaking off** or pulling out of the dive at or above 5,600 feet. (1,707 meters) AGL is recommended. At 310 mph, a jumper travels at 450 feet per second. Slowing down to a safe deployment speed is critical and can be accomplished by transitioning out of the vertical flying orientation to a horizontal one. A jumper may experience a short-lived yet powerful deceleration up to 3.5 times the force of gravity. Speed skydivers should consider the resulting horizontal speed, as well as vertical speed, whether they are at the end of the performance or experiencing spatial disorientation.

A speed skydiver must slow their terminal velocity to deployment speeds. A parachute **deployment**, intentional or unintentional, while performing a speed skydive can result in severe injury or death. Speed skydivers should consider the time it will take to slow down and choose a deployment altitude a safe margin above the minimum deployment altitudes required by the BSRs.

Once **under canopy**, a speed skydiver must take great care to avoid other groups that might still be in freefall. Groups to avoid can include those that exit before or after the speed skydiver. After opening, a speed skydiver should continue flying their canopy along a course perpendicular to jump run to avoid flying underneath a group that might still be in freefall.

# Chapter 6:
# Exhibition Jumping and PRO Rating

One purpose of USPA is to promote successful demonstration jumps as part of an overall public relations program for the sport. These recommendations cover experience, ability and attitude, the Professional Exhibition (PRO) Rating, landing-area size, technical considerations, insurance, and how to complete the FAA authorization request form.

*Note: For all intentional off-airport jumps, USPA recommends submitting FAA Form 7711-2 with the local FSDO to obtain a certificate of authorization (FAR 105.21).*

## 6-1: Exhibition Jumping

*Note: Requirements for obtaining demonstration jump insurance may differ from the recommendations listed in this section.*

### A. Definition

An exhibition jump, also called a demonstration or display jump, is a jump at a location other than an existing drop zone done for the purpose of reward, remuneration, or promotion and principally for the benefit of spectators.

**RELATED READINGS**

FAA Part 105, Parachute Operations

FAA AC 105-2, Sport Parachute Jumping

FAA AC 91-45, Waivers: Aviation Events

### B. Advice and Approval

Jumpers may need to secure approval from federal, state, or local officials prior to a demonstration jump.

Jumpers may need to contact **local authorities** before a demonstration jump. FAR 105.23 requires airport-management approval before jumps onto the airport. USPA recommends that jumpers call the local police, as they might assist with crowd control, and advance notice may make it more likely that they will respond to calls appropriately.

Jumpers may need to contact the **state's** Department of Aviation. Additionally, FAR 105.25 requires that jumpers either notify the FAA or receive air traffic control authorization for almost every jump. At least one hour before any jump, the jumper must notify the air traffic control facility having jurisdiction over the airspace at the first intended exit altitude. Also, FAR 105.21.a. states that no jump be made over or into a congested area or an open-air assembly of persons until a certificate of authorization has been issued (FAA Form 7711-1).

The FAA will determine whether an application for authorization must be filed with the local **Flight Standards District Office (FSDO)**. This chapter contains the FAA's instructions on how to fill out the application for authorization, FAA Form 7711-2. The local FSDO may require an aerial photo and aviation sectional chart marking the location of the jump.

The BSRs **require the organizers** to contact and receive demonstration jump advice from the **local S&TA or a USPA Examiner**, who should be able to assist in meeting all state and federal requirements. The S&TA or Examiner providing this advice should use FAR 105.15.a as a guideline. **Examiners approached for advice should contact the S&TA for the area or the drop zone at which the flight will originate.** The S&TA should assist the jumpers in meeting all applicable state and federal requirements and check that they are met.

The organizer should carry all authorizations and permits on the jump. The S&TA should investigate both the proposed area and the participants. The S&TA or Examiner may recommend the use of specific jumpers or advise the organizer to use only individuals meeting certain experience requirements. The organizer may need flexibility in making last-minute substitutions of aircraft and participants. When consulted for a demonstration jump, the S&TA may also recommend certain additional limitations such as wind speed and direction, altitude, etc.

The S&TA should consider the information in this section when making recommendations and should ask the question, "All things considered, are the chances of performing a safe and professional demonstration jump reasonably good?"

# C. Landing Areas

All FAA-authorized demonstration jumps are classified as Open Field, Level 1, Level 2, or Stadium. With the FAA's concurrence, USPA defines these areas as described in Table 6.A, Size and Definition of Landing Areas.

Minimum landing areas for PRO Rating holders:

- For PRO Rating holders, there should be no less than 5,000 square feet of landing area per four jumpers.
- An additional 800 square feet per jumper is required for any jumper landing within 30 seconds of the last of any four jumpers.

When evaluating a demonstration jump, the jumper must consider alternate landing areas, such as run-offs or escape areas. Open bodies of water may be included when measuring landing-area requirements for open-field, level 1 and level 2 landing areas—however, the vertical and horizontal distance limits from any spectator outlined in Table 6.A still applies.

### Table 6.A— Size and Definition of Landing Areas

**Open Field**
1. A minimum-sized area that will accommodate a landing area no less than 500,000 square feet.
2. Allows a jumper to drift over the spectators with sufficient altitude (250 feet) so as not to create a hazard to persons or property on the ground
3. Will accommodate landing no closer than 100 feet from the spectators

**Level 1**
1. An area that will accommodate a landing area no smaller than 250,000 square feet up to 500,000 square feet
2. Or an area with the sum total that equals 250,000 square feet, up to 500,000 square feet) with a one-sided linear crowd line
3. Allows jumpers to drift over the spectators with sufficient altitude (250 feet) so as not to create a hazard to persons or property on the ground
4. Will accommodate landing no closer than 50 feet from the spectators
5. Many Open-Field athletic areas constitute a Level 1 area.

**Level 2**
1. An area that will not accommodate a 250,000 square-foot landing area but will allow an area no smaller than 5,000 square feet per four jumpers
2. Allows jumpers to fly under canopy no lower than 50 feet above the crowd and land no closer than 15 feet from the crowd line
3. Parachutists who certify that they will use both ram-air main and ram-air reserve parachutes will be permitted to exit over or into a congested area but not exit over an open-air assembly of people.
4. This area would require an FAA Form 7711-2 to conduct an approved demo.

**Stadium**
1. A Level 2 landing area smaller than 450 feet in length by 240 feet in width and bounded on two or more sides by bleachers, walls, or buildings in excess of 50 feet high
2. This area would also require an FAA Form 7711-2 to conduct an approved demonstration jump.

# D. Experience and Ability

Jumpers must have all the following experience and ability when jumping into an Open Field and Level 1 area, as defined by USPA and accepted by the FAA:

- C license or higher
- 50 jumps within the past 12 months
- five jumps within the previous 60 days using the same model and size canopy to be used on the demonstration jump
- For tandem jumps, the above requirements do not apply to the tandem student

Jumpers must have all the following experience and ability when jumping into a Level 2 and Stadium area, as defined by USPA and accepted by the FAA:

- hold the PRO rating (required by the BSRs)
- 50 jumps within the past 12 months
- five jumps within the previous 60 days using the same model and size canopy to be used on the demonstration jump

## E. How to Approach a Demo Jump

On a demonstration jump, as with all jumps, jumpers must consider safety first. The next most important aspect is landing in the target area. Good aerial work is not impressive if the jumpers land out. A stand-up landing in the target area is usually a demonstration jump's most visible and impressive portion.

Jumpers must consider many variables when planning demo jumps, including wind speed and direction, approach types, equipment type, jumper experience, target areas, and alternate landing areas. The organizer must evaluate each proposed demo individually.

While a good demonstration jump provides excellent public relations for the sport, a poorly performed one may severely damage skydiving's image. Therefore, jumpers must recognize and understand that sometimes it may be in the best interest of the individual jumper and skydiving in general not to make the jump at all. Demo jumpers should always exhibit a mature, professional attitude.

Jumpers should promise no more than they can produce and perform with expertise and efficiency, taking no unnecessary chances. Jumpers should prepare in advance, recognize and deal with the air of excitement that surrounds a demo jump, and make mature and professional judgments when dealing with unforeseen circumstances. This may require jumpers to delay or cancel the demo when conditions are not suitable for a safe jump. Jumpers and support staff should have a sharp, clean appearance to make a better impression and present a professional image.

### Equipment

USPA recommends ram-air main canopies for Open Field, Level 1, Level 2 and Stadium jumps. **The FAA requires** ram-air main canopies for Level 2 and Stadium jumps.

The reserve canopy should be steerable for open-field jumps. **The FAA requires** ram-air reserve canopies for Level 1, Level 2, and Stadium jumps.

Jumpers should hand-carry smoke or attach it to an easily ejectable boot bracket. *Warning: military type (M-18) smoke grenades are extremely hot and should not be handheld.*

With very few exceptions, USPA recommends demo jumpers use an AAD and an RSL, preferably with a MARD system. AADs can be set to accommodate differences between the jumper's takeoff and landing altitudes.

### Maximum Winds

When considering wind limits, jumpers should factor in wind turbulence and the capabilities of the reserve canopy. USPA recommends conducting all demonstration jumps with a ground-wind **maximum of 15 mph.** For stadium jumps, jumpers should measure the wind at the top of the stadium, always anticipating turbulence.

### Turbulence and Target Placement

Especially in windy conditions, jumpers must consider recommended minimum distances from major obstacles, including large buildings and trees, which affect air currents and can cause turbulence. A single tree, pole, fence, etc., is not considered a major obstacle. Stadiums often produce turbulence. Jumpers should be thoroughly familiar with their canopies' flight characteristics in turbulent air.

### Aerial Maneuvers

Demo jumpers should rehearse aerial maneuvers, just as any professional would give a show a dry run. Participants should know their exit point, freefall drift, and opening point. Landing on target takes priority over air work. Jumpers should be prepared to break off, track, or pull high if necessary.

Jumpers should not perform radical canopy maneuvers below 500 feet. Demonstration jumpers often use smoke or flags to enhance a show. Before jumping with smoke or an unfamiliar flag system, jumpers should seek out training and advice from a PRO-rated jumper who is familiar with the rigging and associated components.

**Smoke** is usually attached to a foot-mounted bracket or to a line that is dropped below the jumper. The smoke canister is ignited after opening. There are two types of smoke: hot and cold. If using hot smoke, jumpers should ensure that the smoke container won't burn through the line and should use care when crossing over obstacles or spectators during the final approach. Be cautious after landing as the smoke canister may be very hot for a while.

A **flag** may be attached to the rear lines or dropped below the jumper on a weighted line connected to the leading edge. Larger flags typically have the weight attached to or sewn into the leading edge and should be folded into a bag or pouch designed to contain it. Jumpers should deploy flags over uncongested areas to protect people and property in case a weight detaches. Those jumping with the U.S. flag should review Title 4 U.S. Code, Chapter 1 (U.S. Flag Code) so they properly handle it. Ground crew attempting to catch a weighted flag before it touches the ground should be aware of the dangers of being hit by the weight.

Only experienced CF jumpers should perform **canopy formation maneuvers** during demonstration skydives. Efforts to build canopy formations should stop no lower than 2,500 feet AGL. It is much more difficult and dangerous to land a canopy stack on target than it is to land canopies separately.

## Crowd Control

A collision with a spectator is dangerous for both the spectator and the jumper, as well as the well-being of the sport. Ground support should take reasonable precautions to keep spectators out of the landing area. When possible, spectators should be seated, since mobile spectators are more likely to move toward the jump target or into the path of a landing jumper.

Jumpers should pick up their equipment immediately after landing, since it could get damaged, and some spectators may decide that skydiving equipment makes good souvenirs. Jumpers who plan on packing in the crowd should protect their equipment against damage from spectators' drinks and cigarettes.

## Ground Signals

Participants must maintain ground-to-air communication as outlined in the BSRs, using a radio, smoke, or a panel. Ground support should establish a backup to the primary signal in case the primary signal fails. If a Certificate of Authorization (FAA Form 7711-1) is issued, it may require ground-to-air radio communication.

## Announcer

An experienced skydiver on the public address system contributes to a quality demonstration jump. The announcer can point out the aircraft, explain each phase of the jump, give general information, and explain any unusual occurrences, such as a reserve activation or a jumper missing the target. The announcer can also contribute to crowd control by asking spectators not to enter the target area.

## Other Activities

Activities after the jump add to the entertainment of the spectators. For example, after landing, team members may pack their parachutes in view of the spectators. While visiting with spectators after a jump, team members should respond to questions politely and factually, directing persons interested in jumping to uspa.org. Often, team members also distribute brochures advertising a local drop zone.

## Insurance

USPA individual membership liability skydiving insurance (property damage and bodily injury), which is included as a benefit of USPA membership, is not valid for demonstration jumps. Contact USPA Headquarters or visit uspa.org/demo#Demo-Jump-Insurance for information on demonstration jump insurance.

### 6-2: Professional Exhibition Rating

## A. Definition

Working in conjunction with the FAA, USPA issues Professional Exhibition (PRO) Ratings to any USPA member who meets the current requirements. This rating identifies the jumper as highly proficient and accurate in canopy control.

The USPA PRO Rating enables skydivers to perform exhibition jumps in challenging landing areas. To earn this rating, skydivers with a USPA D license must demonstrate landing skills using the parachute they intend to use for exhibition jumps. They also receive training in handling flags and pyrotechnic devices, coordinating with the FAA, and obtaining insurance coverage. The PRO rating allows holders to fly and land closer to crowds than jumpers who have not met these qualifications. Thus, PRO-rating holders must be proficient with various canopy sizes and must be capable of landing in small areas. As such, PRO-rating applicants provide a professional demonstration of skills on a wing loading of 1.5:1 and below. A High-Performance (HP) Endorsement allows PRO-rated members to make exhibition jumps with wing loadings above 1.5:1.

A USPA PRO Rating is not required for all demonstration jumps but may be a valuable advantage in working with the FAA. The FAA recognizes the USPA PRO Rating as a certificate of proficiency.

## B. Qualifications and Procedures

### PRO Rating Qualifications

To qualify for the PRO rating, an applicant must:

- be a current member of USPA
- possess a USPA D license
- have at least 500 jumps on a ram-air canopy

- made two-night jumps in accordance with the BSRs (recommended that the first one be a solo and one in a group) with a freefall of at least 20 seconds. An Instructor with a D license who has completed at least two-night jumps must verify these jumps.
- make a series of 10 solo jumps with a stand-up landing into an area 40-feet long by 20-feet wide using the same model and size canopy at a wing loading 1.5:1 or below.
- The applicant must pre-declare each jump to count toward the requirements for the PRO rating.
  - All declared jumps must be recorded on video that clearly shows the PRO-rating applicant's final approach and landing into a defined area 40-feet long by 20-feet wide. (Both outside and point-of-view footage are acceptable.)
  - The applicant must submit the video footage of each approach and landing to the appropriate USPA Regional Director or to the Director of Safety and Training at USPA Headquarters, along with the PRO-rating application.
  - The applicant may submit the video footage by sharing it online or by sending it on a portable hard drive.
- Once the applicant has started the series, they may make non-declared jumps; however, non-declared jumps may not count toward the accuracy requirements for the rating.
- All 10 pre-declared jumps in the series must be successful for any in the series to count toward the rating. In the event of an unsuccessful jump, the applicant must start a new series. At least two of the landings into an area 40-feet long by 20-feet wide must be crosswind approaches, with the final approach 90 degrees to the direction of the wind. Wind speed must be at least five miles per hour and no more than 15 miles per hour.
- On each declared jump, the applicant must make the first contact and stop within the designated landing area.
- A USPA S&TA, Examiner, Judge or Board Member must witness and sign off on all declared jumps.

## HP Endorsement Qualifications

To qualify for an HP (High-Performance) Endorsement for the PRO rating (fly a parachute at a wing loading greater than 1.5:1), an applicant must:

- make a series of five solo jumps using the same model and size canopy into an area 40-feet long by 20-feet wide.
  - The applicant must pre-declare each jump to count toward the requirements for the HP Endorsement for the PRO rating.
    - All declared jumps must be recorded on video that clearly shows the PRO rating applicant's final approach and landing into a defined area 40-feet long by 20-feet wide. (Both outside and point-of-view footage are acceptable.)
    - The applicant must submit video footage of each approach and landing to the appropriate USPA Regional Director or the Director of Safety and Training at USPA Headquarters along with the PRO-rating application.
    - The applicant may submit the video footage by sharing it online or by sending it on a portable hard drive.
  - At least one landing into an area 40-feet long by 20-feet wide must demonstrate a crosswind approach and landing, with the final approach 90 degrees to the direction of the wind. Wind speed must be at least five miles per hour and no more than 15 miles per hour.
  - At least two approaches and landings must demonstrate a heading change of at least 45 degrees during the final 150 feet of canopy flight. The jumper must start and complete the heading change no higher than 25 feet

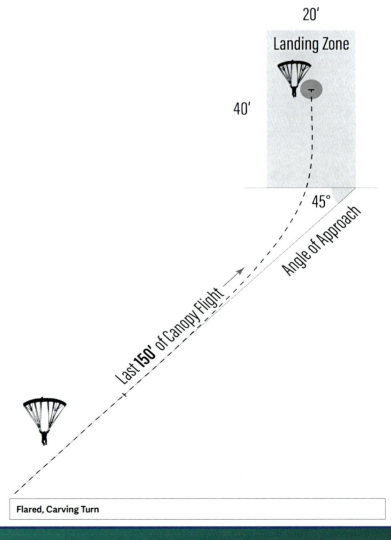

Flared, Carving Turn

# Exhibition Jumping and PRO Rating

AGL. This flared, carving turn demonstrates the ability to change heading during the swoop portion of the landing while still maintaining control of the parachute.
- All five pre-declared jumps in this series must be successful for any in the series to count toward the rating. In the event of an unsuccessful jump, the applicant must start a new series.
- On each declared jump, the applicant must make the first contact and stop within the designated landing area.
- a USPA S&TA, Examiner, Judge or Board Member must witness and sign off on all declared jumps.

## Application Procedures

A USPA S&TA, Examiner, Judge or Board Member can administer the **PRO Rating Exam** online or on paper. Applicants may not use references or other assistance during the exam and must pass with a score of 75% or more. The official will record any passing score on the PRO Rating Application and in the applicant's logbook.

When giving written exams on **paper**, the examining USPA official gives the PRO-rating applicant a blank answer sheet and the questions to the exam. After the test, the examining official collects the materials and grades the exam. An applicant who does not pass will be eligible to retake this exam after seven days.

For written exams taken using USPA's **online** license-testing program, applicants who do not pass may immediately retest using the same method for a total of three attempts per day.

The PRO-rating applicant must send the completed application to the appropriate USPA Regional Director for their signature and include the exam, videos, rating fee, and PRO Rating Proficiency Card signed by a USPA S&TA, Examiner or PRO Rating holder.

Except for the minimum 500-ram-air-jump requirement, the applicant must have completed all training listed on the application within the previous 12 months. The USPA Regional Director will forward the application to USPA Headquarters.

The canopy the jumper uses during qualification will be the smallest size canopy to be allowed for minimum-landing-area (Level 2) jumps, and USPA will note this canopy size on the jumper's USPA Membership Card. USPA will issue an annual PRO Rating with an expiration date that coincides with the applicant's membership expiration date. The PRO-rating holder must renew their PRO rating annually to remain current. If a PRO-rating holder's competence is questioned by an FAA or USPA official such as an S&TA, the PRO-rating holder may be required to reaffirm their proficiency.

## C. To Requalify on Smaller Canopies

### Wing Loading of 1.5:1 or Less

To requalify on a smaller canopy with a **wing loading of 1.5:1 or less**, the rating holder must make three successive, pre-declared jumps, making the first contact and stopping within an area 40-feet long by 20-feet wide.

All declared jumps must be recorded on video that clearly shows the PRO-rating applicant's final approach and landing into a defined area 40-feet long by 20-feet wide. The applicant must submit video footage of each approach and landing to the appropriate Regional Director or to the Director of Safety & Training at USPA Headquarters along with the PRO Rating Application and videos (by sharing them online or by delivering a portable hard drive).

The jumper must stand up all landings, which a USPA S&TA, Examiner, Judge, or Board Member must verify. The applicant must log the three landings on the PRO Rating Application and have the verifying witness sign it. The applicant may then submit the completed application and videos to USPA Headquarters for processing.

### Wing Loading Greater than 1.5:1

To re-qualify on a smaller canopy with a **wing loading greater than 1.5:1**, the rating holder must first meet the qualifications for the HP Endorsement listed above (i.e., must perform the five HP qualification jumps first).

The rating holder must make three successive, pre-declared jumps, making the first contact and stopping within an area 40-feet long by 20-feet wide. All declared jumps must be recorded on video that clearly shows the PRO-rating applicant's final approach and landing into a defined area 40-feet long by 20-feet wide. The applicant must submit video footage of each approach and landing to the appropriate Regional Director or to the Director of Safety & Training at USPA Headquarters along with the PRO Rating Application and videos (by sharing them online or by delivering a portable hard drive).

### Landing Criteria:

- ☐ One landing must be into the wind in any wind speeds up to 15 miles per hour.
- ☐ One landing must be crosswind with a final approach 90 degrees to the direction of the wind. Wind speed must be at least five miles per hour and no more than 15 miles per hour.
- ☐ One approach and landing must demonstrate a heading change of at least 45 degrees during the final 150 feet of canopy flight. The jumper must start and complete the heading change no higher than 25 feet AGL. This flared, carving turn demonstrates the ability to change heading during the swoop portion of the landing while still maintaining control of the parachute.

A USPA S&TA, Examiner, Judge, or Board Member must verify all landings. The applicant must log the three landings on the PRO Rating Application, which the verifying witness signs. The applicant may submit the completed application and videos to USPA Headquarters for processing.

## D. Annual Renewal Requirements

Within the previous 12 months, the PRO-rating holder must perform all the following, verified by the signature of a current USPA S&TA, Examiner, Judge or Board member (the jumper may not sign for themselves) and submit a completed PRO Rating Renewal Application to USPA Headquarters with the current renewal fee:

- Make at least 50 jumps.
- PRO rating for wing loadings of 1.5:1 and less, completed **two** of the following requirements in the presence of a USPA S&TA, Examiner, Judge or Board Member (a requirement can be repeated):
  - perform a stand-up landing, making the first contact and stopping within an area 40-feet long by 20-feet wide with a wing loading 1.5:1 or less
  - perform a Level 2 demo jump (as defined by USPA and accepted by the FAA) with a wing loading 1.5:1 or less
- To renew a HP endorsement for wing loadings of more than 1.5:1, the jumper must meet the requirements for PRO-rating renewal for wing loadings of 1.5:1 or less and complete two of the following requirements in the presence of a USPA S&TA, Examiner, Judge or Board member (a requirement can be repeated) while using a canopy loaded higher than 1.5:1:
  - perform a carving accuracy landing with a 45-degree heading change as outlined in the HP section, making the first contact and stopping within an area 40-feet long by 20-feet wide
  - perform a crosswind accuracy landing 90 degrees to the direction of the wind as outlined in the HP section, making the first contact and stopping within an area 40-feet long by 20-feet wide
  - perform a Level 2 demo jump (as defined by USPA and accepted by the FAA)
- If the PRO-rating holder renews using a canopy size larger than the one originally qualified on, it becomes the smallest-size canopy the jumper may use for demonstrations.

## E. Lapsed-PRO-Rating Renewal Requirements

To reinstate a PRO rating that has **expired less than two years ago**, the rating holder must do the following in the presence of a current USPA S&TA, Examiner, Judge, or Board member:

- for wing loadings of **1.5:1 and less**, perform two stand-up landings, making the first contact and stopping within an area 40-feet long by 20-feet wide.
- for wing loadings **more than 1.5:1**, meet requirements for wing loadings of 1.5:1 or less and perform two landings, one each crosswind and 45-degree heading change outlined in the HP section, making the first contact and stopping within an area 40-feet long by 20-feet wide.

If a PRO-rating holder allows their rating to lapse for **two years or longer**, they must meet the initial landing qualification requirements.

If the canopy size the jumper uses for reinstatement is larger than the one originally qualified on, it becomes the smallest-size canopy the jumper may use for demonstrations.

## 6-3: FAA Form 7711-2

*Parachute demonstration or exhibition jumps conducted into aviation events, congested areas on the surface, or open-air assemblies, require an FAA Certificate of Authorization to be issued by the FAA Flight Standards District Office with jurisdiction where the jump(s) will occur. FAA Form 7711-2 — the application for that authorization — is located on both the FAA and USPA websites. Submit the application to the FSDO after completing the form using the following FAA instructions:*

Organizers should present applications for parachute-jump authorizations made over or into a congested area or open-air assembly of people at least 10 working days before an event, if possible, to allow for processing time. The FSDO provides approval or denial of the application within five working days of receipt.

**Description of items requested on FAA 7711-2 form:**

| |
|---|
| **1. Name of organization** <br> Enter the organization sponsoring the event who retains sole responsibility for safeguarding persons and property on the surface. This person will be indicated as the holder of the Certificate of Waiver or Authorization. |
| **2. Name of responsible person** <br> This individual must have been determined to be competent and knowledgeable concerning the terms and provisions of this Certificate of Authorization. The application may be submitted by the organizer for a sanctioned military team but must be submitted by a team member if not a sanctioned military team. The FAA considers this person responsible for ensuring the operational safety of the event on all authorization matters. |
| **3. Permanent mailing address** <br> This information refers to the holder of the Certificate of Authorization listed in either Item 1 or 2. If no organization is listed in Item 1 then the information pertains to the name in Item 2. |
| **4. State whether the applicant … waiver pending …** <br> Nothing should be entered unless the application is for banner towing. |
| **5. State whether the applicant … waiver denied…** <br> Nothing should be entered unless the application is for banner towing. |
| **6. FAR section and number to be waived** <br> Enter "NONE." |
| **7. Detailed description of proposed operation** <br> Example: "A four-person skydiving exhibition with flags, banners, smoke and pyrotechnics." |
| **8. Area of operation** <br> Example: "1.0 Nm in radius from a point 7.3 Nm on the CVG 270-degree radial from surface to 8,000 feet MSL" or Example: "1.0 Nm in radius from the center of W66 airport from surface to 6,000 feet MSL." |
| **9a. Beginning** <br> Enter the beginning date and time when the jump aircraft will arrive over the jump site; indicate if using local or UTC (GMT aka Zulu time). |
| **9b. Ending** <br> Enter the date and time the last jumper will be on the ground; indicate if using local or UTC. |
| **10. (a) (b) (c) (d)** <br> Enter the aircraft make and model (include N-number if known) to be used, back-up aircraft, pilot(s) name(s) certificate number(s), and home address. |
| **Items 11 through 16** are not required for parachuting authorizations; enter the jumpers' names, license and membership numbers and issuing organization either in the remarks block or on a separate sheet of paper attached. |

# Glossary

## A

**A&P**
1. Assemble and Pack, used on reserve parachute packing record cards.
2. Airframe and Powerplant Mechanic.

**A LICENSE**
The first-level license that signifies that a skydiver has advanced beyond the student phase. Persons holding a USPA A License are able to jumpmaster themselves, perform basic group freefall jumps and water jumps, participate in certain USPA collegiate competition events, and pack their own main parachute.

**AAD**
(see AUTOMATIC ACTIVATION DEVICE)

**ACCELERATED FREEFALL (AFF), USPA**
Harness-hold freefall skydiving student training discipline developed under Ken Coleman and adopted by USPA. AFF-rated USPA Instructors accompany the student in freefall during the initial training jumps.

**AGL**
Above ground level. Refers to altitude, e.g., 5,000 feet AGL.

**AIR**
Acronym for "altitude aware, in control, and relaxed."

**AIRCRAFT**
Any machine or device, including airplanes, helicopters, gliders, balloons, etc., capable of atmospheric flight. For the purposes of regulation, parachutes are not considered aircraft.

**AIRSPEED**
The speed of an airborne aircraft or parachute, relative to the air.

**ALTERATIONS**
Any change or modification to any part of the parachute assembly from its original manufacturer's specifications. (see also MAJOR ALTERATION and MINOR ALTERATION)

**ALTIMETER**
A device that measures height above the surface (altitude); for skydivers, typically above the intended skydiving landing area. (see also AUDIBLE ALTIMETER)

**ANGLE FLYING**
A type of movement jump where skydivers travel across the sky instead of falling straight down. The flying can occur at various degrees of pitch with a diagonal trajectory either in a belly-to-earth or back-to-earth orientation.

**ANGLE OF ATTACK**
The relative pitch (leading edge up or down) angle of a wing measured between the chord line and the relative wind.

**APPROACH ANGLE**
(see GLIDE PATH)

**APPROPRIATELY RATED**
Refers to a USPA Instructor or Examiner rated in the method-specific instructional discipline necessary to perform a particular task in accordance with the BSRs.

**APT**
Acronym for "altitude-position-traffic," the check performed regularly while descending under canopy.

**ARCH**
Position skydivers use to orient the front of their torso to the relative wind. Described, it is hips forward with back arched; legs extended to 45 degrees, toes pointed; knees at shoulder width; arms bent 90-120 degrees at the shoulders and elbows and relaxed; head up.

**ARTISTIC EVENTS**
Skydiving competition events that include freeflying and freestyle skydiving.

**AS 8015 (AEROSPACE STANDARD 8015)**
Standard of tests and minimum safety and performance requirements which must be met to receive approval under technical standard order (TSO) certification. AS 8015A, the standard for TSO C-23c was adopted in 1984 to supersede NAS 804, the standard for TSO C-23b. In June 1994, AS 8015B became the standard for TSO C-23d.

**ASPECT RATIO**
The aspect ratio of a ram-air parachute canopy is the ratio of its length (span) to its breadth (chord).

**ASSISTED DEPLOYMENT**
Refers to a pull sequence prompted or cued by the instructor where the student begins the sequence and is completed by the student but may be assisted by the instructor.

**AUDIBLE ALTIMETER**
An alarm used by skydivers to alert them about reaching one or more pre-set altitudes.

**AUTOMATIC ACTIVATION DEVICE (AAD)**
A self-contained mechanical or electro-mechanical device that is attached to the interior of the reserve parachute container, which automatically initiates parachute deployment of the reserve parachute at a pre-set altitude, time, percentage of terminal velocity, or combination thereof. (FAR 105 definition)

**AUXILIARY PARACHUTE**
(See RESERVE PARACHUTE)

## B

**B LICENSE**
The second-level USPA license. Persons holding a USPA B License are authorized to perform night jumps, and when qualified, apply for a USPA Coach rating.

**B-12s**
Clip hardware sometimes used for leg-strap attachment on a parachute harness. Refers generally to the MS 22044 hardware originally used on the U.S. Army B-12 parachute assembly. (see THREAD-THROUGH)

**BAG**
(see DEPLOYMENT BAG)

**BAG LOCK**
A malfunction of a deployed parachute where the canopy remains in the deployment bag.

**BARREL ROLL**
A maneuver in which a skydiver rolls about their longitudinal axis.

**BASE**
1. When building a freefall or canopy formation, the initial target individual or group of people to which the others fly.

2. Base (leg). The portion of the three-legged landing pattern where the jumper flies across the direction of the wind downwind of the landing area before turning for final approach into the wind toward the target.

**BASE JUMPING**
An activity involving the use of a parachute for descent from fixed objects. The acronym derives from the first initials of four possible launch categories: buildings, antennae, spans (bridges), and earth (cliffs). Because BASE jumping does not meet the FAA's definition of "the descent of an object to the surface from an aircraft in flight," it is not regulated by the FAA or addressed by USPA.

**BASIC SAFETY REQUIREMENTS (BSRS), USPA**
Minimum standards overseen and published by USPA and generally agreed upon as the acceptable standard for safe skydiving activities. The BSRs form the foundation of self-governing by skydivers. USPA oversees the BSRs.

**BELLY FLYING**
Slang for FORMATION SKYDIVING or RELATIVE WORK where jumpers are falling with their bellies facing the earth.

**BOARD OF DIRECTORS (BOD), USPA**
Those representatives elected by the general members of USPA every three years as set forth in the USPA Bylaws; authorized by the bylaws to have general charge and control of the affairs, funds, and property of the organization and to carry out the objectives of the organization and its bylaws; elects officers from among current USPA Board members. The USPA Board of Directors consists of

1. National Directors—those directors elected at large by the general membership;

2. Regional Directors—those directors of a specified geographical area, elected by and responsible for representing the interests of the skydivers in a USPA Region.

**BRAKE FIRE**
A premature brake release during the canopy deployment.

**BRAKED FLARE**
One of the canopy-flight emergency procedures (CEPs) used in several situations such as after flaring too high, after a braked turn to avoid an obstacle on landing, and after a low-turn-recovery CEP. This maneuver generally requires a faster and more forceful flare to get the same response from the canopy as a flare from full flight.

**BRAKED TURN**
One of the canopy-flight emergency procedures (CEPs) used for object avoidance on landing, which may require a turn at a lower altitude. This maneuver slows forward speed, reduces altitude loss, and allows for a heading change while honoring the number-one landing priority of landing with a level wing.

**BRAKES**
1. The steering controls of a ram-air parachute. (see also TOGGLES)

2. The position of the parachute steering controls, measured in relative increments (quarter brakes, deep brakes, etc.), to control speed and descent in a stable state of flight.

**BREAK OFF**
Act of a group of jumpers separating from a freefall or canopy group.

**BREAKOFF**
Procedure in group skydiving where jumpers cease group activity and separate. In freefall, jumpers begin to track at a predetermined altitude for a clear area to open safely; jumpers building canopy formations break off at a predetermined altitude to gain safe separation and allow jumpers to prepare for a landing approach.

**BREAKOFF ALTITUDE**
Planned altitude for initiating separation of jumpers during a group jump.

**BRIDLE**
The device, usually made of webbing or tape, connecting the pilot chute to the deployment bag or the canopy.

**BSRs**
(see BASIC SAFETY REQUIREMENTS, USPA)

## C

**C LICENSE**
The third-level license issued by USPA. USPA C-license holders may apply when qualified for the USPA AFF, IAD, and Static-Line Instructor ratings, ride as passenger on USPA Tandem Instructor training and rating renewal jumps, and participate in intermediate-altitude jumps and Open Field and Level 1 exhibition jumps.

**CANOPY**
The major component of the parachute system comprised of fabric membranes that connect to the parachute harness by suspension lines and provide the means for the jumper to descend safely.

**CANOPY-FLIGHT EMERGENCY**
Any canopy emergency that happens under a fully inflated parachute, anytime during the canopy descent or landing.

**CANOPY-FLIGHT EMERGENCY PROCEDURES (CEPS)**
A set of five skills used in response to a canopy emergency that happens under a fully inflated parachute anytime during the canopy descent or landing. The CEPs are bundled in a safety campaign called "Stay Alive, Practice Five."

# G

## Glossary

**CANOPY FORMATION (CF); CANOPY RELATIVE WORK; (CRW)**
1. The intentional maneuvering of two or more open parachute canopies in proximity to or in contact with one another during descent.
2. The FAI competition discipline involving the building of canopy formations.

**CANOPY WRAP**
When the canopy of one jumper is wrapped around another jumper.

**CASCADE**
The point where two or more lines of a canopy join into one.

**CELL**
Chordwise section of a parachute canopy between the load-bearing ribs. Sometimes, any portion of a canopy separated by vertical ribs.

**CERTIFICATED**
Refers to FAA-approval status of parachute components, technicians, riggers, and aircraft pilots.

**CHECK OF THREES**
Pre-jump equipment self-check performed in the aircraft

check three-ring release system and RSL for correct assembly; check three points of harness attachment for snap assembly or correct routing and adjustment; check three operation handles—main activation, cutaway, reserve—in place.

**CHORD**
The longest dimension from the front to the back of a wing at any given point along the span.

**CLEARED**
Refers to a student who has received a signature from a USPA Instructor to advance.

**CLIMB OUT**
The act of a jumper positioning themself in or near the door or on protuberances or structures outside the aircraft to prepare for launch, usually with a group.

**CLOSING LOOP**
A lace that when threaded through eyelets in the parachute container flaps and locked with a closing pin, keeps the parachute contained until activation.

**COACH**
A non-rated operative who provides advanced skydiving training. (see also COACH, USPA)

**COACH, USPA**
The entry-level USPA instructional rating whose holder may teach the general (non-method-specific) sections of the first-jump course and conduct group-freefall and canopy-skills training and jumps with students, all under the supervision of a USPA Instructor.

**COACH JUMP**
A coach jump is any jump where a USPA Coach jumps with any person and provides instruction and/or critique to that person.

**COLLAPSIBLE PILOT CHUTE**
A hand-deployed pilot chute that automatically collapses after deployment.

**COLLAPSIBLE SLIDER**
A slider rigged so the jumper can compress or wrap it to reduce drag (see also SLIDER).

**COLLINS LANYARD**
A lanyard attached to the reserve static line that is designed to release the non-RSL-side riser in the event the RSL-side riser breaks.

**CONTAINER**
The portion of the parachute system that closes around and stores the folded parachute canopy, deployment bag and pilot chute until deployment.

**CORK**
During high-speed group freefall maneuvers, to lose control and decelerate rapidly.

**CRW**
(see CANOPY FORMATION)

**CROSS BRACED**
Refers to a canopy designed with longitudinal trussing between the vertical ribs to flatten and stiffen the wing in flight.

**CROSS-CONNECTORS**
Straps attached between the risers. Used for canopy formation, they should be from front to rear only to prevent the docked jumper from sliding back up the lines. Especially important for plane formations.

**CROSSPORT**
A vent cut into the structural rib of a parachute canopy to equalize air pressure between two cells.

**CROSSWIND**
Perpendicular to the direction of the wind.

**CUT AWAY** (verb)
**CUTAWAY** (noun, adjective)
Procedure where the jumper releases from the main parachute prior to activating the reserve parachute. Used in the event of a main-parachute malfunction to prevent an entanglement with the deploying reserve; in the event of a canopy entanglement with another jumper; and also in case the wind causes the canopy to drag a jumper after landing.

**CUTAWAY HANDLE**
Pillow or loop handle of a two-handled system, normally located on the right side of the jumper's main lift web, used to initiate a cutaway.

# D

**D-BAG**
(see DEPLOYMENT BAG)

**D LICENSE**
The fourth and highest level or license issued by USPA. USPA D-License holders may participate in all competitions at the national level, apply when qualified for all USPA instructional and proficiency ratings, and participate in high-altitude jumps.

**DECISION ALTITUDE**
A predetermined altitude at which you must decide and act during an emergency.

**DELTA**
Freefall position with legs extended and arms back to initiate a forward dive.

## Glossary

**DEMONSTRATION JUMP (DEMO)**
(see EXHIBITION JUMP)

**DENSITY ALTITUDE**
An expression of air density relative to standard atmospheric pressure at sea level. The pilot calculates pressure altitude and temperature and compares the result with an equivalent altitude MSL at standard temperature.

**DEPLOYMENT**
After activation, extraction of the parachute from the container and full extension of the system prior to inflation.

**DEPLOYMENT BAG**
Intermediate container, also known as a D-bag, for a main parachute or a freebag for a reserve parachute, that contains the folded parachute through complete line deployment.

**DEPLOYMENT DEVICE**
A device that initiates the deployment of a parachute (i.e. static line or pilot chute).

**DESCENT RATE**
The downward horizontal speed of an aircraft or parachute, usually measured in feet per minute.

**DIRECT SUPERVISION**
1. The attentive oversight of an activity taking place in the immediate presence of the supervisor, who is personally responsible for the proper conduct of the activity. (USPA definition)

2. A certificated rigger personally observes a non-certificated person packing a main parachute to the extent necessary to ensure that it is being done properly, and takes responsibility for that packing. (FAR 105 definition) (see also SUPERVISION)

**DIVE BLOCKS**
Hand grips (not loops) on the front risers to facilitate diving the canopy.

**DIVE LOOPS**
Handles on the front risers to facilitate diving the canopy.

**DIVING EXIT**
Launching out of an aircraft without a climb out to achieve a stable entry into the relative wind.

**DIVING (FREEFALL)**
To rapidly descend toward and then make a controlled approach relative to a target.

**DOCK**
To make physical controlled contact with another skydiver while in freefall; or, when building canopy formations, with another jumper's canopy.

**DOWNWIND**
1. The direction toward which the air is moving.
2. positioned farther along the wind's path.
3. a downwind-facing landing.

**DOWNWIND LEG**
The portion of the landing approach flown with the wind blowing from behind the jumper.

**DROGUE**
A trailing drag device used to retard the movement of an object through the air, used in skydiving to regulate the fall rate of tandem skydivers.

**DROGUEFALL**
In tandem skydiving, the portion of the descent where a drogue has been deployed between freefall and main-parachute deployment.

**DROP ZONE**
1. Skydiving establishment or intended parachute landing area. (USPA definition)

2. Any pre-determined area upon which parachutists or objects land after making an intentional parachute jump or drop. The center-point target of a drop zone is expressed in nautical miles from the nearest VOR facility when 30 nautical miles or less; or from the nearest airport, town, or city depicted on the appropriate Coast and Geodetic Survey World Aeronautical Chart or Sectional Aeronautical Chart, when the nearest VOR facility is more than 30 nautical miles from the drop zone. (FAR 105 definition) (see also SANCTIONED DROP ZONE)

**DUAL ASSEMBLY**
Refers to a two-canopy parachute system. Includes the main and reserve canopies, harness-and-container system, and all other components.

**ELLIPTICAL**
Refers to a class of canopies with a tapered or approximately elliptical planform.

**EMERGENCY PARACHUTE**
A certificated parachute which is intended for emergency use; typically, the parachute a pilot wears.

**END CELL**
The last chordwise section of a parachute canopy on either end.

**END-CELL CLOSURE**
Deflated end cell. Routine opening problem, usually correctable.

**ENDORSEMENT**
1. An act of giving approval or support to someone or something.

2. A certification that is an addition to an existing rating, for example a High-Performance Endorsement added to a PRO rating or a manufacturer's endorsement added to a tandem rating.

**EXAMINER, USPA**
The highest level of the instructional rating program. An Examiner is an experienced USPA Instructor who has met additional proficiency requirements and passed a series of written examinations on a wide variety of skydiving-related subjects. An Examiner has all the privileges of a USPA Safety and Training Advisor.

**EXHIBITION JUMP**
An exhibition jump, also called a display or demonstration jump, is a jump at a location other than an existing drop zone done for the purpose of reward, remuneration, or promotion and principally for the benefit of spectators.

**EXIT POINT**
The point on the ground over which skydivers leave the aircraft.

**EXIT WEIGHT**
The combined weight of the jumper and all their equipment for that jump.

**EXTRAORDINARY SKYDIVE**
Night jump, water jump, jump from above 15,000 feet MSL, exhibition jump, pre-planned cutaway jump, and other jumps requiring special equipment and procedures that might be unfamiliar to most jumpers.

**FAA**
(see FEDERAL AVIATION ADMINISTRATION)

**FAI**
(see FÉDÉRATION AÉRONAUTIQUE INTERNATIONALE)

**FARMER MCNASTY**
Slang term for a disenchanted drop zone neighbor with whom communications with jumpers are strained or have broken down.

**FEDERAL AVIATION ADMINISTRATION (FAA)**
An agency of the U.S. Department of Transportation whose primary function and responsibility is to control the nation's air traffic, including the certification of all civil aircraft and accessories, licensing of all civil pilots, mechanics, and riggers, and administration of the Federal Aid to Airports Program.

**FEDERAL AVIATION REGULATIONS (FARS)**
The parts of the U.S. Code of Federal Regulations that apply to aviation.

**FÉDÉRATION AÉRONAUTIQUE INTERNATIONALE (FAI)**
An international organization that governs all aviation sports, certifies all official aviation and space records, and governs official international competitions. Operates through a non-profit National Aero Club in each country.

**FINAL APPROACH**
The final portion of flight before a jumper or aircraft lands.

**FLARE**
1. Under canopy: To convert the downward speed of a parachute momentarily into lift.

2. In freefall: To decelerate prior to approaching a formation.

3. The act of flaring.

4. A membrane used to distribute the load of a parachute at the line attachment points of some canopies.

**FLAT TURN**
A canopy turn performed at braked flight that conserves altitude.

**FLOATER**
A jumper positioned outside the aircraft to leave slightly prior to the person or group designated as the target for the initial freefall formation (see also BASE). A floater maneuvers from a position below the base relative to the horizon.

**FLOATER EXIT**
After a climb out, launching from outside the aircraft to achieve a presented, stable entry into the relative wind. Three common positions in the door are front, center and rear floater.

**FOREIGN PARACHUTIST**
A parachutist who is neither a U.S. citizen nor a resident alien and is participating in parachute operations within the United States using parachute equipment not manufactured in the United States. (FAR 105 definition)

**FORMATION SKYDIVING (RELATIVE WORK)**
1. Aerial maneuvers by two or more freefalling skydivers with each other, usually to form geometric formations.

2. Competition discipline of belly flying.

**FREEBAG**
Intermediate container that contains or constricts the folded parachute through complete line deployment that is not attached to the deploying parachute; generally used with reserve parachutes.

**FREEFALL**
The portion of a parachute jump or drop between aircraft exit and parachute deployment in which the parachute is activated manually by the parachutist at the parachutist's discretion or automatically, or, in the case of an object, is activated automatically. (FAR 105 definition)

**FREEFLY**
1. To exit unlinked with other jumpers.

2. An unrestricted freefall discipline characterized by varied presentations to the relative wind. (see also SIT FLYING and HEAD DOWN.)

3. The competition artistic event of freefly.

**FREESTYLE**
1. A solo freefall discipline that involves choreographed multi-orientation static and dynamic maneuvers.

2. The competition event of freestyle performed as part of a team with a camera flyer (freestyle skydiving).

**FULL FLIGHT**
The stabilized state of input-free canopy flight under an open and fully functioning parachute.

**FUNNEL**
A freefall skydiving formation that has become unstable, usually due to one or more jumpers flying out of position, causing the participants to collapse the formation and land on top of each other.

**GLIDE**
The combined horizontal and vertical movement of a descending canopy.

**GLIDE ANGLE**
(see GLIDE PATH)

**GLIDE PATH**
The trajectory of a parachute as it descends in flight toward a landing point on the ground.

**GO-AROUND**
An in-flight operation where the aircraft circles at jump altitude.

**GOVERNANCE MANUAL, USPA**
The official bound collection of the USPA Constitution and Bylaws.

**GROUND SPEED**
The speed of an airborne aircraft or parachute relative to the ground it traverses in a given period of time.

## Glossary

### GROUP MEMBER
Skydiving centers that have pledged to follow USPA Basic Safety Requirements, including providing USPA-developed first-jump courses, using current USPA-rated instructors and providing USPA-required skydiving equipment. At USPA Group Member skydiving centers, all skydivers cleared for self-supervision must be current USPA members.

### HAALR
A freefall sequence acronym used by students to maintain control and stability

check "heading, altitude, arch, legs, relax."

### HAND-DEPLOYED PILOT CHUTE
A small parachute thrown by hand in freefall to extract the main parachute from its container. (see also PULL OUT and THROW OUT)

### HARD DECK
A predetermined altitude above which an action must occur or below which an action must not occur. For example, the cutaway hard deck is 1,000, below which a jumper should not cut away, unless they are experiencing a downplane.

### HARNESS
The webbing of a parachute system that surrounds and retains a jumper.

### HARNESS-AND-CONTAINER SYSTEM
The major component of a parachute system, usually unitized, which the jumper dons for the jump. It contains the canopies and certain accessory devices.

### HARNESS HOLD
A skydiving training discipline where a student is trained for independent, solo freefall but is accompanied by at least one USPA AFF Instructor until meeting the requirements in the BSRs for self-supervision in freefall. On the initial jumps, the AFF Instructor(s) assist the student on exit via a harness grip.

### HEAD DOWN
Inverted vertical or nearly vertical freeflying orientation.

### HIGH-PERFORMANCE LANDING AREA
An area at a drop zone that DZ management has designated as separate from the landing area where standard landings take place, allowing canopy pilots to perform high-performance landings.

### HIGH-SPEED STALL
A parachute stall in a dive or turn at higher airspeed, induced by applying too much input or input too abruptly with risers or toggles. They happen quickly and less predictably than the low-speed stalls, making them much more dangerous. (see STALL, TOGGLE STALL, and REAR-RISER STALL)

### HOOK KNIFE
A hook-shaped knife with an inside cutting edge. Used in certain emergencies to sever problem lines or components of a parachute system.

### HOOK TURN
Per the FAA:

"A hook turn is a maneuver in any maneuver sequence that causes the canopy to roll at an angle in excess of 45 degrees from vertical and /or to pitch up or down at an angle in excess of 45 degrees from horizontal while executing a turn in excess of 60 degrees."

### HOOKER HARNESS
A single-point aircraft passenger restraint system that integrates with a parachute harness. Designed by Jack Hooker.

### HORSESHOE
A partial parachute malfunction where part of the deployed parachute is entangled with the jumper or his or her equipment.

### I&R
(see INSPECT AND REPACK)

### IAD
(see INSTRUCTOR-ASSISTED DEPLOYMENT)

### INITIATED DEPLOYMENT
Refers to a pull sequence prompted or cued by the instructor where the student begins the sequence but may be completed by the instructor.

### INSPECT AND REPACK
Rigging term used on reserve parachute packing data cards.

### INSTRUCTIONAL RATING MANUAL (IRM), USPA
The teacher's guide for instructional rating holders and training manual for instructional rating candidates.

### INSTRUCTOR RATING COURSE, USPA
A course registered with USPA Headquarters to train, qualify, and test applicants for the USPA Instructor rating.

### INSTRUCTOR, USPA
The holder of a USPA Instructor rating qualified in one or more of four methods of instruction

accelerated freefall (AFF), instructor-assisted deployment, static line, or tandem. The mid-level of the USPA instructional rating hierarchy. A USPA Instructor may train and certify a student for the USPA A License, supervise USPA Coaches, and is eligible for appointment as USPA Safety and Training Advisor.

### INSTRUCTOR-ASSISTED DEPLOYMENT (IAD)
A method of passive deployment used for training skydiving students making their initial jumps. A USPA IAD Instructor controls a hand-deployed pilot chute while a student moves into position and jumps, at which point the instructor releases the pilot chute.

### JUDGE
The official who evaluates a competitor's performance. USPA issues judge ratings at both the regional and national levels. The FAI issues a rating for internationally recognized judges.

### JUMP ALTITUDE
Actual altitude of an aircraft above the ground at the time a skydiver exits.

**JUMP**
(see SKYDIVE)

**JUMP RUN**
The flight of the aircraft prior to exit, generally following a predetermined path.

**JUMPER**
(see SKYDIVER)

**JUMPMASTER**
1. A skydiver, typically a senior jumper or instructional rating holder, who coordinates boarding and exit order, jump flight procedures, spotting, and emergency operations with the pilot.
2. To dispatch jumpers. 3. Prior to 2002, a USPA instructional rating for supervising student jumps.

**JUMPSUIT**
A garment used for protection or to alter performance.

**LANDING PATTERN**
The deliberate flight path, usually rectangular, that a jumper uses in the final phase of descent under canopy.

**LICENSE**
Certificate of proficiency recognizing that a skydiver has met a specified level of experience, skill, and knowledge. There are four classes of USPA licenses A, B, C and D. USPA licenses are recognized internationally through the FAI.

**LINE DOCK**
The docking of two canopies with the docker's canopy above the head of the person receiving the dock.

**LINE TWIST**
A condition of parachute opening where the canopy has attained full or nearly full inflation, but one or more complete twists have developed in the lines and/or risers. Can be dangerous when associated with a spin.

**LINEOVER**
A partial malfunction of a deployed parachute resulting in lines going over the top of the canopy. Also refers loosely to the partial inversion of a round canopy. (see also PARTIAL INVERSION)

**LOW-TURN RECOVERY**
One of the canopy-flight emergency procedures (CEPs) used for quickly neutralizing a turn initiated too close to the ground for the canopy to recover naturally. This maneuver entails neutralizing the turn by pulling the toggle that is still in full flight to match the lower toggle—resulting in both toggles in a braked position—stopping the turn and slowing forward speed before flaring.

**MAE WEST**
WWII term for partial inversion of a round parachute. (see also PARTIAL INVERSION)

**MAIN-ASSISTED RESERVE DEPLOYMENT (MARD)**
A device designed to expedite a reserve-parachute deployment after a cutaway. Upon cutting away the main canopy, the system utilizes the departing main parachute to assist in extracting the reserve parachute, thereby minimizing altitude loss and ensuring a rapid reserve deployment.

**MAIN PARACHUTE**
A parachute worn as the primary parachute used or intended to be used in conjunction with a reserve parachute. (FAR 105 definition)

**MAINTENANCE**
Inspection, overhaul, repair, preservation, and replacement of parts.

**MAJOR ALTERATION**
An alteration not listed in the manufacturer's specifications that might appreciably affect weight, structural strength, performance, flight characteristics, or other qualities affecting airworthiness or that cannot be done by elementary operations. (see also ALTERATION)

**MAJOR REPAIR**
A repair that if improperly accomplished may affect weight, structural strength, performance, flight characteristics, or other qualities which determine airworthiness.

**MALFUNCTION**
The complete or partial failure of a parachute canopy to accomplish proper opening, descent, or flight characteristics.

**MARD**
(see MAIN-ASSISTED RESERVE DEPLOYMENT)

**MASTER RIGGER**
The higher of two certification levels for FAA riggers. May perform more complex repair tasks and approved alterations. (see also SENIOR RIGGER)

**MENTOR (SKYDIVING)**
An experienced skydiver, usually D licensed, who can offer advice and guidance on skydiving-related matters to jumpers with less experience.

**MINI THREE RING**
Refers to a scaled-down version of the original three-ring release system. (see also THREE-RING RELEASE)

**MINOR ALTERATION**
An alteration other than a major alteration. (see also ALTERATION and MAJOR ALTERATION)

**MINOR REPAIR**
A repair other than a major repair. (see also MAJOR REPAIR)

**MOVEMENT JUMP**
A non-wingsuit jump on which a skydiver or group intends to move horizontally off the line of flight during freefall.

**MSL**
Acronym for Mean Sea Level. Altitude measured from sea level.

**NAA**
(see NATIONAL AERONAUTICAL ASSOCIATION)

# Glossary

**NASSER TOGGLES**
Control loops on the front risers attached to one or more A or A-B lines to facilitate diving the canopy toward a canopy formation. Designed by Nasser Basir.

**NATIONAL AERONAUTIC ASSOCIATION (NAA)**
The National Aero Club of the USA which represents the FAI. USPA is a division of the NAA.

**NATIONAL DIRECTOR**
(see BOARD OF DIRECTORS).

**NIGHT JUMP**
A skydive made from one hour after official sunset to one hour before official sunrise. The FAA considers any jump made after sunset and before sunrise a night jump requiring equipment specified in FAR 105.

**NORMAL LANDING AREA**
A landing area at a drop zone that DZ management has designated as separate from the high-performance landing area.

**NOTAM (NOTICE TO AIR MISSIONS )**
An air-traffic advisory or notice filed with an FAA Flight Service Station by an airspace user.

**OBJECT**
Any item other than a person that descends to the surface from an aircraft in flight when a parachute is used or is intended to be used during all or part of the descent. (FAR 105 definition)

**OPEN BODY OF WATER**
A body of water in which a skydiver could drown.

**OPENING POINT**
The ground point of reference over which the skydiver opens the parachute.

**OPENING SHOCK**
The decelerating force exerted on the load as the parachute deploys and inflates. Caused by the resistance of the canopy and items associated with it.

**OSCILLATION**
1. The swinging or pendulum motion of the suspended load under a canopy.
2. In canopy formation, the swaying or swinging of a formation caused by poor docking, turbulent air, or too much movement of the people in the formation.

**OUTBOARD**
Facing to the outside, such as a reserve handle facing to the side of the jumper rather than toward the breastbone.

**PACK**
To fold and close a parachute system in preparation for jumping.

**PACKING DATA CARD**
A card kept with a parachute system that records the maintenance on that system.

**PARACHUTE**
A fabric device that slows the descent of a falling object; derived from the French words "para," to shield, and "chute," to fall. Thus, parachute literally means "to shield from a fall."

**PARACHUTE DROP**
The descent of an object to the surface from an aircraft in flight when a parachute is used or intended to be used during all or part of that descent. (FAR 105 definition)

**PARACHUTE JUMP**
A parachute operation that involves the descent of one or more persons to the surface from an aircraft in flight when a parachute is used or intended to be used during all or part of that descent (FAR 105 definition).

**PARACHUTE LANDING FALL (PLF)**
A method developed by the U.S. military to minimize the chance of injury from a hard landing under parachute. The jumper distributes the force of the landing in an orderly manner over the most robust areas of the body.

**PARACHUTE OPERATION**
The performance of all activity for the purpose of, or in support of, a parachute jump or a parachute drop. This parachute operation can involve, but is not limited to, the following persons parachutist, parachutist in command and passenger in tandem parachute operations, drop zone or owner or operator, jumpmaster, certificated parachute rigger, or pilot (FAR 105 definition).

**PARACHUTIST**
A person who intends to exit an aircraft while in flight using a single-harness, dual parachute system to descend to the surface (FAR 105 definition). (see also SKYDIVER)

**PARACHUTIST IN COMMAND**
The person responsible for the operation and safety of a tandem parachute operation. (FAR 105 definition) Not necessarily a USPA instructional rating holder.

**PARTIAL INVERSION**
Inflation malfunction of a round canopy where one side passes through and inflates between two lines of the other side, resulting in two inflated lobes. (see also LINEOVER)

**PASSENGER PARACHUTIST**
A person who boards an aircraft, acting as other than the parachutist in command of a tandem parachute operation, with the intent of exiting the aircraft while in flight using the forward harness of a dual harness tandem parachute system to descend to the surface (FAR 105 definition). USPA further defines a passenger parachutist as either a licensed skydiver or a tandem student.

**PERMEABILITY**
The amount or volume of air which can pass through a fabric assembly.

**PILOT CHUTE**
A small parachute used to initiate and/or accelerate deployment of a main or reserve parachute (FAR 105 definition).

**PILOT-CHUTE ASSIST**
A method of rigging a static line to a parachute where the static line opens the container and positively extracts the pilot chute before separating from the system. Typically, a strip of touch fastener (Velcro) or break cord of known strength is used.

## P

**PIN**
1. To fly to another jumper and take grips on the jumper (freefall) or canopy (canopy formation).
2. The first jumper to make contact with the base, or target jumper, to begin a formation.
3. Retaining device that, when passed through a closing loop, locks the parachute system closed until activation.

**PIN CHECK**
Inspection of the reserve and main closing pins on a parachute container to ensure they are correctly positioned and secure.

**PLF**
(see PARACHUTE LANDING FALL)

**PLANE**
A compressed vertical canopy formation, where the jumper's feet are docked on the cross connectors below the slider of the lower canopy.

**PLANFORM**
The shape or footprint of a wing surface.

**PLANING**
The act of compressing a parachute stack.

**POISED EXIT**
A departure from an aircraft where the jumper sets up for exit using the aircraft door frame or strut for stability and launches with hips presented into the relative wind.

**POROSITY**
The ratio of open area to closed area in a fabric. Graded as high, low, or zero. Tightly woven and treated material has a lower porosity than loosely woven material.

**PRACTICE DEPLOYMENT**
An in-air exercise used to learn how to locate and operate a parachute deployment handle prior to opening. It may consist of pulling or throwing a practice or dummy handle (instructor-assisted deployment or static-line jumps) or touching the actual deployment handle in freefall or tandem droguefall.

**PREMATURE OPENING**
Unintentional opening of a parachute.

**PROJECTED LANDING POINT**
The expected landing spot on the ground, based on the glide path of the parachute.

**PROP BLAST**
1. The airflow created by a propeller that is developing thrust.
2. relative wind on exit

**PUD**
An aerodynamically low-profile, soft handle that is ergonomically designed to fit into a clenched fist. Used for various parachute operation handles.

**PULL OUT**
A type of hand-deployed parachute activation system. The jumper pulls a handle connected to the container closing pin and the internally packed pilot chute. (see also HAND-DEPLOYED PILOT CHUTE)

**PULL-UP CORD**
A packing aid used to thread the closing loop through eyelets in the container and removed once the closing pin is inserted.

## R

**RAM-AIR PARACHUTE**
A parachute with a canopy consisting of an upper and lower surface that is inflated by ram air entering through specially designed openings in the front of the canopy to form a gliding airfoil (FAR 105 definition).

**RATING-RENEWAL SEMINAR, USPA**
A continuing educational program for USPA instructional rating holders to improve and ensure the quality of skydiving instruction. This seminar can be conducted in a meeting where participants exchange information, introduce and discuss new ideas, and review recent relevant USPA initiatives; or online in the USPA Library consisting of short, interactive lessons reviewing instructional strategies as well as recent relevant USPA initiatives.

**REAR-RISER STALL**
A parachute stall induced by changing the shape of the parachute by affecting the C and D lines (the back half of your canopy), commencing suddenly by pulling down only 5-6 inches on both rear risers. Applying too much input is associated with a slow speed stall. (see STALL, TOGGLE STALL, and HIGH-SPEED STALL)

**REAR-RISER TURNS**
One of the canopy-flight emergency procedures (CEPs) used for canopy-collision avoidance immediately after opening, during the canopy descent, or in the landing pattern. This maneuver is the fastest way to change heading right after opening, even when the brakes are still stowed.

**RECOMMENDATIONS, USPA**
Principles, policies, and concepts applicable to skydiving or a related subject that are derived from experience or theory, compiled by USPA, and offered for guidance.

**REGIONAL DIRECTOR, USPA**
Member of the USPA Board elected from a specified geographical area and responsible for representing the interests of the skydivers in that USPA Region.

**RELATIVE WIND**
The relative airflow opposite a body's trajectory, irrespective of the horizon.

**RELATIVE WORK (RW)**
(see FORMATION SKYDIVING)

**REMOVABLE DEPLOYMENT SYSTEM (RDS)**
Primarily used by high-performance canopy pilots, it is a system that allows the slider, and in some cases the deployment bag and pilot chute, to be removed after opening to help decrease drag.

**RESERVE PARACHUTE**
An approved parachute worn for emergency use to be activated only upon failure of the main parachute or in any other emergency where use of the main parachute is impractical, or use of the main parachute would increase risk (FAR 105 definition).

**RESERVE STATIC LINE (RSL)**
A connection between the main risers and the reserve activation system intended to initiate reserve activation following the release of a deployed main parachute.

**RIB**
A vertical and longitudinal fabric membrane that forms the airfoil shape and primary structure of a ram-air canopy.

## Glossary

**RIG**
1. The complete parachute system used for skydiving.
2. The act of maintaining, repairing, or modifying a parachute system.
3. To don a parachute (e.g., rigging up).

**RIGGER**
An FAA-certificated parachute technician. (see also MASTER RIGGER and SENIOR RIGGER)

**RIPCORD**
An assembly, usually constructed with a metal cable and handle that, when pulled, activates the opening of a parachute.

**RISER DOCK**
In canopy formation, a momentum dock that puts the risers into the hands of the receiver. A very advanced technique.

**RISER LOOPS; RISER BLOCKS**
Gripping loops or devices on a riser that make it easier to grasp.

**RISER(S)**
Webbing straps that connect the main lift webs of the parachute harness to the lines of the canopy.

**RSL**
(see RESERVE STATIC LINE)

**SAFETY AND TRAINING ADVISOR (S&TA), USPA**
A local person appointed by the USPA Regional Director as his or her representative and who is available to provide advice and administrative assistance as the USPA representative at an individual drop zone or specified area.

**SANCTIONED DROP ZONE**
A drop zone that has been verified by a USPA Safety and Training Advisor or a USPA Regional Director as complying with the minimum drop zone requirements as stated in the USPA Basic Safety Requirements section of the USPA Skydiver's Information Manual. (see also DROP ZONE)

**SELF-SUPERVISION**
A term used to indicate an instructor has authorized a student to conduct solo jumps without instructor supervision in the aircraft, freefall, and under the canopy, but before they have completed all the requirements for the A license. Before boarding the aircraft, the student must receive a gear check from an instructional rating holder. At USPA Group Member skydiving centers, all skydivers cleared for self-supervision must be current USPA members. See Category E Academics.

**SENIOR RIGGER**
The initial certification level for FAA riggers that allows its holder to pack and maintain a parachute system and perform simple repairs. (see MASTER RIGGER)

**SHAGG**
Acronym for "shoes—tied, no hooks; helmet—fit and adjustment and buckled; altimeter—set for zero; goggles—tight and clean; gloves—lightweight and proper size (below 40 degrees F)."

**SIM**
Abbreviation for Skydiver's Information Manual (this book). (see SKYDIVER'S INFORMATION MANUAL)

**SINGLE OPERATION SYSTEM (SOS)**
Refers to a parachute harness and container operation system with a combined single-point riser release and reserve handle. Pulling one handle will both release the risers and pull the reserve. (See also TWO-HANDLED SYSTEM)

**SINGLE-HARNESS, DUAL-PARACHUTE SYSTEM**
The combination of a main parachute, approved reserve parachute, and approved single-person harness and dual-parachute container. This parachute system may have an operational automatic activation device installed (FAR 105 definition).

**SIT FLYING**
Head-up vertical freefly orientation based on a seated position.

**SKYBOARD**
(see SURFBOARD)

**SKYDIVE**
1. The descent of a person to the surface from an aircraft in flight when he or she uses or intends to use a parachute during all or part of that descent.
2. To jump from an aircraft with a parachute.

**SKYDIVER**
A person who engages in skydiving.

**SKYDIVER'S INFORMATION MANUAL (SIM), USPA (THIS BOOK)**
The official bound collection of the USPA Basic Safety Requirements, USPA recommendations, relevant FAA references, and other USPA policies and programs that affect the majority of skydivers.

**SKYSURFER**
A skydiver who jumps with a surfboard (skyboard).

**SKYSURFING**
A freefall skydiving discipline using a specially rigged surfboard (skyboard).

**SLIDER**
A device that controls a canopy's inflation by progressively sliding down the suspension lines during inflation. Found on most ram-air canopies.

**SLINKS**
(see SOFT LINKS)

**SOFT LINKS**
Spectra fabric links for attaching the parachute lines to the risers, first developed as an alternative to metal ("hard") links by Performance Designs under the brand name Slinks.

**SOLO DEPLOYMENT**
Refers to a pull sequence not prompted or cued by the instructor, where the student starts and finishes their pull sequence without instructor contact.

**SOLO JUMP**
A jump where a skydiver is not engaged in formation skydiving.

**SOLO JUMPER**
A skydiver who is not engaged in formation skydiving.

**SOLO SKYDIVER**
See solo jumper.

# G

## Glossary

**SOLO STUDENT**
A skydiving student who uses a single-harness, dual-parachute system.

**SOS**
(see SINGLE OPERATION SYSTEM)

**SPACE**
Acronym used to remember what to look for while clearing the airspace and exit separation before exiting "skydivers, plane, airport, clouds, exit light."

**SPAN**
The dimension of a wing measured from tip to tip.

**SPEED SKYDIVING**
Skydiving discipline in which the goal is to achieve and maintain the highest possible speed for a predetermined amount of time.

**SPOTTING**
Selecting the correct ground reference point over which to leave the aircraft, selecting the course for the aircraft to fly, and directing the pilot on jump run to that point.

**STABILITY**
That property of a body that causes it, when its equilibrium is disturbed, to develop forces or movements tending to restore the original condition. In skydiving, control of body position during freefall.

**STABLE FREEFALL POSITION**
A position attained by a freefalling skydiver in which only controlled, planned movements are made.

**STACK**
A vertical canopy formation with the jumpers gripping the canopy or lines just below the canopy.

**STALL**
An aerodynamic event where the parachute loses its ability to produce lift, loses pressurization, and the canopy will no longer support the weight of the jumper. (see REAR-RISER STALL, TOGGLE STALL, and HIGH-SPEED STALL)

**STATIC LINE**
A line of cable or webbing, one end of which is fastened to the parachute and the other to some part of the aircraft, used to activate and deploy or partially deploy the parachute as the load falls away from the aircraft.

**STATIC-LINE JUMP**
A parachute jump during which a static line is used to deploy or partially deploy the parachute. Used for training student skydivers.

**STEP-THROUGH**
Slang for a line continuity issue caused when the container passes through the lines either by a packing error or when the jumper steps through the lines after landing.

**STUDENT**
A skydiver trainee who has not been issued a USPA A license.

**SUPERVISION**
The general oversight of an activity taking place where the supervisor is readily available for counsel and direction and who is responsible that the activity is satisfactorily completed. (see DIRECT SUPERVISION)

**SURFBOARD (SKYBOARD)**
A rigid panel, similar to a snowboard, attached to a jumper's feet.

**SUSPENSION LINES**
Cords, attached from the bottom of the parachute canopy to the risers, that distribute and suspend the weight of a skydiver under the inflated canopy.

**SWOOP**
The controlled flight from above of one body to meet or fly close to another body, a stationary object, or the ground.

**SWOOP POND**
A water obstacle used as a high-performance landing area.

## T

**TANDEM JUMP OR TANDEM SKYDIVE**
Any skydive made using a tandem parachute system with a tandem student or licensed skydiver attached.

**TANDEM JUMPING**
A method of skydiving, typically used for training student skydivers, where one skydiver shares a tandem parachute system with another.

**TANDEM PARACHUTE OPERATION**
A parachute operation in which more than one person simultaneously uses the same tandem parachute system while descending to the surface from an aircraft in flight (FAR 105 definition).

**TANDEM PARACHUTE SYSTEM**
The combination of a main parachute, approved reserve parachute, and approved harness and dual-parachute container, and a separate, approved forward harness for a passenger parachutist. This parachute system must have an operational automatic activation device installed (FAR 105 definition).

**TANDEM STUDENT**
Any person making a tandem skydive who has not been issued a USPA license.

**TARGET**
An area in the landing area on a drop zone where a jumper aims to land.

**TECHNICAL STANDARD ORDER (TSO)**
Issued by the FAA, requires compliance with minimum performance standards and specifications for material and products. Parachute specifications are referenced in TSO-C23.

**TERMINAL VELOCITY**
The equilibrium velocity that a freefalling body can attain against the resistance of the air. The greatest speed at which a body falls through the atmosphere.

**THREAD-THROUGH**
A leg strap configuration on a parachute harness that uses a single piece of adjustable hardware. The leg strap must be un-threaded to be disconnected, or the jumper simply steps into the connected leg straps when donning the rig (see B-12s).

**THREE-RING RELEASE**
A type of single-point release invented by Bill Booth. The system is based on three interlocking rings on each riser held in place by a small loop that is retained by a cable. Pulling one handle releases both main risers simultaneously or nearly simultaneously.

## Glossary

**THROW OUT**
1. A type of hand-deployed parachute activation system. The pilot chute is folded into an external pouch, extracted and thrown. A curved closing pin or equivalent locking device on the bridle is extracted as jumper falls away from the pilot chute and bridle, allowing the container to open (see HAND-DEPLOYED PILOT CHUTE).
2. To initiate deployment.

**TOGGLES**
Handles attached to the ends of the steering lines of a parachute canopy. (see also BRAKES)

**TOGGLE STALL**
A parachute stall induced by slowly pulling the toggles down to full arm extension. The canopy loses airspeed and eventually stalls, which feels like rocking back in a chair and falling backward. Applying too much input is associated with a slow speed stall. (see STALL, REAR-RISER STALL, and HIGH-SPEED STALL).

**TRACK**
1. A freefall position with the legs fully extended, knees locked, arms swept back, elbows locked, and torso fully extended and slightly bowed forward to achieve the maximum horizontal speed.
2. To move at maximum horizontal speed in freefall.

**TRACKING JUMP**
A type of movement jump where skydivers travel across the sky instead of falling straight down. Flying is done in the TRACK body position to achieve the maximum horizontal speed.

**TRACKING SUIT**
A 2-piece inflating suit that transforms the body into a human airfoil.

**TSO-C23**
(see TECHNICAL STANDARD ORDER)

**TURBULENCE**
Disturbed air that can affect canopy flight and integrity.

**TURN REVERSALS**
Also known as "reverse turns." One of the canopy-flight emergency procedures (CEPs) used for canopy-collision avoidance. The maneuver entails a 90-degree turn followed by reversing toggle positions smoothly but quickly for a 180-degree turn in the opposite direction. This maneuver can be practiced as a canopy drill to learn the limits of a canopy related to the maximum speed and depth of a toggle input when reversing a turn to avoid line twists.

**TWO-HANDLED SYSTEM**
Refers to a parachute harness and container operation system that uses separate handles for the canopy release and for reserve activation. (see SINGLE OPERATION SYSTEM)

**UNITED STATES PARACHUTE ASSOCIATION (USPA)**
A not-for-profit, voluntary membership association of skydivers whose purpose is promoting and representing skydiving. As a division of the NAA, it is the official representative of the FAI for skydiving in the U.S.

**UPWIND**
The direction from which the wind is blowing.

**WAIVER**
1. Exception to the BSRs filed by a USPA official indicated in SIM Chapter 2-2.
2. A liability release.

**WATER JUMP**
A skydive which includes intentionally landing in an open body of water.

**WHUFFO**
Term for a non-skydiver ("Whuffo you jump out of airplanes?") Considered insensitive.

**WIND-DRIFT INDICATOR (WDI)**
A device—usually a weighted strip of crepe paper 10 inches wide and 20 feet long—used to determine the wind drift that a descending parachute will experience, so constructed as to descend at a rate comparable to a skydiver of average weight descending under a fully deployed main canopy of average specifications.

**WING LOADING**
The jumper's exit weight divided by the area of the parachute canopy, expressed in the United States in pounds per square foot.

**WINGSUIT**
A gliding jumpsuit designed with fabric membranes between the legs of the jumper and from each arm to the torso.

**ZOO DIVE**
A skydive that becomes chaotically disorganized with many jumpers out of position both vertically and horizontally.

# Appendix: License Study Guide Index

Use this guide to find areas of the SIM to study for USPA license exams. Refer to Chapter 3 for more information on licenses and exams.

## A LICENSE

Chapter 1, all categories
Chapter 2-1 BSRs, FAR 105
Chapter 4 sections 1 & 2
Chapter 5 sections 2 & 7

## B LICENSE

Chapter 1, Categories D, F, G, H
Chapter 2-1 BSRs, FARs 91.17, 91.211, & 119.1
Chapter 4 sections 1, 2, & 3
Chapter 5 sections 2, 3, & 5

## C LICENSE

Chapter 1, Category C
Chapter 2-1 BSRs, FARs 91.15, 91.151, 91.409, & 105.17
Chapter 4 sections 1, 2, 6
Chapter 5 sections 2, 6, 7, 8, 9
Chapter 6 section 1

## D LICENSE

Chapter 1, Categories F, G, & H
Chapter 2-1 BSRs, FARs 91.151, 91.211, 105.17, & 105.43
Chapter 4 sections 1, 2, 3, 4, 5, & 6
Chapter 5 sections 1, 2, 3, 5, 6, 7, 8, & 9
Chapter 6

Made in United States
North Haven, CT
25 May 2025